A Field Guide to
Animal Tracks

THE PETERSON FIELD GUIDE SERIES®
Edited by Roger Tory Peterson

A Field Guide to
Animal Tracks

Olaus J. Murie

Second Edition

*Sponsored by the National Audubon Society
and the National Wildlife Federation*

HOUGHTON MIFFLIN COMPANY
Boston   New York

For information about permission to reproduce selections from
this book, write to Permissions, Houghton Mifflin Company,
215 Park Avenue South, New York, New York 10003

PETERSON FIELD GUIDES and PETERSON FIELD GUIDE SERIES
are registered trademarks of Houghton Mifflin Company.

For information about this and other Houghton Mifflin
trade and reference books and multimedia products, visit
The Bookstore at Houghton Mifflin on the World Wide Web
at http://www.hmco.com/trade

Library of Congress Cataloging in Publication Data

Murie, Olaus Johan, 1889–1963.
A field guide to animal tracks.

(The Petersen field guide series, 9)
Bibliography: p. 359
1. Animal tracks. 2. Zoology—North America.
3. Zoology—Central America. 4. Animals, Habits
and behavior of. I. Title.
QL768.M87   1974   591.5   74-6294

ISBN 0-395-91094-3 (pbk.)   ISBN 0-395-91093-5 (hc)
Printed in the United States of America

VB 33 32 31 30 29 28 27

Editor's Note

WILD ANIMALS are shy, and try to avoid us. A large percentage of mammals are nocturnal, venturing from their dens only after darkness has fallen. We sometimes see their eyeshine in the glare of the headlights as we drive down country roads at night, but in the daytime the most frequent signs of their presence are their tracks — in the snow, in sand, or in the soft mud. Sometimes we find their scats. It is important to be able to recognize these trails and other traces of their presence.

This volume fits well into the *Field Guide* series, for it supplements the volume on mammals and to a certain extent the ones on birds, providing the amateur naturalist (and also the professional wildlife technician and biologist) with a means of identifying the wildlife around him even when he cannot see it. Moreover, it is a bridge between the art of identification and the science of ecology. There is a story behind the tracks in the snow or along the river's edge and study may reveal much about the animal in relation to its habitat.

This book, the only comprehensive one in its category, covers every mammal for which tracks have been obtained in North America, Mexico, and Central America — not only the common ones. It also includes over thirty birds, some reptiles, and a few insects; there is a section on twigs and limbs and one on bone and horn chewing. The abundant illustrations are in line; certainly color is not necessary, because tracks are not colored. Not only are the tracks and trails pictured with measurements, but scats are shown, with variations, and in addition there is a pen and ink drawing of each animal in its habitat. Where peculiarities of the track are not obvious in the drawing they are discussed in the text.

Olaus Murie reminds us very much of an earlier master, Ernest Thompson Seton. Like Seton he was not only an eminent naturalist and an accomplished woodsman but also a fine artist, able to interpret in pen and ink the things he had witnessed. Dr. Murie's drawings in this book were made in the field, except where it was impossible; he used material in museums and zoos only when field specimens were unobtainable.

Dr. Murie was most at home in the wilderness areas of the West. The Red River — with its animals, woods, and waters — was the background of his childhood. After completing his university work in Oregon he went to Hudson Bay for two years and later spent six years in Alaska studying caribou, Arctic waterfowl, and the biology of the Alaska Peninsula and the Aleutians. In 1927 he moved to Jackson Hole, Wyoming, where the elk became the subject of intensive study. Resigning from the United States Fish and Wildlife Service in 1946 he became director of The Wilderness Society and later its president. Modest and very gifted, Olaus Murie dedicated his life to the ideal of wilderness preservation. In this *Field Guide* he shared with others some of his knowledge and love of the natural world.

In the twenty years since the first edition was published there have been many changes in nomenclature. This second edition, completely reset, has attempted to bring both scientific and vernacular names in line with current practice. In addition, there is a new index, and some minor changes have been made throughout the text. We are grateful to the author's widow, Margaret Murie, for her assistance in answering questions and in reading proof, and to the author's brother, Adolph Murie, for his kind help in solving problems of nomenclature.

ROGER TORY PETERSON

1974

Acknowledgments

THIS FIELD GUIDE is based almost entirely on my own field observations and the collection of plaster casts and other material that has been assembled since 1921.

However, I have also studied the extensive mammalian literature, which has been of great value, and a bibliography of some of this literature is given at the end of the book. Moreover, I have had the assistance of a number of persons, and without their help there would have been gaps in my information.

Dr. Hartley H. T. Jackson, with whom I was once associated in the United States Fish and Wildlife Service, many years ago suggested that I write such a handbook, and I began in a small way at that time.

Mr. Ernest P. Walker, Assistant Director of the National Zoological Park in Washington, D.C., together with members of his staff and the staff of the Woodland Park Zoo in Seattle and of the Fleishhacker Zoo of San Francisco have all been of much help. With the help of attendants at the last-named zoo my son, Martin Murie, obtained tracks of the jaguar, which I could not have obtained otherwise.

The entomology department of the National Museum, the United States Fish and Wildlife Service, and the staff at Sequoia National Park have all given me assistance.

Many individuals have furnished valuable material: the late Francis H. Allen of Cambridge, Massachusetts; Dr. E. L. Cheatum of the New York Conservation Department; Dr. C. H. D. Clarke, Department of Lands and Forests, Ontario; Antoon de Vos, Ontario College of Agriculture; Lieutenant and Mrs. H. H. J. Cochrane, Canal Zone; Dr. James Zetek, in charge of the research station at Barro Colorado Island, Canal Zone; Warren Garst, Douglas, Wyoming; Luther C. Goldman, Texas; John K. Howard, who, with co-operation of The American Museum of Natural History of New York, made available to me film on Arctic hares; Dr. William J. Hamilton of Cornell University; William Handley of the National Museum; William Nancarrow, Alaska; Ivan R. Tompkins, Georgia; Dr. Robert Rausch of the Public Health Service, Alaska; Erwin Verity of the Walt Disney Studios; and Dr. Frank N. Young of Indiana University.

My son Donald live-trapped certain mammals for study of their tracks. Howard Zahniser, my associate on the staff of The Wilderness Society, gave me pertinent suggestions. My brother, Adolph Murie, during his long sojourn in Alaska, assembled a mass of valuable data on such animals as the wolf and the wolverine, as well as ptarmigan and other species. This was all put at my disposal.

When I fell ill in May 1954 some illustrations were still needed to complete the manuscript. The warm response of the many people who were asked to help was overwhelming. To every one of them I give earnest thanks, and especially to Mrs. William Grimes of the Massachusetts Audubon Society and Miss Frances Burnett of the Harvard Museum of Comparative Zoology for their helpful research; to Dr. William Burt of the University of Michigan Museum of Zoology and Mr. Bert Harwell of California for their many useful suggestions; to Mr. Richard Westwood of the American Nature Association for taking a personal interest in the project; to the New Hampshire Fish and Game Commission, who obtained from the Blue Mountain Forest Association the feet of a 206-pound wild boar; and to Mr. Ellsworth Jaeger of the Buffalo Museum of Science and Mr. George Mason of The American Museum of Natural History, who both offered their services in finding specimens and making the necessary illustrations.

The seven plates of track drawings were done on very short notice by Mr. Carroll B. Colby of Briarcliff Manor, and to him I owe my deepest gratitude, as I do to my artist friend and neighbor Grant Hagen, who furnished the final sketches for Figure 147 and for the marsh rabbit on page 249.

Finally, I appreciate the cordial and intimate relationship with Mr. Paul Brooks, editor-in-chief of Houghton Mifflin Company, and members of his staff who have taken a genuine interest in the manuscript and whose encouragement has been very stimulating. Among these, I give special gratitude to Katharine Bernard, Helen Phillips, and Anne Cabot Wyman.

Whether in the field of natural history or elsewhere, one does not accomplish a piece of work alone. It must at least in part draw on the experience of others. It is a pleasure to acknowledge such help, and to express my gratitude for such participation in my efforts.

O. J. M.

1954

Contents

Key to Tracks

with General Distribution Areas

Bear Family	see also Fig. 8, 9, 10, 15
Raccoon and Ringtail Families	see also Figs. 16, 17
Weasel Family	see also Fig. 21
5 toes.	
Dog Family	see also Fig. 40
4 toes. Claws usually show in track.	
Cat Family	see also Fig. 54
4 toes. Claws do not show in track.	
Rodents	see also Figs. 63, 64
Only representative or distinctive tracks shown here.	
Rabbit Families	see also Figs. 120, 123, 124, 125, 126, 127, 128, 129
Hoofed Animals	see also Fig. 130

3½ in.   Whitetail Deer (e., s., and cen. U.S., s. Can.,   p. 257
            Mex., Cen. Am.)

6¼ in.   Moose (n. Rockies, Can., Alaska)   p. 278

4½ in.   Elk and Red Deer (parts of nw. U.S., Can.)   p. 271

4¾ in.   Caribou (Arctic)   p. 284

6 in.   Bison (natl. parks, w. U.S., Can.)   p. 308

6 in.   Horse (w. U.S.)   p. 314

3½ in. Mountain Sheep (sw. U.S. up into Canada)   p. 300

3 in. Domestic Pig (U.S., Mex., Can.)   p. 289

1½ in.   Striped Skunk (U.S., Mex., Can.)   p. 77

2½ in. Porcupine (sw., w., n., and e. U.S., Can.)   p. 180
h   f

Bears: Black, Grizzly, Brown   p. 25
                        (mountainous U.S., Can.)
                        Hind foot of Grizzly, about
                        1 ft. long.
h
f

Polar Bear (far n. Can.)   p. 35

6 in. f Sea Otter (western coastal U.S.)   p. 74
h

2¼ in. Kinkajou (Cen. Am.)   p. 42
h   f

7 in. f Beaver (U.S., Can.)   p. 171
h

3¾ in.   Raccoon (U.S., s. Can., Mex.,   p. 37
         h   f   Cen. Am.)

1½ in.   Muskrat (U.S., Can., Alaska)   p. 175
         h   f

⅝ in.   Norway Rat (U.S., Mex.)   p. 193

2¼ in.   Opossum (eastern half U.S., Cal.,   p. 11
         h   f   Mex., Cen. Am.)

2⅜ in.   Marmot (w. and ne. U.S., Can., Alaska)   p. 127
         h   f

2½ in.   Armadillo (Texas, Mex., Cen. Am.)   p. 12
         h   f

1¾ in.   Paca (Cen. Am.)   p. 191

1½ in.   Agouti (s. Mex., Cen. Am.)   p. 189

4 in.   Dog (all over)   p. 85

1½ in.   Domestic Cat (all over)   p. 109

1⅛ in.   Mink (U.S., Can., Alaska)   p. 53

2½ in.   River Otter (U.S., Can.)   p. 69

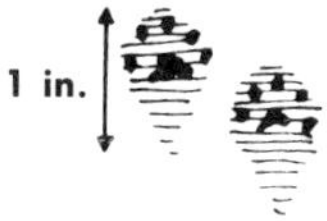

1 in.   Weasel (all over)   p. 46

5 in.   Wolverine (w. U.S., n. and w. Can.)   p. 65

2¼ in.   Badger (n. cen. U.S., sw. U.S. up into Can.)   p. 82

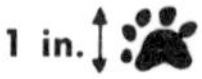

1 in.   Ringtail (Cal. and sw. U.S., Mex.)   p. 44

1¾ in.   Coati (Mex., Cen. Am)   p. 40

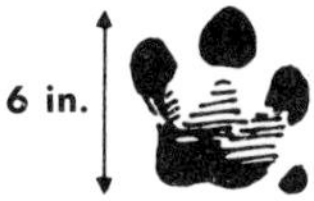

6 in.   Baird's Tapir (s. Mex., Cen. Am.)   p. 317

Seal (coasts and Alaska). Claw   p. 125
marks shown here are over 30 in.
apart. Distance varies greatly
with the species of seal; some
distances are much longer.

Mole (eastern half and western   p. 14
coastal U.S., e. Can.). Mole
house.

Rabbit (all over). The familiar rabbit track   p. 231
pattern shown here applies to all the rabbits,
with some exceptions and with differences in
size.

White-footed Mouse (e., cen., sw. U.S., e.   p. 202
Mex.). Track similar to that of shrew but
slightly larger. This same pattern, in varying
sizes, is common to the pocket mice, house
mouse, grasshopper mouse, and harvest
mouse.

Meadow Vole (n. and cen. e. U.S., Can., into   p. 211
Alaska). Tracks of the voles, including the pine
vole, sagebrush vole, mountain phenacomys,
redback vole, and the lemmings, typically have
this general pattern.

Shrew (U.S., Can., Alaska). Trail pattern up   p. 18
to $1\frac{1}{4}$ in. wide.

5 in.

Red Squirrel (n. U.S., Can., Alaska). This track   p. 147
pattern is common to all the squirrels; smaller
in the chipmunk, larger in the gray squirrels.

6 in.

Ground Squirrel (central and western half U.S., p. 139
s. and n. Can., Alaska, n. Mex.).

Kangaroo Rat (w. and sw. U.S., n. Mex.). Hops   p. 168
on hind feet, leaving a series of twin prints.

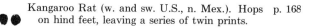

Pocket Gopher (western half U.S., s. Can.,   p. 163
Mex.). Mounds show an earth plug at
one side of the center, not to be found
in molehills.

My Life List

.... Opossum
.... Armadillo
.... Townsend Mole
.... Hairytail Mole
.... Eastern Mole
.... Pacific Mole
.... California Mole
.... Starnose Mole
.... Shrew-Mole
.... Arctic Shrew
.... Northern Water Shrew
.... Pygmy Shrew
.... Least Shrew
.... Gray Shrew
.... Red Bat
.... Hoary Bat
.... Long-eared Myotis
.... Alaska Brown Bear
.... Grizzly Bear
.... Black Bear
.... Polar Bear
.... Raccoon
.... Coati
.... Kinkajou
.... Ringtail
.... Shorttail Weasel (Ermine)
.... Longtail Weasel
.... Least Weasel
.... Mink
.... Marten
.... Fisher
.... Tayra
.... Black-footed Ferret
.... Wolverine

.... River Otter
.... Sea Otter
.... Striped Skunk
.... Hooded Skunk
.... Hognose Skunk
.... Spotted Skunk
.... Badger
.... Dog
.... Gray Wolf
.... Red Wolf
.... Coyote
.... Red Fox
.... Gray Fox
.... Kit Fox
.... Arctic Fox
.... Cat
.... Bobcat
.... Lynx
.... Mountain Lion
.... Jaguar
.... Ocelot
.... Jaguarundi Cat
.... Harbor Seal
.... Sea Lion
.... Woodchuck
.... Yellowbelly Marmot
.... Hoary Marmot
.... Prairie Dog
.... Golden-mantled Squirrel
.... Antelope Squirrel
.... Thirteen-lined Ground
     Squirrel
.... Uinta Ground Squirrel
.... Franklin Ground Squirrel

.... Rock Squirrel
.... Eastern Chipmunk
.... Western Chipmunk
.... Red Squirrel
.... Eastern Gray Squirrel
.... Western Gray Squirrel
.... Arizona Gray Squirrel
.... Eastern Fox Squirrel
.... Apache Fox Squirrel
.... Tassel-eared Squirrel
      Flying Squirrel
.... Pocket Gopher, Genus
      Thomomys
.... Pocket Gopher, Genus
      Geomys
.... Pocket Gopher, Genus
      Papogeomys
.... Pocket Mouse
.... Kangaroo Rat
.... Kangaroo Mouse
.... Beaver
.... Muskrat
.... Florida Water Rat
.... Porcupine
.... Aplodontia
.... Agouti
.... Paca
.... Norway Rat
.... House Mouse
.... Jumping Mouse, Genus
      Zapus
.... Jumping Mouse, Genus
      Napaeozapus
.... Woodrat
.... White-footed Mouse
.... Golden Mouse
.... Cotton Mouse
.... Beach (Oldfield) Mouse
.... Grasshopper Mouse
.... Harvest Mouse
.... Rice Rat
.... Cotton Rat

.... Alaska Vole
.... Mountain Vole
.... Richardson Vole
.... Meadow Vole
.... Pine Vole
.... Sagebrush Vole
.... Bog Lemming
.... Redback Vole
.... Tree Phenacomys
.... Mountain Phenacomys
.... Pacific Phenacomys
.... Collared Lemming
.... Brown Lemming
.... Arctic Hare
.... Whitetail Jackrabbit
.... Blacktail Jackrabbit
.... Antelope Jackrabbit
.... European Hare
.... Snowshoe Hare
.... Washington Hare
.... Rocky Mountain
      Snowshoe Hare
.... Cottontail
.... Marsh Rabbit
.... Swamp Rabbit
.... Pygmy Rabbit
.... Pika
.... Whitetail Deer
.... Key Deer
.... Mule Deer
.... Elk
.... European Red Deer
.... Moose
.... Caribou
.... Reindeer
.... Domestic Pig
.... Wild Boar
.... Peccary
.... Pronghorn
.... Mountain Sheep
.... Domestic Sheep
.... Mountain Goat

.... Domestic Goat
.... Bison
.... Muskox
.... Domestic Cattle
.... Horse
.... Burro
.... Baird's Tapir
.... Willow Ptarmigan
.... Spotted Sandpiper
.... Canada Goose
.... Trumpeter Swan
.... Glaucous-winged Gull
.... Common Teal
.... Sage Grouse
.... Blue Grouse
.... Ruffed Grouse
.... Ring-necked Pheasant
.... Rock Ptarmigan
.... Roadrunner
.... Flicker
.... Scaled Quail
.... Gray Partridge
.... Domestic Pigeon
.... Junco
.... Sandhill Crane
.... Wild Turkey
.... Great Blue Heron
.... Greater Yellowlegs
.... Common Snipe
.... Rock Sandpiper
.... California Condor
.... Bald Eagle
.... Barred Owl
.... Great Horned Owl
.... Raven
.... Crow
.... Magpie
.... *Spruce Grouse
.... *Harlequin Quail
.... *Lesser Prairie Chicken

.... *Sharp-tailed Grouse
.... *Bohemian Waxwing
.... *Townsend's Solitaire
.... *Chukar
.... *White-tailed Ptarmigan
.... *Ferruginous Hawk
.... *Red-tailed Hawk
.... *Prairie Falcon
.... *Swainson's Hawk
.... *Shrike
.... *Sparrow Hawk
.... *Clark's Nutcracker
.... *Short-eared Owl
.... *Long-eared Owl
.... *Burrowing Owl
.... *Great Gray Owl
.... *Goshawk
.... *Golden Eagle
.... Toad
.... Frog
.... Lizard
.... Turtle
.... Sidewinder
.... Garter Snake
.... Kingsnake
.... Hognose Snake
.... Crayfish
.... Clam
.... Mole Cricket
.... Burrowing Beetle
.... Centipede
.... Katydid
.... Mormon Cricket
.... Caterpillar
.... Grasshopper
.... Carrion Beetle
.... Earthworm
.... Twigs and Limbs
.... Bone and Horn Chewing

* Only droppings are shown

A Field Guide to
Animal Tracks

What Has Happened Here?
Introductory

WHO LIVES in the forest? What creatures inhabit the banks of streams, the shores of lakes, or the sands of the desert? What are the animals that leave footprints in the mud, and trails in the snow? What has gnawed the bark, or clipped the twig?

Hunting is about as old as life and tracking is an ancient science, but it would be difficult to determine when land animals began to notice the tracks left by their companions in the mud or sand. It is not likely that the amphibians of prehistory were track-wise. What of the reptiles of the Permian period, and those awkward reptile-mammal creatures who were the forerunners of the graceful present-day mammals? Certainly many mammals are trackers, and they may be the first to have learned the art. But they track by scent. Although a dog assuredly sees the rabbit track, and recognizes it as a track, he can hardly sense that the shape, size, and arrangement spell "rabbit." However, the first whiff with his nose tells him what it is.

I was traveling one day with a cougar hound in a light snow in the deep forest of the Pacific Coast. We found a wolf trail and I was interested in noting the size of the tracks and the stride. The hound poked his nose deep into the footprints to learn their identity. Then as we followed a little way I noticed the dog sniffing curiously at various twigs overhanging from either side. The wolf had merely brushed them in passing, but had left a record sufficient for this master tracker who was with me. What need had he for a knowledge of size or shape of footprints?

Man has lost his power of tracking by scent but has developed greater intellectual refinement. He can read a more complex story in footprints than mere identification and direction of travel. The Indians and Eskimos and the experienced woodsmen have learned to read imperfect track records with remarkable skill, just as a trained ornithologist recognizes a bird without seeing the details of its plumage. The more recent use of tracking ability is in the field of natural history.

It has become a popular pastime to go looking for birds, but what a field there is open to us in becoming familiar with mammals, once we put our minds to it! They are furtive, usually silent, and very often go about at night. You don't find them readily with

1

field glasses, and you don't total up a long list on a "mammal walk," as you do with birds. Nevertheless, their very aloofness is a challenge, and your sleuthing instinct is aroused. Once alerted to this fascinating game, you can never again pass the muddy margin of a stream without instinctively looking to see what has passed by there. You will speculate about every trail in the snow, big or small. You will find that a complex mammal world, which you never suspected, has opened up for you. Driving along a desert road, you can stop and by a five-minute walk in the sand gain some acquaintance with the kangaroo rat, kit fox, or blacktail jackrabbit through the medium of their footprints.

Perhaps it is best for us not to specialize too much. The bird enthusiast can add to his enjoyment and understanding by some interest and skill in reading the record of mammals. The naturalist goes forth to enjoy what he can find, be it bird, mammal, insect, plant, or the music of a mountain stream.

On a wintry day in Wyoming as I was traveling along the foothills in open country, with aspen groves on the hills, dark evergreen forests above, and the Teton mountains across the valley, I came on the tracks of a jackrabbit. Obviously the animal had been in a desperate hurry. How desperate, was soon revealed, for the rabbit track was joined by the track of a coyote. The rabbit had dodged deftly and fast. The coyote swerved too, but had slid in a wider turn. Again the rabbit turned, and the coyote swung in close pursuit. Time after time this was repeated. The rabbit was doing well. Could he gain enough distance to escape by a speedy straightaway?

Suddenly there was a third track. A second coyote had been cruising along a little farther up the hill. His trail of long leaps led diagonally down, just in time to close in when the jackrabbit made one of his desperate uphill turns. A few drops of blood here, and the two coyote trails led off together.

One fall I was looking for elk grazing areas in the upper Yellowstone country. The question was, did the elk summer here, and if so, how extensively? I entered a high basin with open slopes. There were the elk tracks, and there were their droppings. The character of the dung — more or less flattened or formless — revealed that this was summer range, that the animals had found succulent green forage. Winter or autumn droppings would have been hard and pellet-like. Such indications help to build up the facts in the life story of an animal and are useful to the scientist as well as the amateur observer.

Another time, driving along a road in Utah, I glanced at a rocky outcrop with low cliffs. It was possible to know in that glance that woodrats lived in those rocks. Why? Because there were the telltale white spots, visible at a distance, where the little animals had left their excretions. Farther along I could see the location of a nest on a high cliff. This proved to be a raven's home. It had been revealed by long vertical streaks of "whitewash," the smears of guano that accumulate at such nests. They are distinctly different from the marks left by woodrats.

One day in the Wichita Mountains of Oklahoma I watched a flock of sandhill cranes alighting at the marshy shore of a pond. After they had left I looked over the ground. I was struck by certain similarities between the tracks of these cranes and those of the wild turkeys that I had seen nearby. I obtained plaster casts of both for more leisurely study. The casts clearly revealed the trim feet of the crane, with a finer "fingerprint" pattern on the under surface of the toes, in contrast to the coarser aspect of the turkey track.

In April 1949 a friend and I were clambering through the mountains of southern New Zealand, looking for signs of red deer and wapiti. We came on a narrow trail in the moss and litter of the forest floor, leading off from the base of a huge tropical beech. In America it would have been noted as a squirrel trail, but there are no squirrels in New Zealand. We were thrilled when finally it became clear to us that here was the track of the kakapo, a flightless parrot now becoming very rare. Unfortunately we didn't see the bird itself, since it is nocturnal in habit like the owl.

Familiarity with mammal signs — tracks, droppings, gnawings, scratchings, rubbings, dams, nests, burrows — can open up a delightful field for the outdoor traveler. The mountain climber and the touring skier can make interesting observations in far and high places, increasing the pleasure of their excursions afield. The hiker, the visitor to national parks, the wilderness traveler in national forests can add much to their experience by sleuthing about for traces of the unseen inhabitants of the region.

If you are vacationing in Big Bend National Park you will be interested in a possible bobcat track in the mud beside the Rio Grande, or the mountain lion "scratching" in the trail in the Chisos Mountains, or the nibblings on a prickly pear on the desert flatlands. If you spend some days in Mt. McKinley National Park of Alaska, you have a chance to see at first hand the peculiar rounded track of the caribou, the hay piles of the Alaska vole (or "hay mouse"), or the pellets of the gyrfalcon at its aerie in the cliffs. The Boy Scout can enrich his excursions with an interest in animal signs. The serious field biologist requires facility in reading the story left by the passage of mammals. Whatever the purpose, these little stories in wild country can be the means of great esthetic adventuring.

The coyote can read the news of his territory with his nose; and what a wonderfully sniffy time your dog has as he follows you through the woods. It is the purpose of this *Field Guide* to give some aid to man in the interpretation of mammal "sign," not in the manner of the coyote or dog, but by conscious evaluation of what he sees before him. Its object is to encourage the study and enjoyment of the outdoors and the wildlife in it.

Of course mammals are not the only ones to leave sign of their presence. Accordingly, I have included a few tracks and other signs of representative birds, reptiles, amphibians, and some insects. Even the weather leaves a few signs, such as lightning marks, shown in Figure 194, b. The main concern, however, is the mammal world of North America, from Mexico to the Arctic.

Reading the sign. Reading tracks is not easy. Just as a detective, with certain broad principles in mind, finds each situation somewhat different, so the animal tracker must be prepared to use his ingenuity to interpret what he sees. A track in the mud may look different from one in dust, or in snow, even if the same individual animal made them. A track in snow is different after a warm sun has shone on it — enlarging and distorting it. An *average* or standardized track drawing in a book may not look like the one you are trying to identify. The fact is that in many instances the track you find may not seem to fit anything because it is not all there; it may not show all the toes, it may be off-shape because of irregularity of the ground. Then there are the variations due to age of the animal, or the sex. Generally speaking, the front track is likely to be different from the hind track of the same animal, with different number of toes, different shape and size. A perfect track is not always found.

The same applies to droppings. Those of a half-grown coyote may resemble those of a full-grown fox. If a fox or coyote has been feeding on bulky food, with a lot of fur or feathers, the dropping is likely to be unusually large. If the same animal has been eating lean rations, the dropping may be very small.

Therefore, use the material in this book as a guide rather than a rigid key. In the consideration of each species, all possible suggestions will be given to help unravel the story of animal signs. Space does not permit illustration of *all* the variations you will find — and in some cases it has been impossible to obtain any tracks. The policy has been adopted to illustrate, whenever possible, actual tracks, with place and date and character of the snow or ground, and to show several variations. It has been possible to rely mostly on personal experience for the contents of this guide, but no one writer can claim complete information, and there are gaps in the story, which will be pointed out in appropriate places. In some cases I have drawn on the information and experience of others, as indicated in the text.

Now a word of encouragement to the beginner. After you have entered this field of mammal study, you will gradually become conscious of a *knack* in reading signs. In familiar territory you will become adept at interpretation of fragmentary evidence and it will not be necessary to have it spelled out in detail. Even the professional naturalist, if he is honest, however, will freely say that sometimes he is stumped by what he finds.

For the experienced student, I can only hope that this handbook will be helpful. He will recognize the interdependence of those of us who work in this field. I would here express my appreciation of published records, which have been consulted and duly listed elsewhere, and the enthusiastic assistance of co-workers. With humility, and with full knowledge of how great and complex is this field, I offer this guide on animal signs.

Preserving tracks. To the field biologist there may be an advantage in preserving for future study a clear record of tracks in tangible form. To the student or wilderness traveler who might make a hobby of tracking it is also worth while to "take home" souvenir tracks, though this is sometimes awkward. I was confronted by an incredulous customs inspector on my return from Panama. He could hardly believe my sanity when I told him the large crate among my belongings contained "animal tracks."

If one is accustomed to sketching and carrying a pocket tape measure, a good way is to make careful drawings of the tracks, either natural size by the aid of the tape measure (or measured by the pencil) or drawn to scale. One should take note of the lengths of a few sample strides or leaps, as well as the dimensions of individual prints.

Under rare circumstances it is possible to cut around the track with your knife and lift it out intact. I found it possible to do this in the mud of a dried lake bottom in Nevada, where pronghorn and coyotes had left footprints when the mud was just right for leaving a firm, sharp print.

Generally, however, for "take home" tracks I have relied on plaster of paris. I have rarely gone on a field trip during the past twenty-five years without a supply of plaster. The result is an extensive collection of track casts. These, with numerous field drawings, form the basis for the illustrations in this volume.

The method is simple. First, carry your plaster in some tightly stoppered receptacle — a widemouth bottle or jar, or friction-top can, or if in a paper sack, nest two or three sacks inside each other to form several thicknesses of paper. Loose plaster plays havoc if it gets into your packsack.

Upon finding a track in mud, I usually take a tin can, put in a little water, add some plaster, and stir it quickly with my fingers or a stick until the mixture forms a thin batter; or I may put the plaster in first, which is probably a little better. I estimate the amount of "batter" needed for the track or tracks before me. If the mixture appears too thick, I hastily dip in a little more water

with my hand — *not too much* — until it seems right. It is important of course to add water before the mass begins to stiffen, and
to work fairly fast if the first mixture begins to come out thick.
A very thick plaster paste begins to set almost immediately. A
thinner mixture gives you more time. When the plaster has been
poured into the track I wait patiently or busy myself with other
things for ten minutes or more to allow it to set hard. It is not
wise to attempt to pick up the cast too soon. Sometimes, if I am
on the "out trail" I leave the casts and pick them up on my way
back.

If the plaster is too thick so that it does not flow readily, it will
begin to set while being poured and will not enter all the crevices
of the track as it should, perhaps failing to catch sharply enough
the details of feet like those of the porcupine or bear. If too thin
or watery, it will run all over the place, taking forever to harden
and acting queerly in many ways. Sway the solution in the can
as you mix it; when it loses the watery quality and begins to move
a little sluggishly, with the first sign of "reluctance" it is about
ready to pour. Plaster of this consistency, like a thin batter that
pours fairly easily, will make a hard cast. When too thick or if
diluted after it has begun to set, it will harden into a chalklike
consistency that scratches or abrades easily.

You may wish to include in the cast several tracks, the whole
four-foot pattern of a squirrel or weasel or skunk, or you may want
to include two sets of four to show the stride or jump. In that
case pour plaster into one set of tracks, then trail it across the
ground in a strip to the other set. With a long cast of this kind
I often lay one or more sticks or pieces of wire into it for rein-
forcement while the plaster is still soft.

Sometimes when I am short of plaster and want to stretch it,
or when I am greedy and want to get "one more track" with the
batch I have prepared, I pour in enough to cover the bottom to
make sure of the details, then put in sand or stones or sticks and
add the remaining mixture on top. This will do in an emergency.
If you find that you have underestimated the amount needed, more
can be mixed and poured on top of the plaster already there, in
order to make sure the cast will be thick enough for safe handling.

You should be sure that the plaster overflows the margins of
the track to make certain you have all of it, with all its edges and
claw marks. If the track is on sloping ground you may have to
place a dirt ridge, or stones or sticks, on the lower side to keep
the plaster from running away. The proper method is to place
a "collar" of heavy paper or other suitable material around the
track in order to retain the plaster within bounds and make a *thick*
cast that won't break. I confess that, with the urgency of other
work, I have seldom bothered with this detail.

To pick up the cast *after it is hard,* cut around it with a knife,

gouge out some dirt from under the edges all around, then lift out
the piece from a point well underneath. Take it to water and wash
off the mud, using a toothbrush with care, if you have an old one
at hand for such purposes. Should enough water for washing not
be available, simply brush off the surplus mud and wash the cast
later.

These are crude and rough field methods. The serious student
may wish to work out greater refinement. Some naturalists employ
improved techniques. Dr. E. Laurence Palmer of Cornell University, for example, suggested that to delay the hardening of plaster
you might put a little vinegar in the solution.

If the track is in dust great care must be taken. My own method
is to pour the solution directly into the track, but from a point
as close above the track as possible. It should not be dropped in
with any force.

Some naturalists use paraffin or a candle in place of plaster of
paris. It is admittedly simpler to carry some candles on a field
trip. Vernon Bailey recommended dripping a lighted candle into
the track. But one difficulty I have found is that unless there is
an ample quantity of melted paraffin or wax to pour in rather
quickly, you get an irregular surface that does not give continuous
detail, since the paraffin tends to harden while pouring.

Tracks in snow are difficult to cast, and obviously a candle cannot
be used. Even a fairly cold plaster solution tends to melt the
bottom of the track and it is disconcerting to find that the batter
has poured right on through. To avoid this the mixture should
be made as cold as possible by stirring some snow in while mixing.
I have also tried dusting in a fine layer of dry plaster first, as a
base, allowing it to form a slight lining in the track. Dr. Palmer,
mentioned above, devised an excellent method for cold weather.
With an ordinary atomiser containing very cold water, he sprayed
the surface of the track enough to form a thin coating of ice that
would hold the cold plaster of paris mixture.

I have experimented with a substance carried by hardware stores
called water putty. It is a yellowish-brown powder to be mixed
with water into a thick paste for patching cracks and holes in
cement, plaster, and so on. I find that by mixing it thinner, pretty
much as with plaster of paris, it makes excellent casts. Another
advantage is that by mixing in 50 percent of fine sand, or almost
any soil at hand, I have obtained a very hard cast. Perhaps 25
percent of sand is safer to experiment with, though in emergency,
when I was short of material, I have put in much more than 50
percent of sand. However, the more sand, the longer it takes to
harden. If you attempt to lift out this sand mixture too soon, the
cast may break up or crumble. Leave it a long time.

Although this is a material not yet fully proved, some of the
casts I have made, especially those with a moderate sand mixture,

seem very hard and durable and may prove to be less destructible than plaster casts. This is a field for experimentation; but I would offer a word of caution: for small tracks with fine detail, use water putty pure; large coarse tracks are suitable for the somewhat grainy surface you get by adding sand.

Preserving scats. The field biologist may also wish to make a collection of scats as reference specimens, for use in studies of food habits or for any other purpose requiring identification of such material. The first essential is to ensure proper identification in the field, preferably by tracks where the scat is found, or by collection in a locality where it is certain that only one kind of mammal of the type involved is present. For instance, it is helpful if a coyote scat is obtained where it is known that bobcats are absent (though in some parts of the country bobcat scats are fairly distinctive).

The scats, or droppings, if desired as permanent specimens, should be kept in their original shape by suitable packing in the field. In the case of specimens containing animal remains, such as bones and hair, moths or dermestid beetles will destroy them just as they destroy museum skins. I have found it helpful to coat such scats liberally with ambroid, or sometimes glue varnish, using a brush and allowing some of the application to soak into the substance. I have not found it necessary to treat material consisting of plant remains in this way, except to ensure holding the shape.

On several occasions I have found droppings of elk, deer, and mountain sheep formed of pure clay, in the vicinity of mud or clay licks. These make excellent specimens, being perfectly hard and of finely modeled form. Occasionally, too, I have found marmot droppings on arid buttes that appeared to be coated with reddish clay — possibly wind-blown.

Of course there are only special types of scats that can be collected, but a series of typical, well-identified material of this kind, including certain bird droppings and castings, can be a useful aid in certain field investigations and schoolroom projects.

It occurs to me that a scat collection of extant animals, properly identified, should be of importance to the vertebrate paleontologist, who at times has to deal with coprolites found in the fossil record. For such a purpose, particular attention is directed to the difficulty of identification in certain animal groups, a fact emphasized in the following pages.

Stage setting for tracks. Many years ago, in his *Two Little Savages,* Ernest Thompson Seton described a method of getting good tracks by preparing for them. If you know of a place where mammals habitually travel, as on a trail, or near a den tree, or any other conceivable situation, you may prepare a smooth area of dust, or soft mud, as the case may be, over which a traveling mammal will leave good tracks under controlled conditions. It may be possible to use bait to attract certain species over prepared ground. Old tracks may be erased by smoothing over the surface like a clean slate. This general idea has possibilities for expansion and the exercise of ingenuity, not only for the casual student, but also for the field biologist who wishes to delve into the field of population studies and ecology.

Captive animals. Many people find it useful or interesting to keep small mammals in captivity for a short time for close observation, for sketching, or for serious study of mannerisms or other reactions throwing light on their life histories. This subject has many ramifications, and cannot be treated fully here. But the reader will find in the bibliography a few references to articles on live-trapping and types of traps used.

In this connection I would make a few comments. During chilly or cold weather a mouse sitting all night in a live trap without exercise becomes thoroughly chilled, and in really cold weather may die before morning. If a little cotton is placed in the trap chamber the mouse will make a nest and be comfortable. Also, there should be enough bait to serve as food during the night.

When small rodents are being transported, either in a car or by express, the container should have the usual food, and in lieu of water, some form of succulence, such as an apple or potato. It is well to nearly fill the container with excelsior or similar stiff but resilient material, so that the rodents may form burrows and not be injured by heavy food substances rattling about.

Literature. A rather random list of titles has been selected from the literature on mammals and placed at the back of the book. This bibliography may at first glance appear formidable to the beginner. I would suggest that the scientific literature on mammal life history or ecology is not unduly technical, however, and does contain fascinating information on the lives of these creatures that is not suspected by the general public. To the field biologist these titles are familiar, but may be useful as reminders.

For all readers such literature, if sought from time to time, would help outline the broad field of mammals and increase the enjoyment and understanding of the less well known animal life of our country.

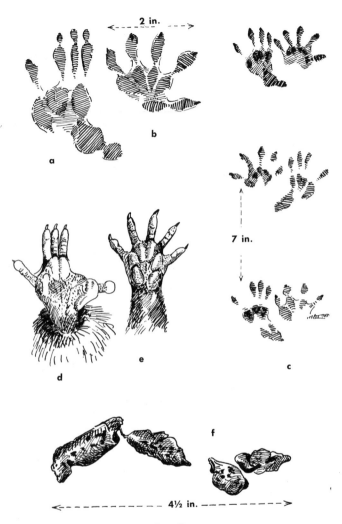

2 in.

7 in.

4½ in.

Fig. 1.   Opossum

a and b. Hind and front tracks, respectively, in mud (Okla.).
c. Trail pattern, walking, in mud.
d and e. Hind and front feet, showing unusual arrangement of the toes on the hind foot.
f. Opossum scat.

10

Opossum Family: Didelphidae

THE OPOSSUM, *Didelphis marsupialis,* is traditionally an inhabitant of the southeastern United States, but has spread as far west as California and Washington, and north to Michigan. Undoubtedly it will eventually occupy the greater part of the country, except the coldest and the most arid regions.

This slow-moving animal is not particular about what it eats. Small mammals, birds, eggs, insects, fruit, carrion, and garbage are all acceptable. Usually found in wooded areas, swamps, along streams or lakeshores, it seeks its shelter in old dens of other animals, in crevices under rocks, in hollow trees or logs, and often seeks safety by climbing a tree. In Texas I found the opossum in rough terrain, in oak forests, and in southern California in arid brushland.

I first found the strange, distinctive opossum tracks (shown in Fig. 1, a, b, c) years ago in Oklahoma, in the mud near a pond. Note the peculiar hind foot, in which the "big toe" is slanted inward, or even backward. There are 5 toes but the 3 middle toes tend to remain in a close group, separate from the others.

A common walking trail pattern (*c*) is similar to that of the raccoon — front and hind tracks side by side. However, this is not always the case. Sometimes the hind foot falls a little posterior to the front, and the steps may vary from 5½ to 11 inches. In snow the tail may leave a steady, sinuous drag mark, or short alternate marks on both sides.

Opossum scats (*f*) are unfortunately not distinctive and will vary in accordance with the kind of food eaten. Figure 1, f, gives the general character.

So far as we know, the opossum has no call beyond a low growl or a slight hissing when disturbed. At any rate it gives out no voice that would help direct attention to it.

Armadillo Family: Dasypodidae

FOR PROTECTION the skunk has adopted an evil smell, and the porcupine a coat of sharp spines, but the armadillo is covered with a coat of mail. The skin of animals is extremely versatile in its functions. It has produced the feathers of birds, the hair of mammals, in great variety of color and form. The horns of the pronghorn and the mountain sheep, and the furry velvet of deer antlers, are special adaptations of the hair-producing function of skin. It would be interesting to know by what long evolutionary steps the skin of the original armadillo ancestors developed, in lieu of the usual hairy coat, the hard shell that today covers most of the body of this strange burrowing nine-banded armadillo.

Dasypus novemcinctus is a product of South America, but has come up from the tropics to inhabit Mexico, most of Texas, western Louisiana and Arkansas, and the southern part of Oklahoma.

In some surfaces the tracks have been referred to as "hooflike." On occasion, too, the reticulated imprint of the "shell" may be seen in the dirt.

The armadillo feeds on insects, but in doing so, like the bear, it eats a large quantity of dirt and other debris. Figure 2, c, shows the droppings, which are mostly composed of clay. They are generally round and marble-like. These clay droppings suggest those of elk and deer after those animals have eaten mud at a mineral lick.

Here is a most efficient digger that can excavate many burrows, 7 or 8 inches in diameter and from about 2 to 15 feet in length. It also uses natural cavities. Since it digs and roots for insects and excavates anthills for food, these disturbances are also evidence of its presence. Note that certain skunks also root after insects, and peccaries seek food underground by rooting. Accordingly, one should try to find tracks or droppings, as aids to identification. Bears also disturb anthills, but ordinarily are not in the same habitat with the armadillos.

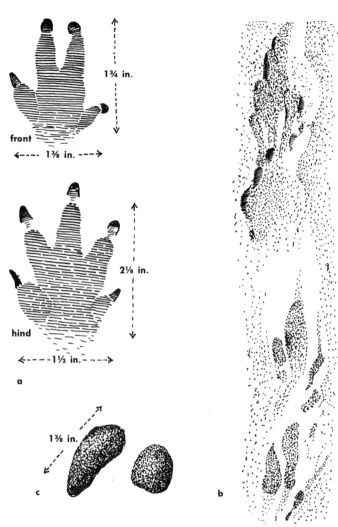

front

1¾ in.

←---- 1⅜ in. ----→

hind

2⅛ in.

←----1½ in.----→

a

1⅜ in.

c

b

Fig. 2.   Armadillo sign

a. Tracks in detail, about ⅔ natural size; these unusual in that all the toes are showing.
b. Tracks faintly shown in dust (from photograph by Dr. W. P. Taylor, courtesy of the U.S. Fish and Wildlife Service).
c. Droppings, about ⅔ natural size.

13

Eastern Mole, Starnose Mole, and Shrew-Mole

Mole Family: Talpidae

THERE IS an amazing confusion about moles and certain rodents. Pocket gophers, and in some places even field mice, are often referred to as moles. Not everything that works underground is a mole! Therefore it is worth while to give some attention to the five groups of moles and the signs they leave for identification.

Moles have soft fur, a compact body with a rather naked snout, minute eyes, and spadelike front feet, altogether well adapted to their subterranean life. You are not likely to find footprints, but the earth mounds and tunnels reveal their presence (Figs. 3 and 4).

The runways consist of raised ridges in the surface of the ground, pushed up as the mole progresses just under the surface. These will vary in appearance with the character of the soil. They must not be confused with the earth cores left in snow tunnels by pocket gophers (for which see Fig. 84, b). Mole ridges have a tunnel underneath; earth cores left by pocket gophers, lying on top of the ground after the snow melts, are solid. In certain types of firm earth there will be tracks in the crust where the mole has raised these ridges. In at least one recorded instance such solid earthen casts were found in an area occupied only by the Townsend mole, *Scapanus townsendi,* pocket gophers being absent. This showed that occasionally the mole too may excavate into snow tunnels. There is also an insect that makes a tunnel like the mole's, but very much smaller; from this it is called the mole cricket (see Fig. 188, a).

In excavating, the mole pushes the dirt out to let it roll where it will. Consequently a molehill has the appearance of an eruption, with no indication of burrow entrance. The pocket gopher pushes the dirt away mostly in one direction, so that the entrance is at or near one edge of the mound, at least off center, and the final earth plug marking the entrance, in a depression, is generally obvious.

The brownish-black scats, or droppings, of the hairytail mole

14

average about 10 x 2.5 mm in size, and are somewhat cylindrical, tapering to points. They dry quickly to a hard consistency with finely pitted surface, composed of soil particles, and chitinous remains of insects, which appear as shiny spots.

The eastern mole *Scalopus aquaticus,* of the East and as far west as southern Minnesota, Nebraska, Oklahoma, and Texas, the California mole, *Scapanus latimanus,* of the Pacific Coast states, and the hairytail mole, *Parascalops breweri,* of the northeastern states and adjacent parts of Canada, are similar in appearance and similar in habits. The mound and runway structure described above apply pretty well to these, though the mounds of *Parascalops* are smaller and the runways less marked than those of the other two. However, there is great individual variation.

The starnose mole, *Condylura cristata,* also of the northeastern

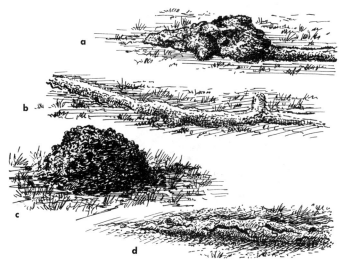

Fig. 3.   Mole workings

a. A runway from the right ending in a small mound, which is 5 x 8½ in. in diameter, and 2 in. high. The runway at the right is 1½ in. wide (Point Lobos, Cal.).

b. Mole runway at Point Lobos, diam. 2 in. In loose sand the diameter varied from 5 to 6 in.

c. Typical molehill.

d. Another type of runway, where the firm crust was raised and cracked as the animal passed underneath (near Redding, Cal.).

Fig. 4.　Molehills in Wisconsin

a. A line of molehills on a golf course.
b. Typical lumpy structure of molehill.

part of the United States and adjacent parts of Canada, differs somewhat in habits, and may come out of subterranean runways and continue them in the grass, or through the snow, and may be found on the snow surface. It also enters water, and may have underwater entrances, and travels under the shore ice of stream borders.

The little shrew-mole, *Neurotrichus gibbsi,* 4½ inches long, of the Pacific Coast from southwestern British Columbia to Monterey County of California, is even less orthodox. Not only is it a good swimmer but it may climb into bushes.

Lloyd Ingles speaks of it thus:

Among the litter of rotting logs and dead leaves in the shady ravines close to the coast of California are little runways that form an irregular but intricate network of semi-subterranean tunnels and passages. . . . If the shade is not too thick, one may possibly catch a glimpse of a tiny mammal, resembling a large shrew, tapping the ground with its long snout, as it walks slowly along in search of food. This is the shrew-mole, which . . . resembles both a shrew and a mole, and is about intermediate between them in size.

This is one of the rare finds for the enterprising naturalist.

Northern Water Shrew, Arctic Shrew, and
Shorttail Shrew

Shrew Family: Soricidae

THE TINY SHREWS, often mistakenly referred to as "those sharp-nosed little mice," or "moles," are active, high-spirited creatures that keep busy hunting insects and other small animal life, or carrion. A large variety of species and subspecies is included in the genus *Sorex,* the longtail shrews, and these range over most of the North American continent. I have found the Arctic shrew, *Sorex arcticus,* of the far north particularly interesting, a handsome morsel of animal life, rich brown above, paler on the sides, white below, in attractive tricolor pattern. In the earlier days of travel by dog team, they used to find our stored feed, dried salmon, and nibble at it persistently. On one occasion on the Alaska Peninsula, I heard thin squeaky voices in the tall grass. I watched quietly and had glimpses of tiny forms flashing by the little open-

Fig. 5 (opposite)

a. Tracks, in snow, showing tail drag. *A, b, c, d, e,* and *f show* tracks from Wyoming.
b. Tracks in light snow, without tail marks.
c. In this snow trail the feet were dragging.
d. Here the tail made a continuous mark.
e. On firm snow the animal didn't flounder; the trail shows common variations.
f. More irregular pattern here, often found even in a short length of trail.
g. Scat of *Sorex,* about natural size (Wyo.).
h. Scat of *Blarina brevicauda,* natural size (New York, furnished by W. J. Hamilton, Jr.).
i. Scat of *Cryptotis parva,* natural size (furnished by E. P. Walker).
j. Track of *Cryptotis parva,* natural size.

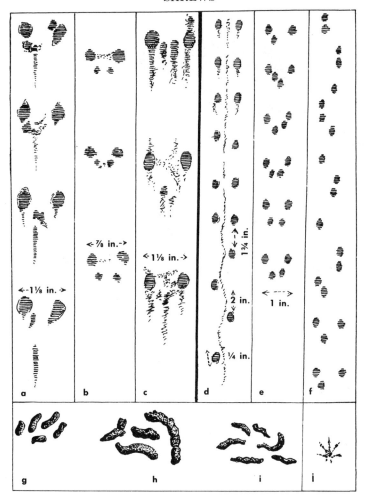

Fig. 5. Shrew tracks and droppings

a

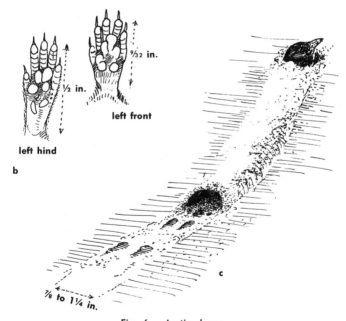

½ in.

⁹⁄₃₂ in.

left front

left hind

b

⅞ to 1¼ in.

c

Fig. 6.   Arctic shrew

a. Arctic shrew.
b. Feet, enlarged to show the tubercle pattern of the underside.
c. The shrew dives into the snow, to come out some distance beyond.

ings in the dense cover. I could only guess what might be the intimate affairs of those diminutive mammals.

Shrews are chiefly nocturnal, but may be found about in daytime as well. These so-called longtail shrews use the tunnels of moles, mice, and the larger shorttail shrews, and they find shelter under bark, logs, and the forest litter. On the Pacific Coast I have found burrows that appeared to have been dug by the shrews themselves, but there is considerable doubt that this is a general practice. Their nests are globular, of shredded leaves or other material, even rabbit hair.

You will seldom find shrew tracks except in snow, though they may be looked for in areas of dust or mud. In snow the shrew trail is much like that of the white-footed mouse, but, at least in the case of the small longtail shrews, the tracks and track pattern are smaller. The shrew trail will measure about 1 inch in width, or straddle, and may reach 1¼ inches, as compared with 1½ to 2 inches of the white-footed mouse. Also, the shrew track pattern appears a little shorter, as if the hind feet do not reach as far beyond the forefoot tracks as do those of the mouse. We must note, too, the depth and texture of snow. In loose fluffy snow the mark of the tail may show, as well as drag marks of the feet. On a thin film of snow over a snow crust or on ice, tail marks are normally lacking and footprints more distinct.

The gait of the shrew varies, even in a section of some 10 or 12 feet of its trail. Notice the many variations shown in Figure 5.

In soft snow the shrew has a habit shared by several other mammals. It will dive in and travel under the surface. The course of such a snow tunnel often may be detected by the slight ridging of the snow. The veteran naturalist Dr. E. W. Nelson reported an amazing incident of following such an under-snow shrew trail on the Yukon River for a distance of a mile or more.

While resting beside a tiny stream in an open mountain meadow in Wyoming, I saw a shrew swimming under water, upstream, encased in a silvery film of air. This was the large northern water shrew, *Sorex palustris,* the one with the pure black and silvery white uniform. It is especially adapted to life around borders of streams and ponds, and takes readily to water. I have never seen its tracks, but they would be larger than those of its smaller relatives, about the size of those of the white-footed mouse.

Blarina brevicauda, the shorttail shrew, represents another group of large size, with tracks somewhat larger than those shown in Figure 5. I found these animals commonly in the plowed fields, and in many other locations in Minnesota and eastern North Dakota. In winter they shared with the meadow voles, or field mice, the space under the shore ice shelf along the Red River, formed when the water had dropped to a new ice level. They have runways in moss and other vegetation after the manner of the field mice, make their own burrows, and also use the burrows and runways of small rodents. These are common throughout the eastern half of the United States, and adjacent parts of Canada.

There are some small species of shrew, slightly over 3 inches long, including the tail. These are the pygmy shrew, *Microsorex hoyi,* and the least shrew, *Cryptotis parva.* The least shrew occupies the eastern half of the United States, and becomes very common in Mexico and Central America. The pygmy shrew is more northern in its distribution, being found in northeastern United States and across the continent from Labrador to Alaska. One should also mention the extremely rare gray, or desert, shrew, *Notiosorex crawfordi.* It is found only among the desert shrubs of Texas, New Mexico, Arizona, southern Nevada and California, and down into Lower California and Mexico proper. Probably these members of the shrew family are the smallest of all mammals, and Figure 5, j, could very well represent the smallest mammal track in the world.

Long-eared Myotis

Bats: Chiroptera

No NEED TO LOOK for the footprints of bats! Their limbs are so enmeshed in a highly developed flight membrane that they do not bother to walk, except for a short distance when they find themselves on a horizontal surface, or when they crawl into hiding in a narrow crevice to roost. But they *can* walk, and I have seen one swim ashore when it accidentally got into the water of a pond. The sketch in Figure 7, a, shows the trail of a long-eared myotis that was turned loose on fine sand. Note the *outside* prints of the front wrist, just outside the print of the hind foot, and the scrape of the wing at the end when it flew off.

Bats may often be detected by the deposit of guano on the ground or floor beneath their roosting places. Figure 7 illustrates bat droppings, which may be distinguished from those of mice by the insect fragments of which they consist. There is also a tendency to be segmented, as shown in the enlarged view.

Looking for bats can be alluring. Some, such as the red bat, *Lasiurus borealis,* and the large hoary bat, *Lasiurus cinereus,* may be found during the day hanging from the twigs of trees. Others hide in crevices behind the bark of trees, under loose shingles, or in cracks in large rocks. It is well known that several species swarm in caves and assemble in attics and barns. They come to life at twilight and swoop through the darkening night after the insects on which most of the bats in this hemisphere feed. Anyone can look for bats, since they occur, in a variety of species, east and west, north and south, though they do not venture north of the northern forests.

23

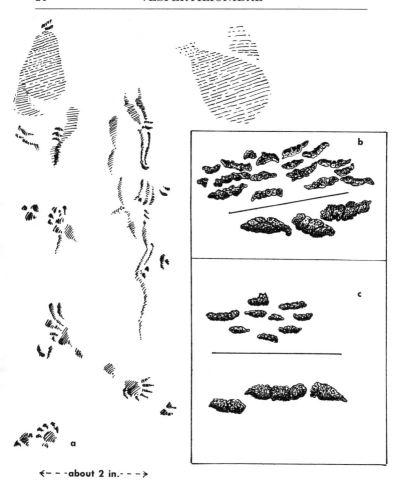

←- - -about 2 in.- - -→

Fig. 7. Bat tracks and droppings

a. Tracks of a bat walking on fine sand, and taking off in flight.
b. Guano, bat of unknown species, probably *Myotis*. Upper samples, natural size; lower, enlarged (Jackson Lake, Wyo.).
c. Droppings of long-eared myotis, *Myotis evotis*. Upper samples natural size; lower, enlarged.

Grizzly with cubs

Bear Family: Ursidae

Black, Grizzly, and Alaska Brown Bears

THESE three bears are discussed together because there are so many similarities. The Alaska brown bear and related species occupy southern Alaska. The grizzly group is found over most of Alaska, western Canada, western Montana, and the Yellowstone Park region. The black bears exist nearly everywhere in wooded areas.

In the spring of 1921 I was camping on Robertson River in the Alaska Range. One morning when I walked over to the river for a pail of water I found grizzly tracks in the sand. They led up to within five yards of my tent, where the bear had been sniffing about during the night. I had plaster of paris with me and took impressions of the tracks, almost the first track casts I had ever made, which are shown in Figure 8, b. These tracks illustrate the long front claws characterizing the grizzly, in contrast to the shorter ones of the black bear (Fig. 8, c). The incident of finding the tracks shows how much can be added to outdoor experience by recognition of animal signs.

To illustrate something else I shall tell of another experience in the same part of Alaska. Prospectors in the Tanana River region spoke of the "glacier bear" and said you could distinguish the tracks, which are "halfway in size between grizzly and black bear tracks." I found this bear, which proved to be a small-sized whitish grizzly, not the true "glacier bear." And indeed it really was possible to distinguish its tracks in many cases. It was definitely smaller than the normal large grizzly whose cast I had obtained. Was this then a different species? Different sex? I still do not know. This experience emphasizes the importance of allowing for deviation in size of tracks due to sex, age, individual

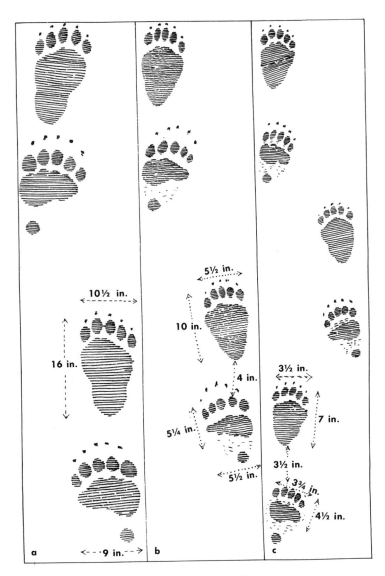

Fig. 8. Walking gaits of bears

a. Alaska brown bear.   b. Grizzly.   c. Black bear.

26

variation, as well as condition of mud, sand, or snow. Remember, too, that the round heel pad of the front foot, shown in these perfect tracks, very often does not register.

The trails of Figure 8 show the typical walking gait, hind foot a little forward of the front foot on the same side. Observations on a cub grizzly showed that when walking very slowly the hind foot registered exactly in the front-foot track, though when stepping out more vigorously the hind foot overstepped the front-foot track to produce the pattern here described.

These variations in track pattern are shown in Figure 9, d. Here the female black bear placed the hind foot squarely in the front print (in the lower part of the figure), then began to overstep the front track (in the upper part) to produce the pattern so often seen. Note that in *c* the cub did not let down the heel of the hind foot, so all of these footprints resemble front tracks.

Notice, too, that the "big" toe of the bear foot is the *outer* one, not the inner one of the human foot. You will find in bear tracking that in dust or shallow mud quite often the "little" inside toe leaves no mark, so the footprint appears to be four-toed. Or the inner toe may be only faintly seen (Fig. 9, a).

In Figure 10 we have the grizzly gallop in *a*, black bear gallop in *e*, with hind feet out in front with each leap. These show two gallop patterns that, with still other variations, may be made by any of these bears.

All three of these bear groups often have well-established trails. Those of the Alaska brown bear, especially on the open tundra of Alaska Peninsula, are striking. They take several forms. In marshy tide flats or along the salmon streams, they appear like any simple trail through heavy vegetation. On the drier tundra of the uplands they take the form of two parallel ruts, made by the right and left feet, where bears had traveled for years (Fig. 10, c). I have walked in such bear trails but found it awkward, for the

Left hind foot and
right front foot of
Alaska Brown Bear

Fig. 9

Tracks of yearling grizzly and black bear cub and mother

a. Yearling grizzly.   Hind track, 6½ in. long by 3¾ in. wide; front, 4 in. x 4 in.
b. Cub's front track, 2½ in. both length and width.
c. Trail of cub, in erratic pattern.
d. Trail of mother, showing two pattern types.

brown bear's hips and shoulders are much greater than a man's, and I found it necessary to spraddle widely to keep in the ruts.

There is still another type of brown bear trail, shown in Figure 10, d. Sometimes these big brown bears get the habit of stepping repeatedly in the same footprints, until a series of pits in zigzag fashion are developed. In order to travel in these I found it necessary to make a half hop from one to the other. It is interesting to note that on mossy tundra this type of trail, if abandoned for some years, grows up in grass because the seeds find bare soil available in the bottom of the pits. So you may find a zigzag line of grass clumps marking an old brown bear trail. In the trails of both the black bear and the grizzly you will also occasionally find a tendency toward the formation of zigzag pits in locations where the bears have stepped in each other's footsteps for years.

During June, and on through the summer, the salmon ascend the streams to spawn. Then the brown bears come into the lowlands to feed on the salmon. You find their trails, well worn, along the banks of the streams, and find resting places scooped out in the vegetation among the willows and alders. Sometimes there are beds specially prepared by scraping together a pile of moss, perhaps a dozen feet in diameter and apparently to serve as a mattress. Once when I found some of these piles of vegetation I wondered if they had served to cover some stored food, but did not find evidence of it. Rather, these seemed to serve as comfortable mossy mattresses.

In wooded country it will be noticed that a bear trail will go under obstructions that an elk, for example, would have to go around.

Then there are the bear trees. Bears will bite and pull off strips of bark from the trunks of pine, spruce, and fir trees, sometimes girdling the trees. Having pulled away the bark, they will scrape off the juicy substance on the wood with their incisor teeth, leaving vertical tooth marks (Fig. 11, a). I tasted some of this. At first there was syrupy sweetness, followed immediately by turpentine! But the bears like it.

Sometimes a young black bear will climb an aspen tree. The claw marks remain in the soft smooth bark and a scab forms on each, so that the climb remains recorded for the life of the tree (Fig. 11, b).

There is still a third tree. Bears like to rub themselves, usually on a tree, but occasionally on a bush or stump. They will rub and rub, sometimes grasping the tree and clawing it, sometimes biting it as they stand on their hind legs. Often this tree is in a prominent place, on a point or beside the trail, where it easily comes to the notice of the bear, and it is rubbed and scratched repeatedly until we recognize it as an established "bear tree" (Fig. 11, c, and Fig. 12, a). Generally pitch oozes out and you will find hairs stuck in

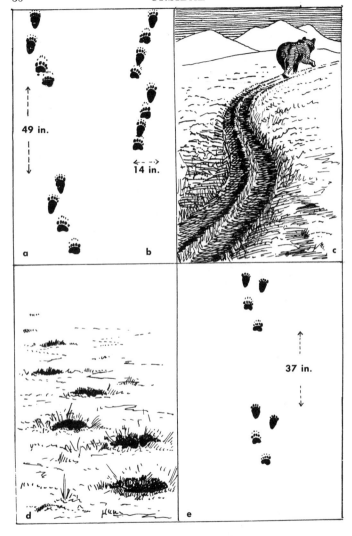

Fig. 10

Grizzly, Alaska brown bear, and black bear tracks

Fig. 11.   Bear trees

a. Tree stripped for the juicy pulp under the bark.
b. Old healed scars on an aspen, where a bear had climbed.
c. A grizzly rubbing tree (Alaska).

it, or clinging to the bark. Such hairs should not be confused with buffalo hairs in places like Yellowstone Park, for instance, since the buffalo also rubs trees (see p. 311). This type of bear tree has been construed as a signal tree, a means of showing the height of the bear and serving as a challenge to rivals. Undoubtedly it can serve secondarily as a "sign" post, similar to the scent post of the dog tribe, but it is primarily a place for comfortable rubbing. In national forests or in national parks you will often find trail signs chewed up by bears. Bears like to "fool around," I suppose, like a boy walking along and idly rubbing the pickets of a fence. Often I have seen a black bear straddle a small pine sapling, letting it rub his belly as he walked over it until it sprang up behind.

Bear droppings may be confusing at times, though generally they have a distinctive form, with a tendency to maintain a fairly even

Fig. 10 (opposite)

a. Grizzly tracks, fast lope, in snow (Yellowstone Natl. Park).
b. Grizzly tracks, slow lope, in snow (Alaska).
c. Double-rutted trail of Alaska brown bear on high tundra.
d. Staggered prints of Alaska brown bears, each bear stepping in the same place repeatedly over a long period of time.
e. Fast lope of a black bear.

diameter (Fig. 13). Bears will eat meat whenever they can, killing animals as large as a moose — or feeding on carrion. On such a diet the scats are likely to consist chiefly of hair. Remember, however, that a bear is pretty much of a vegetarian, and a large proportion, probably the majority, of the scats you find will consist of grass, sometimes roots. There may be a mass of wood debris mixed with ants, or a mass of pine nuts, or berries in season. Coyotes eat pine nuts too, but their droppings are smaller. A straight diet of strawberries may produce a semi-liquid mass. The same applies to a diet of fish, as with the big brown bear of southern Alaska. Grizzly and brown bear droppings are larger than those of the black bear, but they do occasionally overlap in size.

There are other feeding signs. You may find an old log turned over or torn apart where a bear has been looking for beetles or ants (see Fig. 12, b). Rocks are turned over for the same purpose. Anthills are scooped out, so that the swarming ants can be licked up in quantity. In Yellowstone Park I found spots in meadows torn up where a bear had scented an underground ant colony, and in the same park my brother found them turning over buffalo chips for beetles. Once in Alaska I found a bank swallow nest clawed out of a bank by a black bear, the claw marks being obvious. Bears dig for plant roots, and sometimes their diggings are

Fig. 12.   Bear trees and black bears foraging

a. A tree clawed by a black bear (Great Smoky Mts., Tenn.).
b. Black bear tearing open a rotten log for insects. An anthill in the foreground has been scooped out for the same purpose.

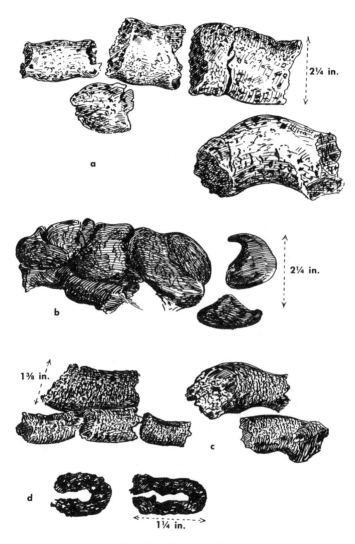

Fig. 13.   Bear droppings

a and b. Grizzly scats.
c and d. Black bear scats, d being that of a cub.

33

very prominent, as if someone had been sporadically digging a garden plot. Or you may find an excavation where a bear has dug a ground squirrel from its burrow, or a pocket gopher's root cache.

Occasionally you might find a food cache where a bear has covered part of a carcass of a deer or other animal for future use. This is very similar to the cache of the mountain lion, and I know of no way of distinguishing the two except by finding an occasional track or some other sign of the animal nearby.

There is another indication that comes very close home. If you are camping in certain of the national parks or if you are living on a ranch or in a camp in black bear country and find a garbage can tipped over and the contents scattered, you may know that you have been visited by a black bear.

Dens for hibernation are not often found. They may be in a hollow under an upturned root, in the case of black bears, or in any of many natural cavities. On Unimak Island, Alaska, I found big brown bear dens in long underground tunnels which were natural cavities in the lava beds. In interior Alaska I found grizzly dens excavated in the base of a hill. One day my brother showed me a den, excavated in August, that he had found high on a mountain slope. We crawled inside to see what it was like, feeling quite certain that the bear was not at home. (See Fig. 14.)

Bears leave plenty of sign, and its interpretation furnishes a good story. They also produce sound to express a variety of emotions. If you find yourself near a bear, whether black, grizzly,

Fig. 14.   Grizzly bear den
on a high slope (Mt. McKinley Natl. Park, Alaska)

or brown, and he makes a coughing sound or "chops" his jaws,
look out! The bear is in a threatening or surly mood. Sometimes
when the animal is more mildly annoyed, it will growl in a low,
smooth-voiced manner that is hard to describe. The most pitiful
sound I have heard in nature has come from a bear in great trouble,
as when it is wounded. It is a strong, variable, moaning sound,
so realistically human in its quality that it is heartrending to listen
to. The bears, then, express themselves with a considerable variety
of growls, coughs, sniffs, and certain whining or bawling sounds.
Ordinarily, however, as you find these animals in the field, you
are not likely to hear their voices.

Polar Bear

Few of us have the chance to trail the polar bear of the genus
Thalarctos. The only time I ever saw one in the wilds was at
Hudson Bay in 1915, and it was on mossy tundra and left no tracks.
The footprint shown in Figure 15, a, was obtained in the Woodland
Park Zoo in Seattle, where a polar bear was induced to step in
moist sand. The polar bear soles are extremely hairy, hence the
various pads are not clear-cut. Figure 15, b, from a photograph,
shows the over-all shape of some tracks but does not reveal details
of foot structure.

Any bear tracks that you are likely to see on the ice of the polar
sea or the islands of the Arctic coast, or on the islands of Bering
Sea, should be those of the polar bear.

The droppings of this bear consist of vegetation or remains of
seal, fish, or other carnivorous fare. Contrary to traditional natural
history, the polar bear has been found to feed on vegetation as
well as meat, specifically in the Bering Sea and on the Arctic
islands.

Available photographs suggest that occasionally the polar bear may produce a simple alternating print pattern, as in the right-hand trail in Figure 15, c, in which case the hind and front foot tracks would register. No doubt the patterns vary, sometimes with the hind foot registering in the front track as noted above, sometimes overstepping, just as the black bear's does.

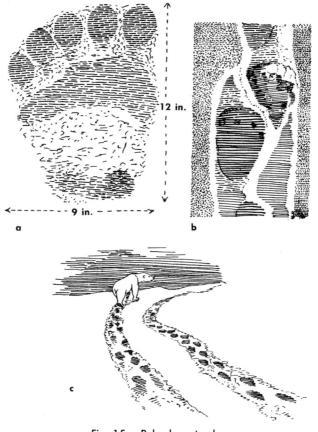

12 in.

9 in.

a

b

c

Fig. 15. Polar bear tracks

a. In sand (Woodland Park Zoo, Seattle).
b. In snow (Arctic Is., Canada, from photograph by C. O. Handley, Jr.).
c. The snow trails.

Raccoon and Ringtail Families:
Procyonidae and Bassariscidae

HERE IS an interesting little group in our animal world. Its members inhabit the southern portion of our continent, though the raccoon finds its way north into southern Canada.

The tracks of this group tend to be plantigrade, or flat-footed, like those of the bears, only in miniature. The ringtail cat, however, does not follow this pattern. Figure 16 shows the tracks and scats of this group, drawn to scale for comparison.

Raccoon

The well-known raccoon, *Procyon lotor,* may be found from the Atlantic to the Pacific, from the southern states to lower Canada. It generally avoids the dry desert, but I saw its handlike tracks at a watering hole among the cacti in southern Texas. On the sandy beaches of the Pacific Coast you may find it beachcombing.

The track is distinctive and easily identified, as shown in Figure 17. It has five toes on front and hind feet and, lumbering, rolypoly animal that it is, its plantigrade feet leave a track pattern some-

37

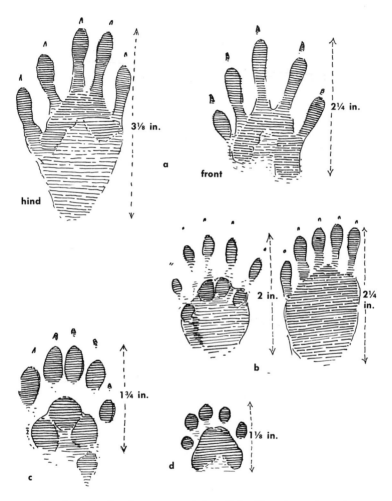

Fig. 16. Tracks of raccoon and ringtail families, drawn to scale

   a. Hind and front tracks of raccoon.
   b. Track of kinkajou.   c. Track of coati.
   d. Track of *Bassariscus astutus*, or ringtail.

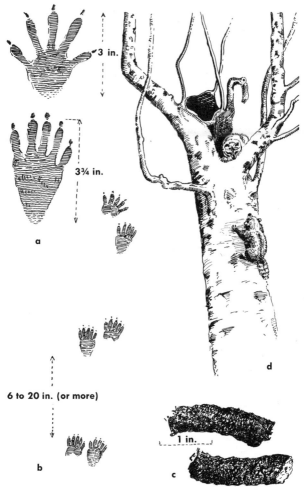

Fig. 17.   Raccoon

a. Typical tracks in mud, the front track above.
b. The track pattern, walking.
c. Rather typical droppings, with lack of taper at the ends.
d. Raccoon tree, a sycamore (Ariz.).

what suggestive of that of the bear's in miniature. Raccoon tracks, however, are usually paired, with the left hind foot placed beside the right forefoot as the animal walks along (see Fig. 17, b). As pointed out in the discussion of the opossum, the track patterns of these two animals are similar, and in soft sand, where toes do not show, identification is difficult.

Raccoon scats are by no means as readily identified as the tracks. They often have a granular appearance, tend to be even in diameter. In color they range from black to reddish, sometimes bleached to white. Many samples are irregular in shape. On the whole they may be confused with those of the larger skunks or opossum. In some areas scats may be deposited on large limbs of trees or logs, in which case that fact is indicative. This animal is omnivorous, and relishes flesh, fruit, nuts, corn and other garden crops, and carrion.

In Minnesota along the Red River, we used to identify the raccoon trees by the claw scratches on the bark, made as the animal climbed. They were usually elm trees, but occasionally an oak or basswood. First we looked for a hole in the trunk, where a large limb had broken away and a cavity had been formed *downward* into the trunk. Having found a big tree with such an apparent cavity high on the trunk, we would check by looking for the scratches on the bark. In more southern woods the sycamore may be the raccoon tree, as in Figure 17, d. Raccoons also utilize a variety of dens in the ground. They may use a hollow log, or cavities among rocks. A most unusual instance is reported by W. H. Bergtold, who found a raccoon with a family of young housed in a magpie nest!

Although I have lived in raccoon country many years, I cannot describe the call from personal experience. Yet several writers have described this animal as quite vocal, and Seton, referring to its call as the "whicker," describes it as a "long drawn tremulous 'whoo-oo-oo-oo.'" He compares it with a querulous call he says it may be confounded with, the call of the screech owl.

Coati

Related to the raccoon, and sharing its inquisitive traits, is the coati, *Nasua narica*. Its true home is the southern tropics, but its range extends north through Mexico, into the southern border of Texas, and the southeastern quarter of Arizona and southeastern corner of New Mexico.

This venturesome long-tailed and long-snouted animal is a successful inhabitant of the jungle, and with encouragement be-

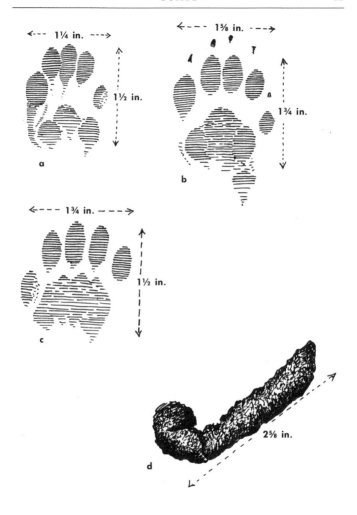

Fig. 18.   Coati tracks and scat

a, b, c. Tracks in mud. In a the toes are held unusually close together.
d. Dropping, about ⅔ natural size.

Coatis

comes very friendly with people. At the headquarters of Barro
Colorado Island, in the Canal Zone, some of these coatis had
learned to walk on a slack wire, balancing precariously with the
agile body and long tail, to seek the pieces of bread suspended near
the middle of the wire. In the wild, their food habits appear to
be similar to those of the raccoon. They are fond of fruits and
other vegetation, and pick up any birds' eggs or young birds they
may find, as well as insects or other small creatures they are able
to capture.

As with the raccoon and opossum, the scats will vary in appearance in accordance with the type of food eaten.

The tracks shown in Figure 18 are from captive animals, since
I failed to find them in the jungle. Possibly at times the long heel
shows in the track, but I did not find it so in the samples I had.

Kinkajou

Kinkajou, *Potos flavus,* is only a name to most of us, suggesting
that vague world we know as the tropical jungle — and perhaps
suggesting the traditional "tooth and claw" so commonly associated
with that lush green world. As a matter of fact, when kept as a
pet the kinkajou has a genial, friendly disposition.

This animal ranges northward into tropical regions of Mexico,
and thus becomes a member of the North American fauna. During
a few days spent in the Panama Canal Zone I had hoped to have
a glimpse of a kinkajou, possibly among the limbs of a tree, using

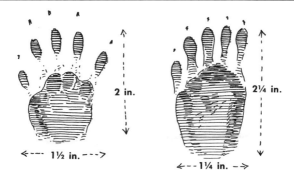

Fig. 19

Front and hind tracks of captive kinkajou, in mud

its prehensile tail as I saw the white-faced monkeys doing. But I saw none, nor did I find the tracks.

For the tracks in Figure 19 I called on a cooperative kinkajou in the National Zoological Park which allowed itself to be handled, and accommodatingly stepped in some mud. The tracks suggest those of the raccoon; not surprising in view of its close relationship.

Ringtail or Cacomistle

The secretive ringtail, *Bassariscus astutus,* known also as caco-mistle, is a warm-climate animal of Central America and Mex-ico. In the United States it has found congenial habitat in the West and Southwest — southern Oregon, California, southern Nevada, Arizona, parts of Utah and Colorado, and parts of New Mexico and Texas.

The ringtail is strictly nocturnal and seldom seen, and in its dry habitat the tracks are not readily found. However, in Cottonwood Cave, New Mexico, in 1939, by the light of a candle I found many of its footprints in the loose dirt on the rock ledges, and some of the scats shown here. In this cave the ringtail had been feeding on bats almost exclusively. The tracks are quite catlike and there is not a noticeable difference between front and hind tracks. This is one of the animals that have all five toes.

The food is quite varied, and includes rodents, bats, insects, and fruit. Consequently the scats vary. In Texas, where miscella-neous food was eaten, the scats were often found broken up in short lengths, and crumbled easily when dry (see upper sample, Fig. 20, d).

The ringtail finds shelter, and makes its nest, in hollow trees, cavities in rock piles or cliffs, and in caves.

Little seems to have been reported on the voice of the ringtail, although it is known to produce a bark like that of a small dog. I have never heard it.

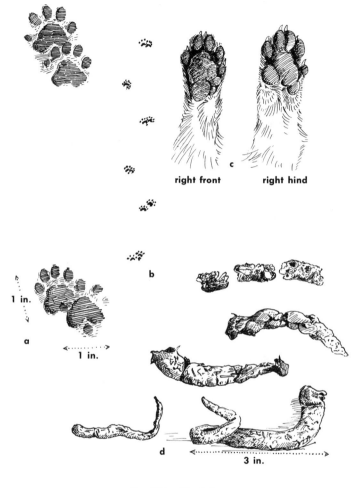

Fig. 20. Ringtail

a. Typical tracks, in soft dirt, hind track partly covering front track.
b. The trail pattern.   c. Feet (after Seton).
d. Scats, showing great differences in size and shape. Upper sample, from Texas (1950), contains insects; other samples, from New Mexico (1939), contain mammal remains.

Weasel Family: Mustelidae

IN THE game, or profession, of animal tracking it will add interest and value to your efforts to keep in mind group characteristics. The skunk, for example, is far different from the slender weasel, yet both can produce an offensive odor. The weasel family is a vigorous group of animals that have dispersed themselves into all conceivable niches of our natural environment. The otter and the mink took to the water, the sea otter developed a marine life, the fisher and marten found the coniferous forests, the wolverine developed a powerful physique and took to timberline and the sub-arctic. The skunk concocted a vile smell for protection so that it could poke leisurely about in the leaves of the woods or in the meadows for insects and other easy game. The badger, with the powerful forelimbs, explores underground. And the agile little weasel, a bold and persistent hunter with a great zest for life, explores everywhere.

The feet of this family have five toes, both front and hind (Fig. 21), though the fifth toe track may not show. There is a tendency in the group to form a twin-print pattern in the snow (Fig. 23, b).

Perhaps the scats shown in Figure 22 illustrate again how similar they are. There is much overlapping in size among some of them.

As you note the differences in the tracks of this weasel group in the field, you will be able to read in the trail something of the diverse characters and mental traits of the animals that left the footprints.

Shorttail (Ermine), Longtail, and Least Weasels

Weasels are distributed over the whole continent and are familiar to most people. Familiar, too, should be the twin prints of their feet in snow country. Weasels traveling in search of prey leap here and there in energetic fashion, and you will find their slender snow trails suddenly changing direction, doubling back, looping around here and there, disappearing under a half-buried log to re-appear farther on. Weasel tracks are eloquent. Looked at knowingly, they reveal the character of the nosy, eager little hunter.

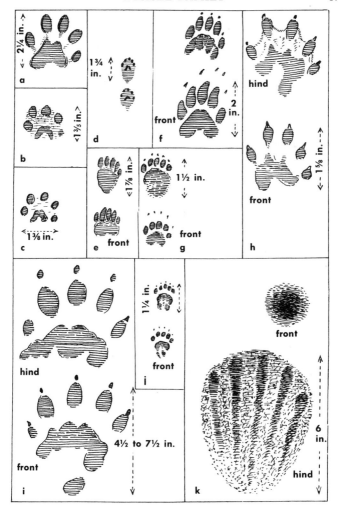

Fig. 21. Tracks of Mustelidae, approximately in proportionate sizes

a. Fisher.   b. Marten.   c. Mink.   d. Weasel.
e. Hognose skunk.   f. Badger.   g. Striped skunk.
h. River otter.   i. Wolverine.   j. Spotted skunk.   k. Sea otter.

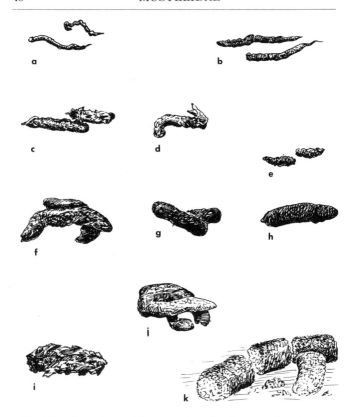

Fig. 22. Droppings of the weasel family, in proportionate sizes. The diameters given are variable.

a. Shorttail weasel, *Mustela erminea muricus.* Diam. ³⁄₁₆ in.
b. Longtail weasel, *Mustela frenata nevadensis.* Diam. ¼ in.
c. Mink, *Mustela vison.* Diam. ⅜ in.
d. Marten, *Martes americana.* Diam. ⅜ in.
e. Spotted skunk, *Spilogale* sp. Diam. ¼ in.
f. Wolverine, *Gulo luscus.* Diam. ⅝ in.
g. Badger, *Taxidea taxus.* Diam. ⅝ in.
h. Striped skunk, *Mephitis* sp. Diam. ⅝ in.
i. River otter, *Lutra canadensis.* Diam. ½ in.
j. Fisher, *Martes pennanti.* Diam. ⅝ in.
k. Sea otter, *Enhydra lutris.* Diam. 1½ in.

Shorttail Weasel (Ermine)

When running in snow the weasel's hind feet usually register in the front tracks, nearly or completely, so that the trail appears as a line of twin prints (Fig. 23, b). Usually, though not always, these fall one slightly ahead of the other. Often, too, one leap is short and the next one long, producing an irregularity in spacing — alternating short and long. In deeper snow the footprints of the short leap are connected by a drag mark, thus producing a very characteristic pattern (see Fig. 24).

One day we were walking through the winter woods in Wyoming when my companion said, "Look at the weasel!" Some hundred feet away, a white face accented with the black eyes and dark nose protruded from the snow, regarding us intently. It ducked out of sight, then reappeared a few feet away. This was repeated several times, and then we saw it no more. This is characteristic, the weasel readily diving into snow as if it were water. Often the trail will disappear into a neat round hole in the snow, to reappear some distance beyond.

Although the twin-print pattern is a common one, there are many variations. See Figure 23, d, for these.

The accompanying sketches of tracks require interpretation. Space does not permit inclusion of tracks of the numerous species, which vary enormously in size. The three basic species are: shorttail weasel (ermine or weasel), *Mustela erminea* (about 15 inches long in the North to about 9 inches in the Southwest); longtail weasel, *M. frenata;* and least weasel, *M. rixosa.* The least weasel is about 6 to 9 inches long, and the longtail weasel may be from 12 to 20 inches long. Each group has a variety of subspecies of different sizes, and often the two sexes of the same form are strikingly different in size. Add to this variations due to the character of the snow, and you have a complex scale of size values. However, weasel tracks fall into a general pattern, and if one determines which weasel forms occur in a given locality, tracks of the two basic species may be distinguished fairly well.

Some large weasels will leap upward of 6 feet, and an 8-foot leap has been recorded in western Wyoming. *M. frenata* can leap 20 to 51 inches, while in the same locality *M. erminea* leaps 13 to 40 inches. In Alaska some least weasel tracks showed leaps up to 23 inches.

There is also a difference in the width of the track pattern, or straddle. For the least weasel it will be about 1¼ to 1⅝ inches in soft snow. For *M. frenata* in Wyoming it may be as much as 3 inches in width.

Weasels have five toes, but the fifth toe does not always show. In fact, it is only under exceptional circumstances that the toes will show clearly.

The scats are long and slender, dark brown or black in color. They vary in size between subspecies, but may overlap in measurements. In practice, a large collection of weasel scats may be assorted between larger and smaller forms, probably with few errors. But it would be difficult to allocate properly a single scat specimen in the intermediate size range. Scat contents may be expected to consist of rodent fur and bits of bone, more rarely feathers.

An occasional dropping may be found by following a snow trail. An accumulation will be found at a den or near a winter nest under the snow. In summer droppings are deposited along trails or roads, often on rocks or other prominent objects in or beside the trail. Such places are often used repeatedly so that three or four may be accumulated in one spot. I have found weasel droppings on or near coyote droppings.

Dens may be in the ground (in a mole or pocket gopher hole), under a barn, in a pile of stored hay, under rocks, or in similar safe retreats. On several occasions I have found a winter nest of the field mouse appropriated by a weasel, and lined with the fur of its victim.

Weasels store food for future use. A heap of dead mice may be uncovered in a shed of baled hay, where a weasel had found a safe

Fig. 23 (opposite)

a. Tracks of longtail weasel, *Mustela frenata,* in wet snow. Leaps were 29 to 34 in.
b. Tracks of shorttail weasel, *Mustela erminea,* in snow, carrying a lemming (Hudson Bay, 1915).
c. Tracks of shorttail weasel, *Mustela erminea richardsoni,* on sand (Kodiak I., Alaska, Sept. 1936).
d. Tracks in snow of longtail weasel (Wyo., 1949).
e. Feet of shorttail weasel, about natural size (Cascade Mts., Ore., 1913).
f. Droppings of *M. erminea,* about natural size (Wyo.).
g. Droppings of *M. frenata,* about natural size (Wyo.).

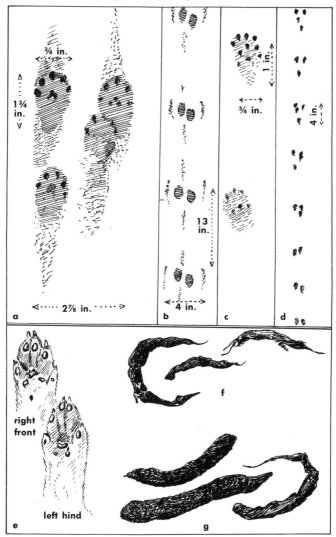

Fig. 23.   Weasels

Fig. 24. Short leaps of shorttail weasel in deep snow, showing drag marks, alternating with long leaps entirely clear of the snow. The weasel also dives into the snow, to emerge some distance away.

retreat, or stored mice may be found under a stump or in a burrow. Figure 23, b, shows shorttail weasel tracks with drag marks in the snow on either side. This was sketched in the Hudson Bay area, where I followed the trail nearly half a mile to find that the animal had stuffed a lemming down in the snow beside a bush.

Weasels are inquisitive animals, and often, when you have seen one disappear in a rock pile or a hollow tree, he will reappear to have another look if you make a mousy squeak. When greatly disturbed a weasel will also emit a characteristic odor, to some as disagreeable as that of the skunk.

In summer you may hear a noisy outcry among birds. Note in which direction the birds are looking, and move cautiously. You may see the creature they are mobbing, possibly an owl or a crow, and again it may be a weasel. One should always listen to the warnings of birds.

It is on occasion helpful to the naturalist to know the killing technique of a carnivore. The weasel apparently prefers to seize its prey at the back of the skull, sometimes the neck or throat. Small tooth marks there would suggest the work of a weasel.

Mink

Like the weasel, the mink, *Mustela vison,* occurs over most of North America, but is more restricted to forest cover and water.

The mink and the weasel are fashioned after a similar pattern, and their tracks are similar in form. Mink tracks are generally in the familiar double-print pattern, a larger edition of those of the weasel. This pattern is made by the hind feet almost registering in the front track (Fig. 25, c). The mink too, will go down under the snow on exploratory dives. When traveling along, the mink will occasionally push itself forward in the snow, leaving a trough, and it will sometimes coast down a slope like an otter. It is obvious that these dives into snow and the coasting on the level or downhill on snowy surface reveal in the mink a degree of the exuberant playfulness we find in the otter.

Along a river in winter you may find a smooth round hole down through the snow and through an air hole in the ice, where the mink has been foraging under water. The hole may be more or less muddy, for the animal has been on the stream bottom, and may have left fragments of frogs or other food nearby.

As in the case of the weasel, the male mink is larger than the female and their tracks differ correspondingly in size. Trappers often attempt to distinguish tracks of male mink from those of females, and to some extent this may be possible, with experience. Condition of snow and age of animal as well as sex affect the size of tracks. A number of individual mink tracks on mud and sand have measured about 1¼ inches in width, and about the same in length, exclusive of claws. However, when the heel of the hind foot shows, as in Figure 27, the hind track may be 1¾ inches long. In snow, tracks have been as much as 2 and 2½ inches long. The width of the track pattern, or straddle, varies from 2¼ in mud to 3½ inches in snow. Running gaits in mud and on firm snow are illustrated in Figure 25, d and e. Note similarity in mink gait, *d*, to skunk gait in Figure 37, d.

Mink scats are of course somewhat larger than those of the weasels, though an occasional small one will fall within the weasel size, just to confuse matters. When consisting of fur, as the dark one in Figure 25, f, they are irregularly segmented, or folded, and are blackish in color. The light-colored one in this figure is characteristic of those consisting of feathers. If the contents are fish remains or similar food, the scat is rough, and usually black and glistening.

Mink dens may be dug into banks, in which case they will be approximately 4 inches in diameter. The mink may also use muskrat burrows, holes in logs or stumps, or other ready-made shelters. The nest is made of leaves, in some instances at least,

Fig. 25 (opposite)

a. Typical mink tracks in mud.   b. Mink feet.
c. The common mink trail, twin prints made by the hind feet registering in the front tracks, or nearly so.
d and e. Running track patterns.
 f. Mink scats, about ⅔ natural size.

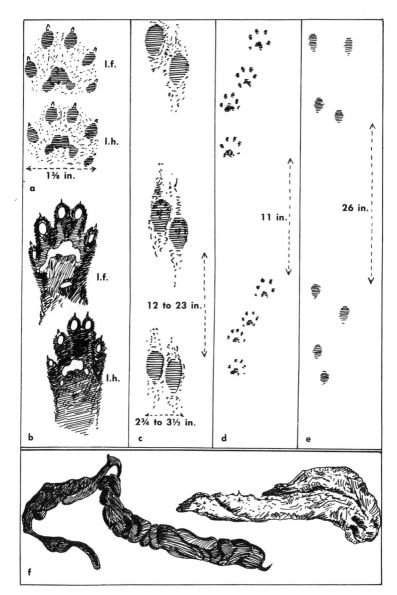

l.f.

l.h.

1⅜ in.

a

l.f.

l.h.

b

12 to 23 in.

2¾ to 3½ in.

c

11 in.

d

26 in.

e

f

Fig. 25.   Mink

55

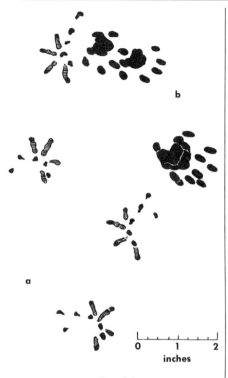

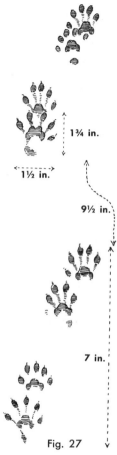

b

a

0   1   2
inches

Fig. 26

Tracks of mink and toad traveling in opposite directions, in soft mud

a. Toad tracks, walking gait showing the toe tips, only, of the hind feet superimposed on the four-toed front-foot tracks. b. The mink also had stepped in or nearly in the front-foot tracks with the hind feet. Here again is illustrated the making of the "two-two" pattern, the four feet making what appears to be two tracks when details are lost in snow.

1¾ in.

1½ in.

9½ in.

7 in.

Fig. 27

Running pattern of mink, in mud (Wyo.). This is similar to the trail shown in Figure 25, d, but note that the individual tracks tend to segregate into pairs, approaching the two-and-two pattern shown in Figure 25, c.

and is about a foot in diameter. It may be lined with feathers, when these are available.

A beaver pond often gives us a story of adaptation. The beaver has furnished the engineering skill to create a pond. The muskrats take advantage of this and make their home in the same pond, often with shelters within the outside structure of the beaver house itself. Then along comes the mink, which is fond of muskrat meat, and preys upon some of these animals. On several occasions I have found on the beaver house a collection of mink droppings consisting of muskrat fur and bone.

Like the weasel and the skunk, the mink produces a strong scent, but not as disagreeable as that of its two relatives. As boys, some of us used to poke a long switch into a suspected mink den. If we then caught the scent given off when the mink is disturbed, we knew that the animal was at home.

Marten

The marten, *Martes americana,* is a dry-land counterpart of the familiar mink, inhabiting the boreal forests of the continent, and forested mountain ranges of the West.

Marten tracks may be confused with the slightly smaller mink, and the larger fisher. All of these, as well as the weasel, have similar track patterns, varying, and overlapping in size. For example, Antoon de Vos, of Canada, finds that the walking stride of a male fisher is 13 inches, of the female 9 inches; the similar stride of the male marten is about 9 inches, that of the female 6 inches.

Compared to the mink's, the marten's feet are larger, yet there

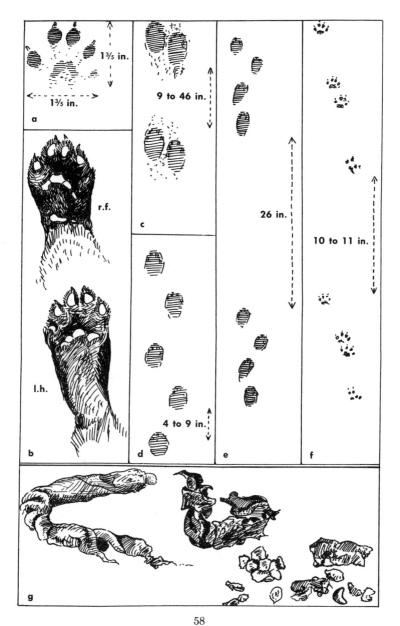

a

1⅗ in.

1⅗ in.

b

r.f.

l.h.

c

9 to 46 in.

d

4 to 9 in.

e

26 in.

f

10 to 11 in.

g

is much variation in size of footprint. One on hard snow was 1½ inches long and wide, only slightly larger than a mink track on firm snow surface, and smaller than mink tracks in loose snow. In softer snow the marten track varies from 2½ to 4½ inches in length. One was 6 inches long, but some of the longer measurements include the combined front and hind tracks registering imperfectly. The straddle of the marten trail varies from 2½ to 6 inches, the greater width being in loose snow.

In midwinter the under surface of the marten's feet is so heavily covered with hair that the toe pads do not show. Toward the end of winter the toes appear, and in summer they are prominent.

I have not seen evidence of the marten coasting on the snow, as for the mink and the otter, although it has been reported that they will tunnel under the snow.

Marten scats are confusing. They are similar in shape to those of mink and weasels, are about the size of those of the mink, and sometimes may overlap in size with those of a large weasel. One circumstance that is helpful is the fact that martens are fond of blueberries, huckleberries, mountain ash berries, and pine nuts, which apparently mink and weasels do not eat, and these fruit contents characterize many marten scats. In Alaska it was found that the lips of marten were stained blue in berry time. Marten scats may be found on rocks along mountain trails, and in the trail itself. Often several are found together, showing the marten's tendency to deposit them where others have already been left, as many other animals do. Weasel and marten droppings will also be found together.

Marten dens are normally in a tree, in a convenient cavity, though dens in the ground have been reported. The marten will also bury surplus food, as do weasels and mink.

The marten has no prominent characteristic call, though in distress it will hiss, or growl, and sometimes "scream." In the wild, it has no call that is useful as a guide to its whereabouts.

Fig. 28 (opposite).   Marten

a. Print on hard snow.
b. Feet in summer (Wyo., Aug. 1, 1928). In winter thick hair on the soles conceals the toe pads, though they begin to show again in late winter.
c. A common form of track when marten is running easily, hind feet registering in the front tracks.
d. Walking tracks.   e. A running gait seen on harder snow.
f. Tracks on crust, toes showing. The rear track reveals an injured foot (Teton mts., Feb. 24, 1946).
g. Three samples of scats, about ⅔ natural size.

As in the case of weasels, birds such as magpies, jays, robins, and other small birds in the vicinity may assemble to scold a marten prowling in the daytime.

Fisher

The fisher, *Martes pennanti,* is a larger relative of the marten which has become very scarce. It is still found in fair numbers in a few parts of Canada and in adjacent parts of some eastern states, and rarely in the Coast Ranges of Washington and Oregon; it also is found in parts of the Sierras of California.

This is another lithe member of the weasel family, and its tracks may at times be confused with marten tracks. As Antoon de Vos of Canada puts it: "The average walking stride of a large male fisher is 13 inches, that of a large male marten around 9 inches, while that of a female fisher is about 9 inches and of a female marten 6 inches. The average jump of a large fisher is around 26 inches and that of a large marten 24.5 inches."

Stride and size of tracks are extremely variable, depending on snow condition and gait. Fishers have been reported leaping 3 to

Fig. 29 (opposite). Fisher

a. Track in sand, about ⅔ natural size (Vanderhoof, B.C., June 1934).
b. Front and hind left feet.
c. Walking tracks, in mud (Olympic Mts., Wash., April 5, 1934).
d. Common running gait in snow (Sequoia Natl. Park, Cal., 1941).
e. Scat, reduced about ⅓ in size (Brit. Col., 1934).

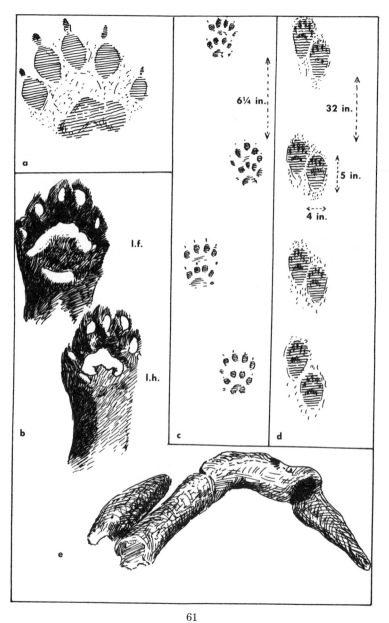

a

b

l.f.

l.h.

c

d

6¼ in.

32 in.

5 in.

4 in.

e

61

5 feet. A fisher will also leap with all four footprints separated, as in the case of the marten and mink (see Fig. 28, e).

On firm mud or sand footprints will measure approximately 1½ x 2 inches, excluding claws. In snow, however, the individual track will be 2 x 2½ inches at least, and has been reported 4 x 5 inches, indicating rather loose snow.

Fishers have a habit of climbing trees, and can readily travel from tree to tree. Under such circumstances it is necessary to circle widely to pick up the trail in the snow farther on. In the Sierra Nevada, at least, the fisher has been found to burrow in the snow after mice, but apparently such under-snow travel is rare in Ontario.

The droppings may be confused with those of the marten, though they are usually larger. The fisher is quite omnivorous and feeds on berries and nuts as well as flesh, in this respect resembling the marten. The fisher also feeds on porcupines, and swallows a certain number of quills. The coyote does the same, so that the scats of both of these animals may contain porcupine quills. Coyote scats, however, are larger, except in the case of small pups.

The fisher has no outstanding call aside from the usual growls of animals that are threatened.

Their dens may be either in trees or in the ground.

Tayra

The tayra of the American tropics, *Tayra barbara,* reminds one of the marten and fisher of the North, and the track, shown in Figure 30, is much like that of the fisher. They need not be confused, however, for the fisher is confined to the snow countries of part of

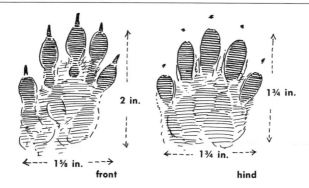

Fig. 30. Front and hind tracks of a pet tayra
(Canal Zone, Sept. 1952)

the Rocky Mountains and the northern forests, while the tayra lives in South and Central America, and comes north only as far as parts of Mexico.

I had not found the tayra or its tracks in the jungle of the Canal Zone, but Lieutenant H. H. J. Cochran of the Air Corps, who was stationed there and had a pet tayra, and his wife saw to it that I got the tracks. Mrs. Cochran works with ceramics. After she had mixed some clay in two dishes, they maneuvered the unruly, lively pet until it pressed its feet in the clay, front foot in one dish, hind foot in the other. So, through the enthusiastic help of two animal lovers, I was able to get at least a couple of samples of tayra tracks.

This animal, like so many of the weasel tribe, is inquisitive, full of vitality, and certainly becomes a fascinating pet.

Black-footed Ferret

This may be the rarest North American mammal. *Mustela nigripes* science calls it, denoting its close kinship within the weasel group. At one time it was found generally throughout the prairie dog country of the West, though apparently it was never really abundant. With the drastic poisoning of prairie dogs, on which the ferret largely depended for food, it was reduced to near extinction. This endangered species survives mainly in South Dakota. Comparatively few people now living have seen this animal alive.

Through the kindness of Mr. Warren Garst, who had the privilege of studying a few captive animals in eastern Wyoming, tracks and

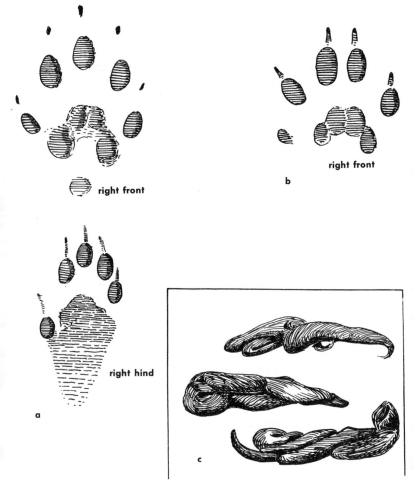

Fig. 31.   Black-footed ferret sign, all natural size (Douglas, Wyo.)

       a. Front and hind tracks.
       b. Front track of mink for comparison.
       c. Black-footed ferret scats.

Black-footed Ferret

droppings were made available to me. (These animals were later released in a national park.)

Figure 31, a, illustrates the tracks in natural size. Note the close resemblance to the mink track, shown for comparison in *b*. Probably it would be very difficult to distinguish them in the field. The droppings, too, are similar to those of mink, and have the same type segmentation when composed largely of hair.

However, if you come upon tracks like these in a prairie dog town in Wind Cave National Park, for example, or in pariie dog towns elsewhere in the West, they will probably be those of the black-footed ferret.

Wolverine

The most powerful and picturesque character of the weasel tribe is the wolverine, *Gulo luscus,* whose home is the boreal and Arctic regions of the Northern Hemisphere, and some of the western mountain regions of the United States.

Few have seen this elusive animal of the wilderness, which has now become exceedingly scarce south of Canada. Therefore its tracks assume all the greater importance. As shown in Figure 32, perfect tracks reveal the five toes characteristic of the weasel tribe, though the small toe does not always show. There are many track patterns: walking or trotting, as in *b;* a little faster, *c;* loping, *d;* galloping, *e*. It is interesting to note some similarities with other members of the weasel family. Observe the "mink" pattern in *c;* compare with the similar double-print pattern in the mink, weasel, marten, and fisher. Again, compare the loping pattern, *d*, with similar pattern of the skunk, mink, and marten — even to some extent similar patterns of the red fox and wolf. In *f*, the tracks show that the left hind foot is injured and not being used. The

Wolverine

size of the tracks varies, of course, with the size of the animal and condition of snow. The front track may vary in length from 4½ to 7½ inches; in deep snow there will only be a series of deep holes, as in Figure 33.

Wolverine tracks may be confused with those of the wolf at first glance, but the wolf has four toes, the wolverine five, and the heel pads are different. The wolverine trail tends to wind around, the wolverine nosing about in an inquisitive manner, alert for any tidbit of game or carrion.

Wolverine scats have the usual elongated weasel shape, but are larger than those of the other Mustelidae, except for the distinctive scats of the sea otter.

The wolverine has been referred to as "skunk bear." In fact, in shape it does resemble a diminutive bear, and it has two pale brown stripes on the sides that are somewhat skunklike, reaching to a bushy tail. Moreover, it has well-developed anal glands that produce a disagreeable odor.

The only sounds I have heard from wolverines were growling and snarling, among a group of captive ones in a zoo.

The wolverine has a notorious personality that has been a popular subject in journalistic writing. There is no question about its ferocity and strength. I wonder if there is another inhabitant of northern wilderness that so excites the imagination. One time I came on a wolverine trail in an early winter snowfall in central Alaska. So eager was I for "wolverine lore" that I laboriously

Fig. 32 (opposite).   Wolverine tracks and scat

a. Typical tracks, which show all five toes.   b. Walking or
   trotting gait.   c. A little faster gait.   d. An easy lope.
e. A gallop.
f. Track of wolverine with crippled left hind foot. (Note that there
   are only 3 footprints, signifying that it must have been holding up
   the injured foot.)
g. Typical scat.

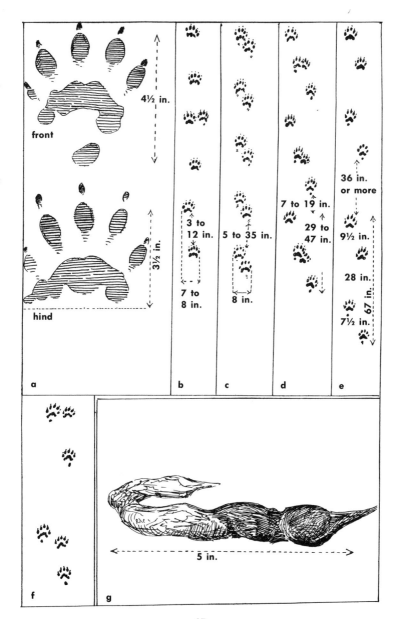

a

front

4½ in.

hind

3½ in.

b

3 to 12 in.

7 to 8 in.

c

5 to 35 in.

8 in.

d

7 to 19 in.

29 to 47 in.

e

36 in. or more

9½ in.

28 in.

7½ in.

67 in.

f

g

5 in.

67

Fig. 33.   Wolverine running in deep snow

tracked the animal a long distance to see what it had been up to.
Merely seeing those tracks in the snow made it a red-letter day.
Its keen nose had discovered something under the snow, which
proved to be a raven wing. At another place it had uncovered some
caribou bones. Thus there unrolled a record of seeking and finding
animal remnants that evidently mean so much in the economy
of the wolverine.

   At another time I shot a mountain sheep ram for a museum
specimen. It was a bitterly cold winter day, and dusk was falling.
There was not time to completely skin the animal and get back
to my tent. I had seen wolverine tracks on that mountainside,
and I knew what could happen to my specimen if I left it there.

So I made a bargain with the wolverine. I didn't want him to spoil the head of the sheep. In great haste in my race with darkness, I partly skinned the ram back from the rear, laid the loose skin back over the head to protect it, and left exposed for the wolverine's feast the hind quarters and the belly, with its choice internal organs.

Next morning I went back. There were the wolverine tracks all around the carcass. Great chunks of the best meat had been taken out, but my specimen, the skin and head, was untouched.

River Otter

Though not commonly observed in the wild, the river otter, *Lutra canadensis,* is a fairly familiar animal to most people. Its original range covered most of North America. It is one of the larger of the weasel tribe, its recorded weights running over twenty pounds, though I do not have at hand weights of the large Alaskan subspecies.

The otter is agile, fluid in its movements as the water that is its favorite element. Yet on the land it is not as light on its feet as the weasel or marten and seems almost to plow through the snow. This is revealed by its tracks, which sometimes appear in a snowy trough. Characteristic, too, is the long mark in the snow where the otter has slid. Coasting is enjoyed occasionally by the mink, but the sport is developed to the extreme by the otter (Fig. 35).

One wintry day in southern Hudson Bay territory I was snowshoeing up a small stream when I spied a movement on the snowy

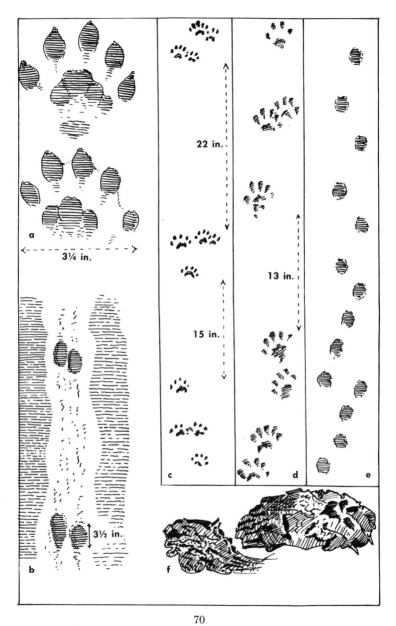

a

‹ ─ ─ ─ ─ 3¼ in. ─ ─ ─ ─ ›

22 in.

15 in.

13 in.

b

3½ in.

c

d

e

f

Fig. 35.   The otter slide

streambank ahead. I realized that it was an otter, and the next moment it slid down the bank. Another one appeared, clambered up the bank, and slid down. A third appeared from a hole in the ice, and for several minutes I watched these frolicsome animals, climbing, sliding, climbing, sliding, over and over again — until they all disappeared under the ice. Their playtime was over, and they went on their way beneath the ice, as so often they do.

When coasting thus the front feet are held back along the sides, and the hind feet trail out behind, in a streamlined arrangement. These marks in the snow are sure evidence of the otter's presence. Some of these slides may be as much as 25 feet long, or longer. The otter will also slide on the level, giving himself a forward push as he travels along. Furthermore, both the otter and the mink may dive into loose snow when closely pursued, to come up some distance beyond. Severinghouse and Tanck (1948) recorded level slides on ice as long as 20 to 25 feet, when the otter's speed was 15

Fig. 34 (opposite).   River otter tracks and scat

a. Tracks in wet sand (Wyo., 1937).
b. Tracks in deep snow trough.
c and d. Tracks of otter running in soft mud (Wyo., 1936).
e. Mixed gait, slowing to a walk, in soft sand (Yellowstone Lake, 1937).
f. Otter scat, about ⅔ natural size.

to 18 miles per hour. The slides were shorter on well-packed snow. The late Francis H. Allen kindly furnished the following incident:

On March 7, 1937, I found otter tracks on the snow-covered ice at the edge of a pond in Cohasset, Massachusetts. The ice extended only a little way out into the pond, and there was no snow on the land, so that the only tracks I could see were those in the thin coating of snow on the ice. The ice was too thin to bear me, but, standing on the shore, I estimated that the otter, after a run ending a few feet from the shore, slid for about two and a half feet, then ran for about nine feet, then slid about twenty feet, then, after a run of six feet or so, slid two or three feet to the end of the snow, with open water only a few feet ahead. What was particularly astonishing to me was the length of the twenty-foot slide after so short a run. The final spring before the long slide seemed to be from all four feet at once and was evidently very powerful.

Like the mink, too, the otter will spend much time under the ice of a stream, evidently finding air space near the shore, where the ice often slopes down from a previous water level. There are usually air holes in the ice through which mink or otter can go in or out. Such holes, leading down through the covering snow and through an opening in the ice, have been described for the mink. Those used by otters are of course correspondingly larger.

The "slip," as the otter travels in the snow, may be a foot or more wide, and is easily distinguished from the one made by mink. However, it should be remembered that a beaver will also come out of the water into the snow, and will make a wallowing trough. But, a close study should reveal some sign of the beaver's large webbed hind feet. In the distance I have seen such a beaver mark on a snowy bank and mistaken it for that of an otter.

The porcupine is another animal that will wallow out a trough in deep snow. A close study should reveal some marks of the stiff hairs of the tail, and the toed-in foot marks. Of course there will be no slide. When there is doubt in such cases, follow the trail a distance to find some indication in a better spot of snow, or to see whether the animal climbed a tree, or did any other un-otter-like thing.

The otter track is similar to that of the mink, on a larger scale, as shown in Figure 34, a. In the hind track especially the inner toe is often conspicuously out to one side. On a firm surface the web does not leave a noticeable mark, but appears particularly in soft mud. Very often the gait is in the two-and-two pattern of the mink, either in the wallowing trail, shown in Figure 34, b, or on firmer surfaces. Various other gaits are shown in c, d, and e.

In addition to the slides, which may be in snow or wet mud, the

Forefoot and hind foot of River Otter

otter also leaves indications in "rolling" places. The otter loves to roll, whether in the water or on land. Evidence of such activity on land is revealed by the disturbed vegetation.

David B. Cook published a significant experience that took place in December 1938, in New York State, when he was walking up Kinderhook Creek: "Glancing upstream, I noticed a dark object floating down in midstream. As it came nearer, it resolved itself into an otter. I watched the animal come down through two riffles, with head well up, body and tail held stiff and hind legs wide apart, very obviously enjoying a free ride. It skillfully avoided boulders and kept itself in the swiftest current."

There is another sign that I have not seen, but which is described by Grinnell, Dixon, and Linsdale (1937). To quote them:

River otters have a unique way of twisting up tufts of grass to mark selected points where scent from their anal glands is regularly deposited. A. H. Luscomb, who has long been acquainted with the river otters in the Suisun Bay region, says that he knows of several such rolling places and "sign heaps" that have been visited regularly by almost every otter passing along a certain slough during a period of fourteen years. It is thus likely that otters, like beavers, maintain certain signposts and that these stations are visited by any adult otter that passes through the neighborhood.

Otter droppings may be found at these signposts, or on logs or rocks adjacent to or extending out into the water. The boat concessioner at Yellowstone Lake sometimes has been troubled by the otters thus defiling the rowboats during the night.

The droppings are likely to be irregular in form, sometimes

merely a flattened mass of fishbones and other undigested matter. Often they consist of short pieces. The color varies greatly with the type of food eaten.

The otter den may be merely a convenient resting place under roots or other suitable shelter. The permanent den is dug into a bank, with both underwater and outside entrances. They have been found also in a hollow log; Audubon and Bachman reported them in cypress roots, one in a hollow tree that stood at the edge of the water, with an entrance beneath. The nest consists of sticks, leaves, and grass.

Trails lead off from slides, or between two bodies of water, or to a "rolling place." Such rolling place in tules is described as a flattened-down area some 5 or 6 feet in diameter (Grinnell et al.).

Here, then, we have a member of the weasel family specialized for aquatic life; but more significantly, specializing also in the enjoyment of life in play — whether it be rolling in the grass, rolling, diving, and gliding in the water, riding on the surface of a swift-flowing stream, or coasting on mud or snow. Surely here the superabundant energy of the weasel tribe has been directed to esthetics of a sort.

Sea Otter

Sea otters, *Enhydra lutris,* formerly ranged along the Pacific Coast from California to the Aleutians and into the Bering Sea, as well as on the Siberian side. Today on the American side they occur along the coast of southern California south of Monterey, and throughout the Aleutian Islands.

Detecting the presence of sea otters usually means seeing the animals themselves, rather than their tracks, for these are the most aquatic members of the weasel family. They eat and sleep and breed in the water, and need not often come ashore. A male otter may be as much as 5 feet long and weigh 80 pounds or more. The hind feet are developed into seal-like flippers.

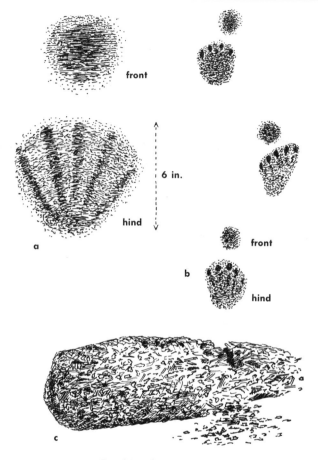

Fig. 36. Sea otter sign

a. Tracks in sand, showing the round front track and the large track of the webbed hind foot.
b. Sea otter trail pattern on sand.
c. Sea otter scat, about ⅔ natural size.

There is one sea otter sign that may come to your attention. In the Aleutian Islands I had often heard a rapid tapping sound coming across the water from where the sea otters were feeding. This was puzzling. Months later, two friends and I were watching the sea otters on the California coast and there found the solution. We heard the same sound repeatedly, and with binoculars saw what was happening. A sea otter would dive, then come up with a clam or mussel and a small rock. The rock was placed on the stomach as the animal floated on its back, then, holding the clam with both hands, it pounded it against the rock to break the shell! If you hear the tapping sound, therefore, coming from feeding sea otters, train your field glasses on them and you may witness an amazing performance — an animal deliberately picking up a tool, in this case a rock, on which to break open clamshells.

Sea otters prefer the kelp beds, which are present in the Aleutian area in summer only. They do come ashore at times, preferably on rocky beaches, and there can be found the unmistakable droppings — consisting of bits of sea urchin tests, pieces of shells, remains of crustaceans, altogether a compact mass of broken bits of hard material. Sometimes you may find only the scattered grains of this material on the rocks, when the scats have crumbled. Also note that gulls will regurgitate the same kind of material. Crumbled gull casts contain but a tiny portion of the volume of sea otter droppings. Where only fragmentary remains of such material are found, there must be some doubt about identification.

Tracks are rare indeed. Once, on Ogliuga Island, a sea otter had been on a sandy beach, where footprints could be seen, as shown in Figure 36.

It is often confusing to pick out a sea otter in a kelp bed, for the sea otter's head protruding from the water may be mistaken for one of the large bulbs or "floats" of the kelp.

This animal of the sea has the agility and playfulness of the river otter to a considerable degree. While lying on its back nibbling at a treasured clam or mussel, it may suddenly swirl in the water, with a combined dive and spin, then come back belly up and continue eating. Such maneuvers seem to be done just for the fun of it.

A baby will often lie curled up to doze on the stomach of the buoyant mother, while she rests on the water. When she wants to go off in a hurry, she puts an arm around the baby and swims off smoothly and powerfully, apparently with great ease.

Hognose Skunk (foreground) and Striped Skunk

Striped Skunks: Striped, Hooded, and Hognose

Under this heading are included for convenience the common striped skunk found over so much of North America, *Mephitis mephitis,* with its many related forms: the hooded skunk, *Mephitis macroura,* found in southern Arizona and Mexico; and the hognose skunk, *Conepatus leuconotus,* found in the Southwest in and near Mexico.

Their well-known defensive weapon of odorous spray from the anal glands has given these lowly animals a poor reputation. Actually skunks are interesting and need not cause any difficulty if approached quietly. Consider the significance of the facts. Here is a member of the weasel tribe, a group of animals noted for agility and fierce hunting instincts. But the skunk chose to find its living by grubbing for insects, catching frogs, eating what eggs or carrion it could find. All the weasels have the anal glands, but the skunk specialized in producing a vile liquid spray for defense.

As a result of these developments and habits the skunk did not need agility. Like all sedentary creatures, including some people, it grew paunchy and stodgy. This whole history is revealed in the skunk trail. See those short steps and close pattern illustrated in Figure 37.

I found that the tracks of the hognose skunk in southern Texas showed somewhat longer toes than in the tracks of the striped skunk (see Fig. 37). In the arid country of Big Bend National Park I had to rely on dusty parts of roads or other dusty spots for tracks, and there was little chance to find continuous trails. The striped skunks agree in the general pattern. Note the variations in pattern of the shuffling run in Figure 37. The greatest speed, with hind feet in front, is shown in *f.*

In snow country, from New England to the Pacific, the skunk goes into the long winter sleep. But occasionally during warm

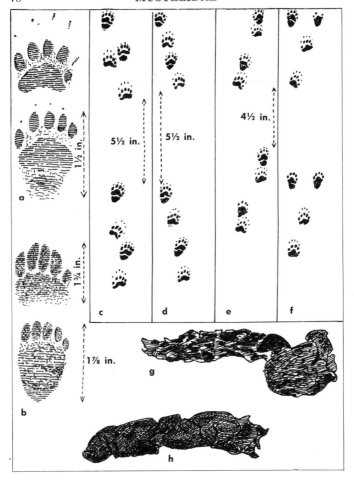

Fig. 37.   Tracks and droppings of striped skunks

a. Tracks of *Mephitis* sp., in mud.
b. Tracks of hognose skunk, in dust; in both cases the top figure
   represents the front foot (Big Bend Natl. Park, Tex.).
c, d, e, f. Various gaits of the striped skunk; note variations in place-
   ment of hind feet, which can be recognized by the heel.
g. Scat of striped skunk.   h. Scat of hognose skunk.

Hind foot and forefoot of Striped Skunk, ⅔ size

spells, especially in late winter, you may find the trail of a wandering skunk winding over the snow, ending up in some den or hollow log, or under a building. Why had it shifted to another resting place? And did it later go back to the original winter nest? Does it have in its memory a series of convenient refuges? Surely it must doze a good while longer. At any rate, attention to this short-gaited line of tracks reveals interesting actions of a newly awakened sleeper.

All skunks root after insects or grubs, but this habit is more pronounced in the hognose skunk, which has developed the snout for that purpose. Therefore the diggings or extensive rooted-up places are a good indication of the presence of this animal, which in parts of New Mexico and Texas is known as the "rooter skunk." The striped skunk also digs after insects and grubs, but its work appears more as little pits. Such sign is admittedly difficult to distinguish from other disturbances.

Here again we have an auditory sign. When a skunk is under a floor, or in a similar refuge, and is disturbed or otherwise is in a nervous state, you may hear a thumping sound, made by a foot. For some time we had one under our house and in the stillness of the night we would hear these loud thumps beneath the floor. We marveled how such a loud sound could be made by a skunk. (We finally managed to plug the entrances when we were sure the skunk was away, and no doubt it has found a more remote thumping place.)

Skunks seek almost any cavity for a den — an abandoned

ground burrow, hollow log, or rock crevice (even under a building!) — where they make grass nests, such nest remnants by the
den sometimes revealing that it is occupied. In the case of a
long-haired animal like the skunk, look also for traces of hair about
the burrow entrance. Occasionally a faint smell is an indication,
though normally the violent skunk odor is not emitted except when
the animal is disturbed.

Spotted Skunk

This skunk, known as *Spilogale putorius* to the scientist, with
several related species, is an attractive little animal, more agile than
the striped skunk; in fact active enough to climb trees to some
extent. It shares with the larger skunks the repelling odor, and
is found in varied scattered habitats from the eastern and southern
states through the Southwest, and Mexico, to the rain forests of
the Northwest.

The much smaller tracks of this animal follow a pattern quite
different from that of the larger skunks, as shown in the illustrations. Its walking gait produces a "puttering" style of track
pattern, as in Figure 38, f.

The droppings are small and irregular in shape, about ¼ inch
in diameter.

The dens are in all kinds of places — in burrows, among rocks,
or under buildings. To my regret, once I disturbed a spotted skunk
that had come into my cabin in the woods and sought a dark corner
under the bed as a refuge!

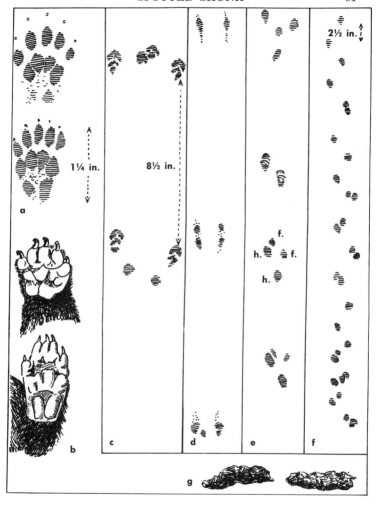

Fig. 38.   Spotted skunk

a. Tracks in mud (Olympic Mts., Wash.).
b. Feet of spotted skunk (Olympic Mts.).
c, d, e. Various running track patterns.   f. Walking pattern.
g. Droppings, about ⅔ natural size; diam., ¼ in.

Badger

This weasel became burly and strong, spurned the trees and the water, and decided to gain his living underground. The badger, *Taxidea taxus,* is short-legged, flat to the ground, with powerful front feet and claws for digging. Unlike the nocturnal English badger, who lives in the woods, the American badger is characteristic of plains country, from Mexico north into southwestern Canada, from the Pacific Coast eastward to the Middle West, including parts of Ohio, Indiana, Illinois, Kansas, Oklahoma, and Texas. To some extent it also ventures into high mountain country and into woodland.

The badger hole, the most prominent sign, is a feature of the western landscape, known to the early riders of the range as a hazard for their saddle horses, since stepping into one unknowingly could cause a broken leg for the horse and a bad fall for the rider. Abandoned holes also furnish nesting places for burrowing owls, and refuge for other animals.

The burrows are conspicuous, with entrances from about 8 inches to a foot in diameter, elliptical in shape, as one would expect from such a flattened digging dynamo. A large mound of earth is thrown out, for the tunnel is big and a great deal of earth is moved. There may be many holes in a given area, since the badger seeks food by digging for one ground squirrel or other rodent after another. In prairie dog towns, numerous burrows are enlarged by the badger, who is after these rodents.

Badger tracks, shown herewith, are extremely toed-in, and the

Fig. 39 (opposite)

a and b. Tracks in dust (Jackson Hole, Wyo., 1931).
c. Tracks on hard snowdrift, fragmentary type often found (Jackson Hole, Dec. 22, 1927).
d. Badger trail in snow.
e. Badger scat, about ⅔ natural size.

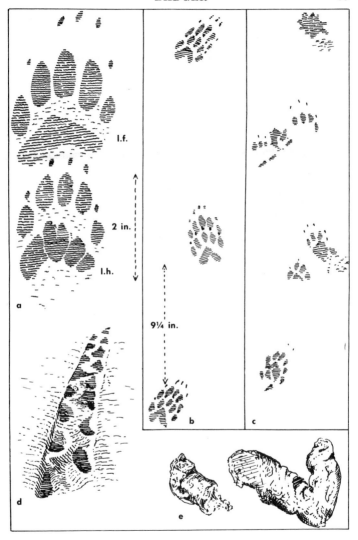

Fig. 39. Badger tracks and scat

long claws of the front feet generally leave marks. Figure 39, c, illustrates a badger trail of a fragmentary nature on hard snow-drift. The stride varies from about 6 to 12 inches, the straddle is about 4 to 7 inches, though the width of the badger trail appears greater in loose snow. The front track is approximately 2 inches wide, the hind track slightly less. Sometimes the hind-foot track is behind that of the front foot, as in Figure 39, b and c, but at other times it is in front.

I have not found the scats prominent, at least to casual observation. Nor have I discovered any outstanding characteristic that would distinguish them readily from those of other carnivores of equal size. Again, one must be alert for accompanying signs that give additional clues, and keep in mind what animals are known to occur in a given place.

Whenever you meet a badger you will be impressed by its definite character. The only sound I have heard it make is a growl, or a hissing sound, as it faced me, daring me to come closer. At other times, when it poked its head out of a hole to have a look at me, its striped face has had an almost clownish look.

Once a badger started to dig into the ground to escape. I seized it by the hind legs and tried to pull it out of the hole as the hind quarters were disappearing, just to have another look at it and to see what it would do. But the badger held fast. I felt as if I were trying to pull out a big plant by the roots. In a few moments I noticed the muzzle coming out, doubling back under the belly, reaching for my hands. I promptly let go and watched it disappear into the ground!

Dog Family: Canidae

RELATED TO the domestic dogs in America are the wolves, coyotes, and foxes. Their tracks have a similar pattern, with four toes, the toenails usually showing in the track (see Fig. 40). The front foot is slightly larger than the hind foot (see Fig. 40). The heel pad, when shown clearly, has a fairly distinctive outline, the front one differing from the hind one, with some differences in shape among the members of this family. Note the more pronounced three-lobed hind margin of hind-foot pad, as compared with the front pad, in both the dog and wolf. In the coyote the outlines are different. The red fox has a curved ridge of callus across the pad, showing through the hair, and this may appear in a clear track, though generally the full outline of the hair-covered pad appears. In the gray fox the pads have a more pronounced hook-like projection on each side. Generally the Arctic fox does not show pronounced pad peculiarities, nor have I found it in the kit fox tracks.

The droppings of the dog tribe are remarkably similar. There are average differences in size, but the variation is so great that there is much overlapping in measurements and one cannot be certain of identification in some cases. Aside from variations due to types of food and quantities eaten, there is the confusing fact of smaller size among young animals in each species.

The samples illustrated in Figure 41 are offered as average or typical, for a guide to intelligent guesses in some instances, or more positive identification where it is known what animals are in the area and when one has gained familiarity with the animals' characteristics.

Dog

Dogs are of such great variety of size and shape that it would be hopeless to characterize the tracks of all of them. In Figure 42 are shown the tracks of the Alaskan malamute (a Husky dog) from

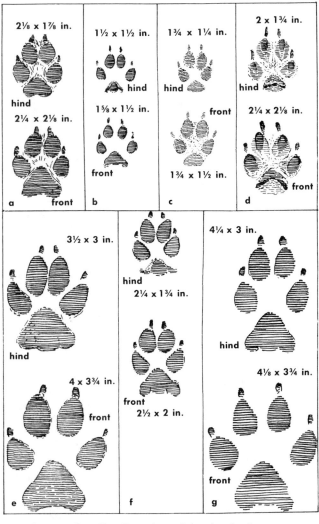

Fig. 40.   Footprints of the dog family

a. Arctic fox, in sand.   e. Alaskan malamute, in mud.
b. Gray fox, in mud.   f. Coyote, in mud.
c. Kit fox, in snow.   g. Gray wolf, in mud.
d. Red fox, in mud.

86

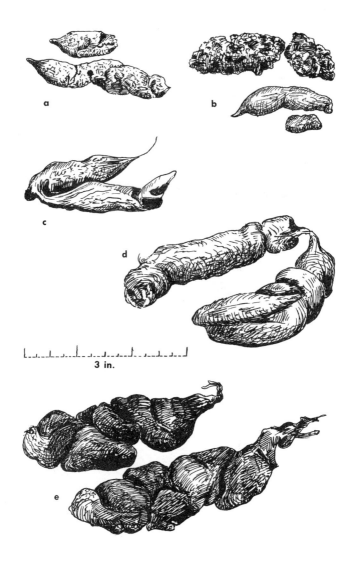

Fig. 41.   Scats of the dog family

a. Gray fox or kit fox (Texas).   c. Red fox (Alaska).
b. Arctic fox (Aleutians).   d. Coyote (Wyo.).
        e. Wolf (Mt. McKinley Natl. Park, Alaska).

87

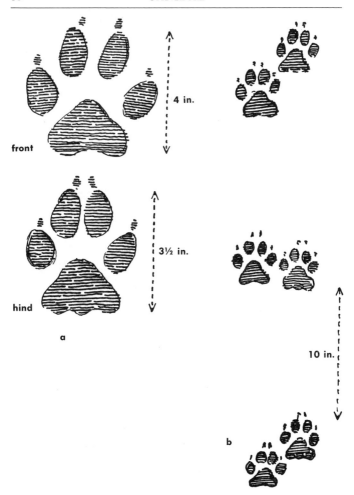

front

hind

4 in.

3½ in.

a

10 in.

b

Fig. 42. Tracks of Alaskan malamute
a. Front and hind foot.   b. Walking track pattern.

Port Moller, Alaska. These could be confused with the gray wolf tracks, since both are found in the same territory. Figure 43 shows tracks of a cocker spaniel and a mongrel dog, for comparison.

There are certain features in the tracks of the dog family, common to dog, wolf, and fox which might be stressed here. The heel pads of front and hind feet have distinctive outlines, but as you find the tracks in snow or mud there is a difference somewhat unrelated to the actual shape of the pad, a difference that helps to distinguish front and hind tracks; front and hind feet are held at somewhat different angles as they strike the ground. Perhaps it is more important that the front paws in this group of animals are more mobile than the hind ones; and their toes tend to spread

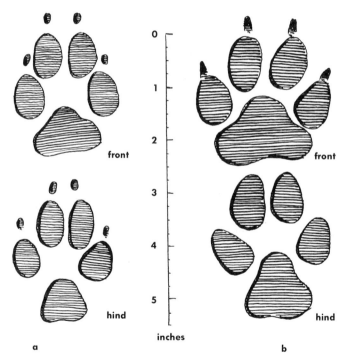

Fig. 43.   Cocker spaniel and mongrel dog tracks

a. Cocker spaniel, about   natural size.
b. Mongrel dog, about ⅗ natural size.

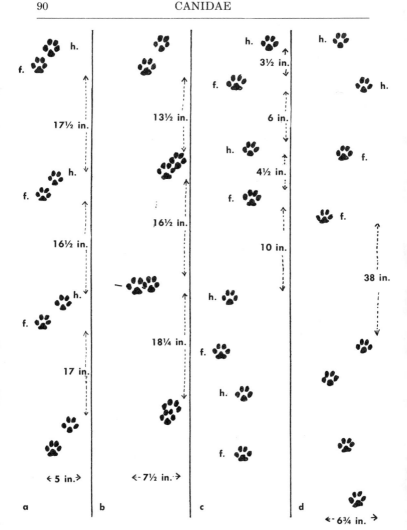

Fig. 44.   Mongrel dog trails in mud

a. Slow trot; 5-in. straddle.
b. Similar gait, with hind foot almost registered in front track.
c. Slow lope.   d. Gallop.

more. At any rate, the front heel pads make a fairly clear imprint, while the heel pad of the hind foot does not completely register in mud or snow, leaving out, or but faintly showing, its lateral lobes. Thus the hind-track heel pad tends to be merely a roundish or oval depression.

In Figure 43 this is illustrated in both the cocker spaniel and mongrel dog tracks. Hind and front tracks can be distinguished also in the dog trails in Figure 44. The same features can be found in coyote and fox tracks.

Note how in Figure 44 the hind foot commonly oversteps the front track, though in *b* it tends to step in the front track at times. These gaits, from *a* to *d*, show a transition from a slow trot to the gallop in *d*, with *c* being an intermediate stage from *a* to *d*.

Compared to a coyote, a dog of like size would tend to have a shorter stride and larger tracks.

Dog droppings are very similar to those of the wolf, coyote, or fox, varying in size with the breed of dog and character of food. For distinguishing scats of the dog and cat families, we have relied to some extent on the fact that cats, large and small, have the habit of meticulously covering their dung by scraping together mud or debris with their forepaws. However, after voiding dung, dogs and coyotes at least, and possibly others in the group, are likely to give some vigorous backward scrapes at random with the hind legs. So even in the case of some of the dog family there may be some scratch marks nearby.

Wolf

The gray wolf, *Canis lupus,* with its several subspecies, once ranged widely over North America and far into the Arctic. Now this glamorous animal has been almost crowded out of the United States. It is still to be found in small numbers in northern Minnesota, Wisconsin, and possibly Michigan (where it is referred to as the timber wolf), but occurs more commonly in Canada and Alaska, where it reaches a large size. The smaller so-called red wolf, *Canis niger,* with the black color phase, can be found in Texas, parts of Louisiana, Arkansas, and Missouri, probably also in northern Mexico. This little wolf approaches the coyote in size, at least in some specimens.

In these times of disappearing wilderness, to have heard the howl of the wolf in wild country is a memory to be cherished. I recall seeing some wolf sign in central Labrador many years ago, in company with an Indian. Even then the wolves were becoming scarce in that country, and we were impressed by the fact that a wolf had been at the spot where we were standing.

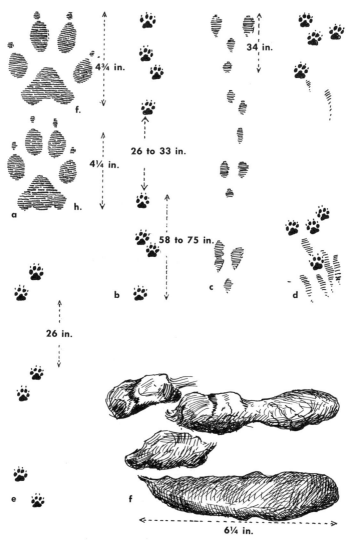

Fig. 45. Gray wolf tracks and droppings

a. Tracks in mud (Alaska).
b. Easy gallop.
c. Irregular run.
d. Faster gallop.
e. Slow trot.
f. Droppings (northern Minn.).

Gray Wolf

One night four of us, including our year-old baby, were encamped on a gravel bar of the Porcupine River, in northeastern Alaska. It was clear September weather, and we slept that night in the open without tent. At dawn we were awakened by a voice across the river. Soon we realized that we were being serenaded by two wolves, one upstream, the other below our camp. First one, then the other, raised its muzzle and howled. Apparently we were intruding on their home ground. At any rate, we lay there in the crisp autumn morning, comfortable in our sleeping bags, and listened to this song of the Arctic wilderness with a feeling of awe.

The wolf song is a long monotone, lacking the "yapping" and tremolo of the coyote. It is very similar to the howling of the Alaskan malamute and other deep-chested breeds.

For further contemplation of the probable significance of the wolf howl and its ceremonial actions, I would refer to Chapter 2 of the monograph *The Wolves of Mount McKinley* by Adolph Murie.

The tracks figured here are those of the large Alaskan variety. The front foot is larger than the hind foot and in mud or wet sand will measure 4 to 5 inches long (without the claws) by 3¾ to over 5 inches wide, depending on the speed, and spread of the toes. The front toes tend to spread much more than the hind ones. The hind tracks measured were 3¾ to 4¾ inches long by 3 to 4½ inches wide. In snow the tracks tend to be somewhat larger, the front track reaching 5½ inches in length. The largest track measured was one in wet sand, on the Porcupine River, Alaska, which with toes widely spread measured slightly over 6 inches in

Right front and hind feet of male Gray Wolf,   size

length and width. Note the difference in the outline of the foot pads in front and rear tracks. A similar difference can be seen in the dog tracks, Figure 42.

Figure 45 illustrates various gaits, which are quite like those of a dog of corresponding size. In fact, in the North wolf tracks can easily be confused with those of Alaskan malamutes.

Wolf droppings are illustrated here, but there is such variation in size that many could be confused with those of the dog, as well as with larger ones of the coyote.

Coyote

The coyote, *Canis latrans,* with its many varieties, known also as brush wolf and prairie wolf, is widespread and well known.

I sometimes think that the most conspicuous coyote sign is his night song. Certainly a camp on the plains in the Southwest or in the western mountains is cozier when enhanced by the serenade of coyote in the moonlight. He who would follow the mammals in the wilds should know something of the significance of this. Unac-

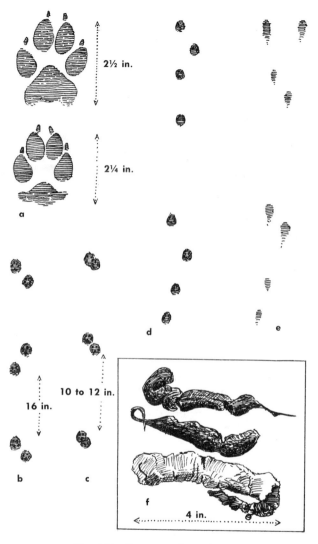

Fig. 46.   Coyote tracks and scats

a. Tracks in mud.   Upper, front; lower, hind (Okla.).
b and c. Easy lope.   f. Two types of scats.
d and e. Gallop.

Coyote

customed ears, trained by traditional journalism, might interpret
the coyote voice as something doleful, a sad requiem that makes
one crowd closer to the campfire. Or a flippant tongue might speak
of the "yapping" of the coyotes.

But if the coyote could reflect and speak he would say this is
his song, simply that. However it may appear to human ears, to
the coyote it satisfies the universal impulse for expression of emo-
tion, simple as that may sometimes be among the furred animals.

The coyote song is much higher pitched than that of the wolf.
It is the soprano of this tribe. It may begin with a long clear call,
breaking into a violent tremolo, these alternating irregularly. It
may begin with a few barks that merge into the long call.

In our family we have used the coyote call as a signal. One
evening as I approached within a quarter of a mile of camp I gave
the coyote call to let them know in camp that I was coming. On
an open hillside nearby a coyote replied with a lusty outburst!

Coyotes, and dogs that still retain this unsophisticated urge in
their being, will often respond to such a call. Also coyotes may
sometimes approach to investigate a simulated mouse squeak if
they are within hearing, or the louder cry or scream of an animal
in distress, if it can be imitated, and if you are in the lee of the
coyote. In this instance, of course, it is the hunting instinct that
is aroused.

When you happen to approach a coyote den, you may hear the
parents bark, much like a dog.

The tracks follow the general pattern of the large wolf, and dogs,
as shown in the accompanying sketches. As in the other Canidae,
the front foot is larger than the hind foot. Front tracks, in soft
mud, are 2¼ to 2¾ inches long, 1¾ to 2⅜ inches wide. The hind

tracks in mud have measured 2 to 2⅜ inches long, 1½ to 1⅞ inches wide. Note the differing patterns in the heel pads of the front and hind tracks, Figure 46, a. This clear outline, however, rarely appears in the tracks you find. In loose snow and many other surfaces the heel-pad pattern is only suggested and usually appears roughly like that of the front foot. It is on firm snow, and mud, that this outline may appear.

One wintry day I followed a coyote trail in the snow for a short distance. Where the trail crossed an opening in the woods, the coyote had at several places turned aside to dig in the snow. Finally, at one place, he had been rewarded by finding the remains of a ruffed grouse. Some feathers were strewn about near the hole in the snow (see Fig. 48, a). At first I thought the coyote had pounced on a grouse, resting in its burrow under the snow, as grouse do, but the coyote had dug much too deeply for that, and there was no blood on the snow. So it would have to be the remains of a bird lying far beneath the snow. Was it originally

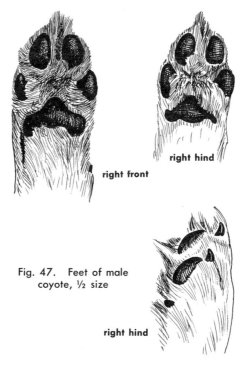

right front

right hind

Fig. 47.   Feet of male
coyote, ½ size

right hind

left there by the coyote for future use, or did the coyote's keen
nose detect it under several feet of snow? I don't know.

This same coyote gave me the track patterns shown in Figure
48: walking in *b*, trotting in *c*, and with a slow lope in *d*. The

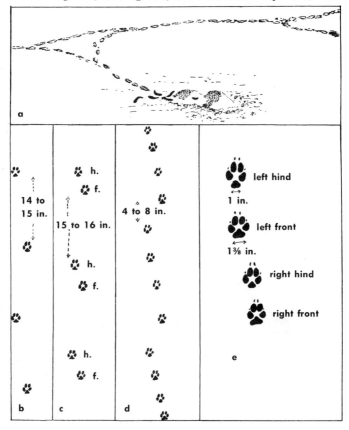

Fig. 48.   Coyote tracks in Wyoming

a. Coyote trail, showing excursions to one side of route to dig in the
   snow.
b. Walking gait.   c. Trotting gait.   d. A slow lope.
e. The lower series in *d*, to show details and order of front and hind
   feet.

width of the trail, or straddle, was 4 inches in *b* and *c*, and 6 inches in *d*. In *e* we have an enlarged view of the lower track series of *d*. The hind pad of the hind foot generally registers in a somewhat circular form in snow, and smaller than the well-lobed front pad.

In the track patterns *b*, *c*, *d*, and *e* of Figure 46, the hind prints are forward of the front prints. When the coyote was galloping fast the leaps here figured measured 32 to 61 inches, in snow. In other cases they leaped 51 to 120 inches.

Coyote scats are extremely variable in size. The residue from pure meat is likely to be semi-liquid. The scats consisting of much hair are likely to be large. Those resulting from a diet of pine nuts or chokecherries are likely to crumble. In size, coyote scats overlap those of the wolf and the red fox, and those of pups are of course much smaller.

Scats are likely to be deposited along trails. In the western mountains they will be found where a trail comes over a little knoll, or level place, or any other point of special interest to the coyote. There is likely to be an accumulation where two trails cross — as when a ridge trail dips down a slope and crosses a trail coming over a saddle.

Such accumulations may be at the scent post used by dogs, wolves, and foxes. This may be a rock, a prominent tuft of grass, a stump, or almost anything that stands out, where urine is deposited by members of the dog family who casually investigate it when passing by.

Red Fox

The red fox, *Vulpes fulva,* is one of the best-known characters in history and legend, widely spread over the temperate and northern regions of the world. For its combination of beauty and grace and intelligence it has had the attention of artists, poets, and natural-

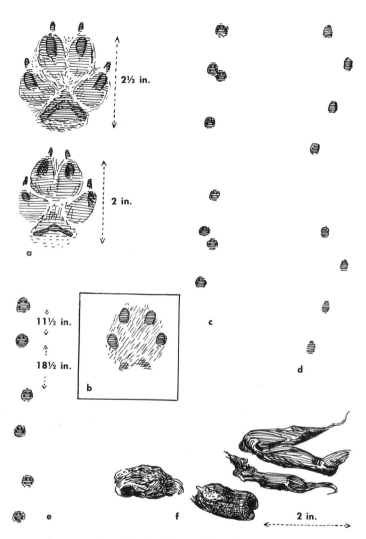

Fig. 49. Red fox tracks and scats

a. Tracks in mud. Upper, front; lower, hind (Alaska Peninsula).
b. Track on firm sand (Alaska).   c. Loping gait.
d. Running, with hind tracks out in front.
e. Walking gait.   f. Scats.

ists, and merits the attention of those who would read the signs
of the out of doors.

On January 30, 1841, Henry Thoreau wrote in his journal:

Here is the distinct trail of a fox stretching a quarter of a mile
across the pond. Now I am curious to know what had determined
its graceful curvatures, its greater or less spaces and distinctness,
and how surely they were coincident with the fluctuations of
some mind, why they now lead me two steps to the right, and
then three to the left. If these things are not to be called up
and accounted for in the Lamb's Book of Life, I shall set them
down for careless accountants. Here was one expression of the
divine mind this morning. The pond was his journal, and last
night's snow made a *tabula rasa* for him. I know which way
a mind wended this morning, what horizon it faced, by the setting
of these tracks; whether it moved slowly or rapidly, by the greater
or less intervals and distinctness, for the swiftest step leaves yet
a lasting trace.

The red fox has a variety of calls, variously described as squalling,
screaming, and barking, and of course each has its own significance.
I do not know the purpose of the red fox bark, unless it may
correspond to the howl of the coyote. At least on one occasion,
when three of us who were boys in Minnesota came upon a fox
den in the woods, the outcry from the parent foxes was clearly
a protest, an expression of alarm at our intrusion. It was a combination of a sharp bark and scream, harsh and penetrating. This
was quite different from, more shrill than, the regular bark.

The trail of the red fox is traditionally known as a line of dainty
footprints in an almost straight line. This is largely true; but, as
in the trails of other animals, the pattern varies greatly with the
gait and speed. In the almost "straight line" of the walking pattern
the trail may be not more than 3½ inches wide; sometimes, at
a different speed, about 4 inches. The width of the coyote trails
in similar patterns is from 4 to 6 inches.

When contemplating the "dainty" form of the red fox tracks,
note also the difference between the wide, sprawling front-foot
print as contrasted with the narrower, more pointed hind-foot
print. Some prints, especially in a shallow, firm snow or similar
medium, show only the portion of the toes and heel pad that
protrudes from the hair (Fig. 49, b). In such prints the heel pad
appears to lie far behind the toes, without the lobe extending
up between the two hind toes as in dogs and wolves. However,
in deeper snow and in soft mud, the entire pads, including the
portion covered with hair, make an impression, and then we get
a track (Fig. 49, a) quite comparable to that of a small dog or
coyote, or other foxes.

The red fox track has one good characteristic that is distinctive, if you have a track showing details. The heel pad has a transverse, arched, raised bar protruding from the hair of the foot, as shown in Figure 49, a. In shallow snow, or otherwise a firm surface, this bar may show without the rest of the pad. Then you get a print something like Figure 49, b, with the whole bar, or only two ends. In deeper material the bar makes a little groove in the bottom of the heel-pad print.

It is important to keep in mind this foot structure in order to interpret red fox trails properly.

Red fox scats vary greatly in size and appearance, depending on the quantity and kind of food eaten. The samples illustrated in Figure 49 are representative, showing that they have the general form of the scats of any of the Canidae. The variation in size, moreover, makes it difficult to identify some samples, for they may be confused with those of the gray fox in the eastern states, or with the Arctic fox in some parts of Alaska, not to mention the coyote in the lands in between. Normally, however, coyote scats will be definitely larger.

Foxes dig their dens in a variety of places; in the woodlands of the eastern states or on the open plains of North Dakota. They have been known to make their home in a hollow log, and sometimes they excavate an old woodchuck burrow. Such dens may be identified by tracks in the neighborhood, or by fox hairs clinging to the entrance. There is also a distinctive scent that some people

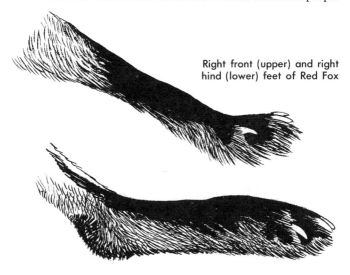

Right front (upper) and right hind (lower) feet of Red Fox

are able to catch. I, for one, am not able to distinguish it from the coyote scent, though of course it must be different. Francis H. Allen once told me: "I have often smelled the fox scent at some distance from any den. It resembles skunk but has a different quality and is not so strong."

Gray Fox, Long-eared Kit Fox, and Kit Fox

Gray Fox

The gray fox, *Urocyon cinereoargenteus,* with its related species and subspecies, ranges throughout most of the United States *except* the north-central and northwestern states (including the Dakotas, Nebraska, Wyoming, Montana, Idaho, most of Washington, and parts of adjacent states). These areas are either open plains country or high mountain country, and such environment is shunned by the gray fox. Its chosen country is the woodland of New England, the brushlands of the Southwest, the chaparral and woods of the Pacific Coast, and its congenial environment down through Mexico and Central America.

In the Southwest, the gray and kit foxes often occupy the same general areas. And here we have some difficulty in distinguishing their signs.

The gray fox tracks measure:

     front — length, $1\frac{1}{4}$ to $1\frac{7}{8}$ in.; width, $1\frac{3}{8}$ to $1\frac{1}{2}$ in.

     hind — length, $1\frac{1}{8}$ to $1\frac{3}{4}$ in.; width, $1\frac{1}{8}$ to $1\frac{1}{2}$ in.

However, on islands off the coast of southern California the gray fox is considerably smaller than its New England species.

Tracks are imperfect, and it is to be noted that where the imprints of the gray fox feet are not detailed, the heel pad of the hind track may appear chiefly round and small, the lateral portions failing to register as readily as in the heavier front track. There is the same tendency to be found in the coyote tracks.

It should be remembered that the gray fox is the only fox that climbs trees readily, especially leaning trees, a fact that may possibly be revealed in its trail at times.

I have not been able to distinguish the droppings of the gray and kit foxes. Those shown in Figure 50, i, could be either. Such small droppings in the eastern states, where the kit fox is not found, would of course be those of the gray fox.

The dens may be in any of a great variety of places, in the ground, among rocks, or even in a hollow tree.

I have not heard the voice of the gray fox, but it is known to be a bark, after the manner of the red fox. Apparently it is not well known, for it has seldom been referred to in the literature.

Kit or Swift Fox

The kit fox, with two species (*Vulpes velox and V. macrotis*) and several varieties, is chiefly a desert animal and is found only in the arid Southwest and in northern Mexico. The names kit fox and swift fox are used interchangeably.

These trim graceful creatures are the smallest of our foxes, and the trail is correspondingly dainty. Kit fox tracks measure:

front, length — 1⅛ to 1¾ in.; width, 1⅛ to 1½ in.

hind, length — 1¼ to 1¾ in.; width, 1⅛ to 1¼ in.

At least three kit fox tracks have been found to be 2 inches long.

When dealing with such close distinctions in the tracks from relatively small feet, it must be kept in mind that there will be considerable differences of measurements on different surfaces, whether it be loose or firm sand, wet or dry, or snow. In loose sand the details of kit fox tracks are blurred. Therefore, in sand dune country of the Southwest, you will find a kit fox trail composed of a line of depressions, in which sand has slid down to conceal the toe marks (Fig. 50, e), and you will only be able to identify it by the size of the footprint as a whole and the track pattern in general.

Fig. 50 (opposite)

a. Tracks of gray fox.
b. Tracks of kit fox, in snow.
c. Feet of gray fox.
d. Track of kit fox, in dust.
e. Track of kit fox, in loose sand.
f. Kit fox trail.
g. Tracks of kit fox when leaping.
h. Trail of gray fox.
    i. Droppings of kit fox or gray fox (Texas). These are often indistinguishable.

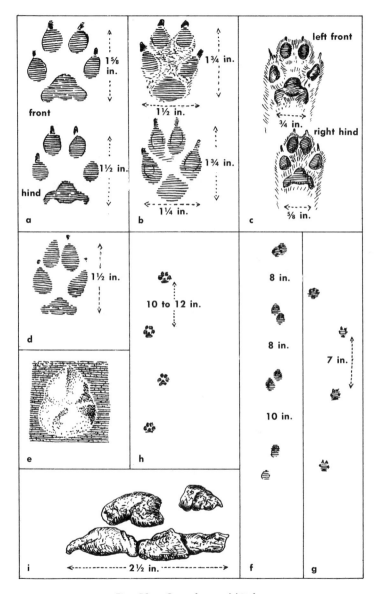

Fig. 50. Gray fox and kit fox

105

The kit fox scats (see Fig. 50, i) are similar to those of the gray fox. If such droppings are found in a strictly desert area, they are most likely to be those of the kit fox.

The burrow is often out on the sandy plain and may have several entrances, which measure approximately 8 inches in diameter, sometimes larger. It is said that the kit fox uses its den as a refuge the year round.

I have never heard the voice of the kit fox. Ernest Thompson Seton has described it as a bark much like that of the red fox, but on a smaller scale.

Arctic Fox

The Arctic fox, *Alopex lagopus,* ranges throughout the Arctic regions, and comes as far south as the Aleutian Islands in Alaska. It has two winter color phases, white and blue. The majority become white in winter, but some members of the family turn a bluish gray, from which the furriers derive the term "blue fox." All Arctic foxes are brownish in the summer.

Fig. 51 (opposite)

a. Tracks in sand. Upper, front foot; lower, hind (Aleutians). Some tracks in sand were as much as 2¾ x 2½ in.
b. Trotting or walking pattern.　　　c. Running pattern.
d. Well-furred left hind foot, in winter (Hudson Bay, 1915).
e. Arctic fox droppings; those containing feathers (two upper samples) were stringy and thin.

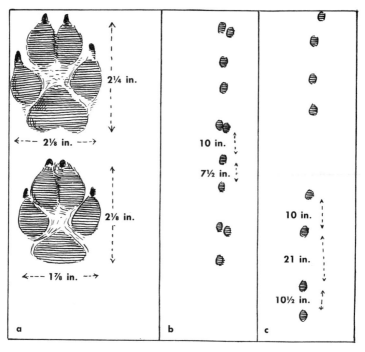

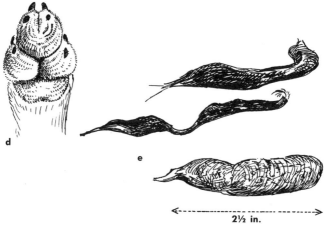

Fig. 51. Arctic fox

107

We have here a fox that is far different from the traditional Reynard of the fairy tales or the sly fox of numerous stories. One day I was sitting on a knoll on one of the Aleutian Islands, watching a pair of blue foxes below me on the beach. One of them spied me and, to my surprise, came charging all the way up the hill, bumped me in the knee with its muzzle, and hurried back to the beach. History tells us that when Vitus Bering camped in the Commander Islands, where these foxes were unusually plentiful, the animals would come into the tents and would sometimes nip the men resting there. In Greenland, too, the Arctic foxes live near human habitations. Accordingly, except where they are intensively trapped and therefore frightened by men, you may expect to find the Arctic fox easy to approach and to observe.

The feet of this fox are hairy underneath, especially in winter, more so than those of other foxes. However, an orthodox canine track, with impression of toes and heel pad, is produced in spite of the hair, particularly in summer when the hair is less dense. When the imprints are clear the track of the Arctic fox may be distinguished from that of the red fox by the absence of the barlike impression that appears in the heel pad of the latter. It may be difficult to distinguish this feature in light or loose snow, or other unfavorable surface.

In general, the droppings are similar to those of the red fox, but often, when feeding on crustaceans, the Arctic fox will leave droppings pinkish in color and tending to bleach out white. In the Aleutian Islands I occasionally found gull castings that somewhat resembled blue fox droppings, especially when the bird had fed on crustaceans.

The call is a raucous cry or bark, a rather harsh sound.

Cat Family: Felidae

CAT AND DOG TRACKS show considerable resemblance, but there are significant differences if the tracks show details. The cats normally keep their claws retracted, hence under usual circumstances claw marks do not show in their tracks. In the cat tracks, too, the heel pads appear relatively larger, and the toes tend to be arranged somewhat as a curved row in front of the large pad, more so than in tracks of the dog family.

The droppings are difficult to identify, for the food is quite similar. The cat family has the strong habit of scraping together dirt or rubbish to cover the dung, and these scratch marks are useful when present for identifying the tracks. Nevertheless, not all droppings of any one of the cats are covered. It should be noted that coyotes and others of the dog family will give random scratches with the hind feet after voiding dung, but they do not deliberately cover it.

Domestic Cat covering dung

Domestic Cat

The domestic cat, referred to as *Felis domestica,* comes in a variety of breeds, sizes, and colors, but so far as the tracks are concerned they are fairly uniform. The tracks are too small to be confused with those of the bobcat and are rounder than those of a gray fox or small dog. Absence of claw marks distinguishes the domestic cat track from that of a fox or dog, and also from mink, which

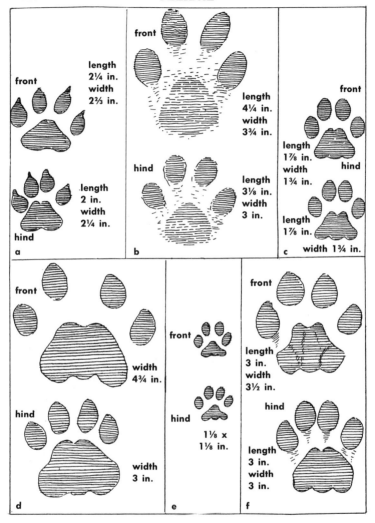

Fig. 52. Cat tracks

a. Ocelot.   b. Lynx.   c. Bobcat.   d. Jaguar.
e. Domestic cat.   f. Mountain lion.

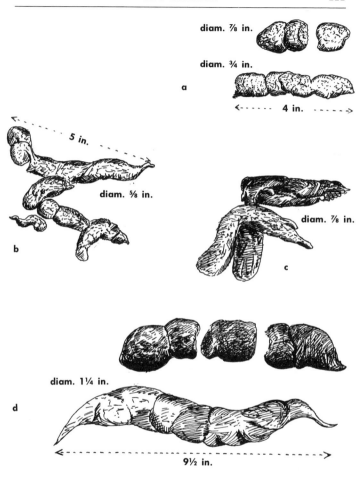

diam. ⅞ in.

diam. ¾ in.

a

← - - - - - 4 in. - - - - →

5 in.

diam. ⅝ in.

b

diam. ⅞ in.

c

diam. 1¼ in.

d

← - - - - - - - - - - - - - - - - 9½ in. - - - - - - - - - - - - - →

Fig. 53.   Scats of the cat family

a. Bobcat.   b. Ocelot.   c. Jaguar.
d. Mountain lion (upper sample, Chisos Mts., Tex.; lower, Olympic
Mts., Wash.).

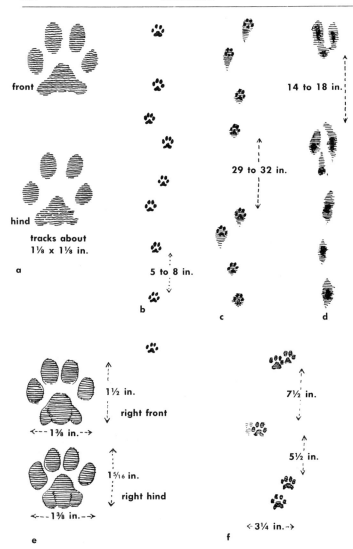

front

hind

tracks about
1⅛ x 1⅛ in.

a

b

5 to 8 in.

c

d

14 to 18 in.

29 to 32 in.

1½ in.

right front

<---1⅜ in.--->

1⁵⁄₁₆ in.

right hind

<---1⅜ in.--->

e

7½ in.

5½ in.

< 3¼ in. >

f

Fig. 54. Domestic cat tracks

shows five toes as opposed to the cat's four. Cats walk neatly and leave a fairly straight trail (see Fig. 54, b).

The cat follows the traditions of its family by covering its dung, a habit of cleanliness shared by the cat's wild relatives.

Bobcat or Wildcat

The bobcat, or wildcat, *Lynx rufus* and several related species, ranges throughout the United States and much of Mexico.

Since it is chiefly nocturnal the bobcat is seldom seen, but its tracks are distinctive. The track is more rounded than that of the coyote or dog and shows no claw marks. When the imprint is imperfect, coyote and dog tracks may not show the claws, either. The ball pad of the bobcat is distinct from that of the coyote (or any of the dog tribe) in that the anterior border is two-lobed (compare Figs. 55, a, and 40).

Fig. 54 (opposite)

a. Typical tracks.
b. Walking, showing an irregularity in the gait.
c. Galloping in shallow snow.
d. Walking, and breaking into a gallop, in deep snow.
e. Tracks in dust, showing details.
f. Walking, in dust; varying positions of front and hind feet, when they do not register.

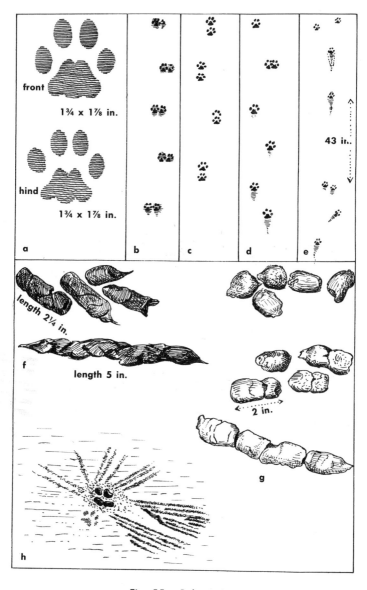

front
1¾ x 1⅞ in.

hind
1¾ x 1⅞ in.

a   b   c   d   e

43 in.

length 2¼ in.

f   length 5 in.

2 in.

g

h

Fig. 55.   Bobcat sign
114

Tracks from the Olympic Mountains and North Dakota measured as follows:

front — length, 1¾ to 2⅛ in.; width, 1⅞ to 3⅜ in.
hind — length, 1¾ to 2¼ in.; width, 1¾ to 1⅞ in.

A set of tracks from southern Texas varied. In firm mud they were
2 inches long and 2 inches wide. In softer mud the same feet made
tracks 2¼ inches long and 2⅜ to 2⅝ inches wide.

Apparently the front foot tends to spread the toes more than
the hind foot when the animal is speeding. The principal difference
between the front and hind tracks is the somewhat smaller ball
pad of the hind foot. Tracks tend to be slightly longer than wide,
though this is not always evident, as it depends on the spread of
the mobile toes.

In walking or trotting, the tracks are spaced about 8 to 16 inches
apart. In running, the leaps vary greatly, and may be from less
than 4 to more than 8 feet, depending on the urgency of the
moment and the depth of snow. As in the case of other winter
travelers, in deep loose snow the trail may be a deep trough, with
tracks obscured. Look for a favorable location where the individual
track is revealed.

The dens may be in a number of places, which vary with the
character of the country. They may be in rock crevices or caves,
in hollow trees, or hollow logs, or in suitable protected places in
thickets.

Scats can be confused with those of coyotes and dogs. In the
Pacific Coast rain forests they resemble those of the coyote, and
this may apply to other humid areas. However, in the arid Southwest the scats tend to become definitely marked off in short
segments by constrictions, and sometimes are deposited as pellets
(see Fig. 55, g). This characteristic is useful for identification in
these arid regions.

Contrary to the habit of the dog tribe, cats tend to cover the
scats. Sometimes the effort is perfunctory, but if the dung is
covered, or if there are scratch marks, one may conclude that it
is bobcat sign. If the scats are old and scratch marks are obliter-
ated, one must depend on extreme segmentation of the scats for

Fig. 55 (opposite)

a. Typical tracks.
b. Walking track pattern, stride 9 to 14 in. (No. Dak.).
c and d. Other variations in walking patterns: c, stride 10 in., d, stride
      13 to 16 in. (Olympic Mts., Wash.).
e. Galloping pattern (Olympic Mts.).
f. Two scat samples (from Wash.).
g. Three samples (Nev.).
h. Bobcat "scratching" (Palm Canyon, Cal.).

Bobcat claw marks on a tree trunk,
where animal had been scratching
(Olympic Mts., Wash., 1934)

identification, at least in arid regions. Elsewhere, if coyotes are known to be present, mark it doubtful!

Sometimes a bobcat will stretch and scratch a tree, just as the domestic cat will.

So far as the voice is concerned, again we must say that the bobcat is simply a large pussy cat, with the growls, yowlings, and hissing and spitting we are familiar with in the house cat just correspondingly stronger. The first time I heard a bobcat, in Oregon, I was startled by the deep low sound of its growl.

Lynx

Lynx canadensis is a close relative of the bobcat, but since it lives primarily in the north country it has adapted itself to cold and deep snow by growing a warm coat of fur, and by having large feet that serve as snowshoes. It inhabits the boreal regions of

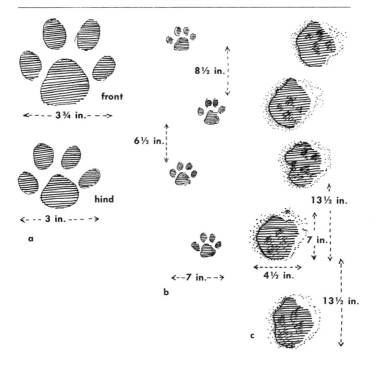

Fig. 56.   Lynx tracks

a. On hard snow.
b. In snow, showing toes; the lynx sank 2 to 3 in. into the snow.
c. In deep snow, toes indistinct.

North America, down into some of the northeastern states and along the Cascades and the Rocky Mountains.

The tracks are larger than those of a bobcat, and even approximate those of the mountain lion, but the lynx does not sink as deeply in the snow as a mountain lion. At times, also, the mountain lion's tail drag shows in the trail. The width of trail, or straddle, of the lynx represented in Figure 56, b, was 7 inches. The straddle of the mountain lion, in the few trails thus measured, has been from 8 to 13 inches.

The lynx is, of course, physically much like the bobcat, but has more wide-spreading toes and hairy feet. I have not been able to distinguish their droppings.

The lynx is very vocal, indulging in the growls and yelling described for the bobcat, being a much magnified version of the calls of the domestic cat. Various calls have been referred to as "mewing," "yeowing," screaming and moaning, and growling. John Burroughs has referred to one midnight serenade as "a shrill, strident cry, ending in this long-drawn wail."

Mountain Lion or Puma

The mountain lion, or puma, *Felis concolor,* at one time ranged over all of the United States, within suitable habitats, into lower Canada and in the Northwest well up into British Columbia, and southward through Mexico into South America. Now it is gone from much of this territory.

This American lion, called cougar on the Pacific Coast, is nocturnal and so secretive that the sight of one in the wild is a rarity, and a choice experience. The signs of its presence, then, have added significance. And merely finding the tracks in the

Fig. 57 (opposite)

a. Tracks in mud (Olympic Mts., Wash.).
b, c, d. Track patterns of walking or trotting gaits.
e. Mountain lion wallowing in deep snow.
f. Tracks in snow, showing foot drags.
g. Another view in snow, leaping gait, showing tail marks (Canada, from photographs by Dr. C. H. D. Clarke).

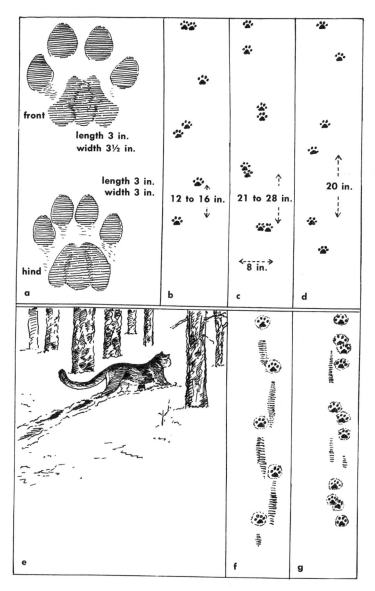

Fig. 57. Mountain lion

119

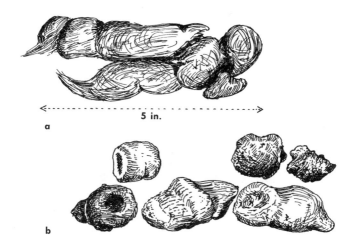

Fig. 58.   Mountain lion scats

a. From Olympic Mts., Wash.   b. From Diablo Mts., Texas

snow gives you a thrill second only to glimpsing the animal itself.

The track rarely shows the claws. As with other cats, the front foot is the larger and the toes tend to spread widely with speed. The width of tracks varies from 3 to over 4 inches, and can be much greater in certain types of snow. Pumas of the tropics may be expected to produce smaller tracks.

A distinguishing characteristic in some snow areas is reported to be the tail marks in the snow (see Fig. 57, f and g). This is not always present, however, and was not observed in my studies on the Pacific Coast.

As in the case of the bobcat, the droppings of the mountain lion tend to have deep constrictions, or may even be in pellet form in the arid Southwest (see Fig. 58). Mountain lions also share with other cats the habit of covering the droppings with earth, and the scratchings are a characteristic sign. In some areas it is said by "lion" hunters that, when scratching, the mountain lion usually faces in the direction it is traveling.

It also shares with the wolf and the bears the habit of burying surplus food for future use.

One day I was going up Pine Canyon in the Chisos Mountains of Texas. The ground was deeply carpeted with oak leaves. I had stopped at one point to photograph a brightly colored butterfly and then had noticed a disturbance in the ground over at one side. I walked over and found a mound of leaves, and under them the remains of a young deer. A little farther on I caught a faint odor of meat and noticed flies buzzing around a certain place, where I found the partial remains of another deer. There was an over-abundance of whitetail deer at that time and the mountain lion was thus helping to keep them in balance. It was impressive to find such tangible evidence of the presence of this great cat.

Mountain lion dens are generally in caves when caves are available, or in any spot that gives natural shelter.

The voice of the mountain lion has been a subject of controversy. The call has been variously described as screaming, caterwauling, roaring, like the moaning of a woman, yelling, or growling. When we consider the variety of calls of our common house cat, it is easy to understand the diversity in the calls of the mountain lion as they have been described. The few times that I have heard them convince me that they are more or less similar to those of the house cat but magnified many times in volume and depth of tone.

Jaguar

I should have liked to see the jaguar in its South American jungle home, with parrots in the trees, and perhaps a monkey up among the limbs. In Mexico we would have found it far from the jungle, in the arid brush country and in the mountains. A jaguar track in the dust or on a muddy water margin where we searched would

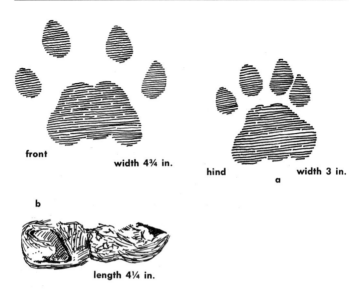

front

width 4¾ in.

hind   width 3 in.

a

b

length 4¼ in.

Fig. 59.   Jaguar tracks and scat

a. Tracks.   b. Dropping.

have made an exciting discovery. But I do not have the track from the wild to offer here. Instead, my son, with the cooperation of the attendants, obtained the tracks shown here at the Fleishhacker Zoo in San Francisco (Fig. 59).

In general, jaguar tracks are much like those of the mountain lion, and approximately the same size. I think they would be difficult to distinguish in southern regions where both occur together. The scats, too, are similar.

El tigre, as he is known in Mexico, or the *Felis onca* of science, ranges up through Mexico and has been known to enter Texas, Arizona, and California.

The call has been referred to as a roar, but in a series of short coughlike sounds, and not at all like the roar of the lion.

Ocelot

This beautiful cat, known to science as *Felis pardalis,* is at home in the South American tropics but occurs also in Mexico, and at one time had ventured into the southern United States.

I have had no opportunity to track this animal in the wild and so had to fall back on the director of the Woodland Park Zoo in Seattle, who helped me get the tracks in wet sand (Fig. 60, a). These tended to show the claws, giving a very uncatlike picture. This may possibly be the result of abnormal claw development in captivity, or of the ocelot's excitement in being driven across the prepared wet sand.

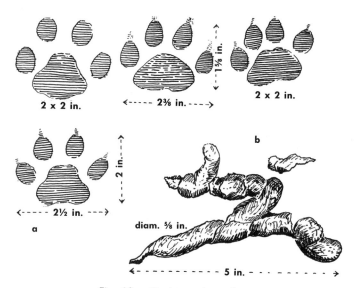

2 x 2 in.

←----- 2⅜ in. ----→

1⅞ in.

2 x 2 in.

←----- 2½ in. ---→

a

2 in.

b

diam. ⅝ in.

←- - - - - - - - - - 5 in. - - - - - - - →

Fig. 60.   Ocelot tracks and scat

a. Tracks in sand (Woodland Park Zoo, Seattle).
b. Dropping.

Jaguarundi Cat or Eyra

This small, slender cat, known as *Felis yagouaroundi,* is another product of the South American tropics which has found its way up through Mexico into southern Texas. It is one of those animals, like the screech owl, the red fox, and black bear, which may be born blond or brunet. That is, there are two color phases, a "red" type, generally rusty brown, and a "gray" type, which is mostly dull gray. In Texas and Mexico, it lives in the arid brushlands. This is one cat that not only climbs trees but readily takes to water as well.

Figure 61 shows the imprints of the front and hind feet of a jaguarundi cat.

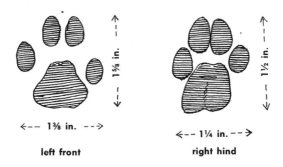

1⅝ in.

←-- 1⅜ in. --→

left front

1½ in.

←-- 1¼ in. --→

right hind

Fig. 61.   Front and hind feet of jaguarundi cat, about ⅔ natural size (furnished by Mr. Luther C. Goldman of the U.S. Fish and Wildlife Service; obtained near Harlingen, Texas, July 1952).

Sea Lion

Seals: Pinnipedia

AQUATIC ANIMALS like seals and sea lions naturally do not leave traces except when they come ashore. The common short-flippered harbor seal, *Phoca vitulina,* hitches along awkwardly on land. If this happens in mud or sand, the drag marks of the body may be seen, as well as the holes made by the nails of the front flippers (see Fig. 62, a). If the seal hauls out on ice or another hard surface covered with snow, the scrape marks appear as in Figure 62, b.

Hair seals generally deposit scats in the water, but when they are found on land they appear claylike or pasty, about 1½ inches in diameter.

On Arctic ice floes seals are readily discovered in the distance, since their dark color contrasts vividly with the snow and ice. They have the habit of sleeping intermittently, raising their heads to look around every few minutes. Eskimos often approach a seal by crawling up during the intervals when the head is down, timing it so that they are motionless when the seal is on the lookout. On the winter ice the seals keep open breathing holes in the ice. When the snow forms a mantle on the ice, the seal comes out of the hole but not through the snow, thus virtually forming an igloo for itself under the snow crust.

A sea lion rookery is easily detected at some distance by the raucous roaring; at a closer distance by the strong smell of ammonia. Sea lion droppings are similar in substance to those of the seal, but larger, about 2 to 2½ inches in diameter, depending on sex and age (see Fig. 62, c). They may also be soft and formless.

125

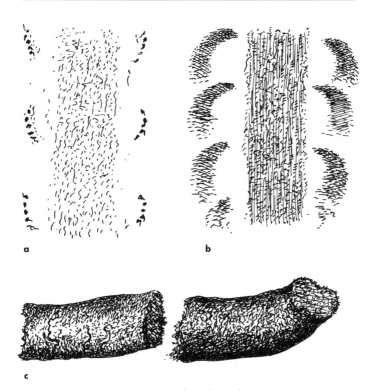

Fig. 62. Seal tracks and scat

a. Tracks of harbor seal in mud (after photograph by Dr. Victor B. Scheffer).
b. Tracks of seal in ½ in. of snow (Natl. Zoological Park, Washington, D.C.).
c. Droppings of northern sea lion, *Eumetopias jubata,* diam. about 2 in. (Aleutians).

Rodents: Rodentia

THE ANIMALS we classify as Rodentia, the chisel-toothed animals that gnaw and live on vegetation, are extremely numerous and extremely varied. They include large creatures such as the beaver, agouti, paca, and marmot, as well as the hordes of mice of many species. There are those that eat leafy vegetation, those that live mainly on seeds, even those that fell trees and eat bark. These varied habits are reflected in the signs they leave in the mud or snow, or in the flora.

In Figures 63, 64, 65, and 66 are assembled for handy reference representative tracks and droppings of the rodents exclusive of the rabbits. So far as possible they are drawn to scale on each page. The pages on scats are presented about natural size.

For more detailed study refer to the discussions of the species which follow.

Woodchuck; Yellowbelly and Hoary Marmots

The common woodchuck, *Marmota monax,* is the lowland marmot and is found in the eastern half of the United States (except the southernmost states), across the southern half of Canada (except the western coast), and on into easternmost Alaska.

The yellowbelly marmot, or rockchuck, *Marmota flaviventris,* is the common marmot of the western United States, living mostly in and near the Rocky Mountains, the Cascades, and the Sierras.

The hoary marmot, *Marmota caligata* (with two other species, *M. olympus* and *M. vancouverensis*), is the large marmot of the high mountain country, most often found in the mountains of western Canada and Alaska but appearing also in some of the mountains of western Montana, Idaho, and Washington.

The tracks of all these marmots are quite similar, though slightly larger in the case of the big hoary marmot. For example, note in Figure 67 the similarity of the track patterns of the Nevada yellow-belly marmot, *Marmota flaviventris* (*e*) and the Minnesota woodchuck, *Marmota monax* (*f*). Measurements of the individual tracks

127

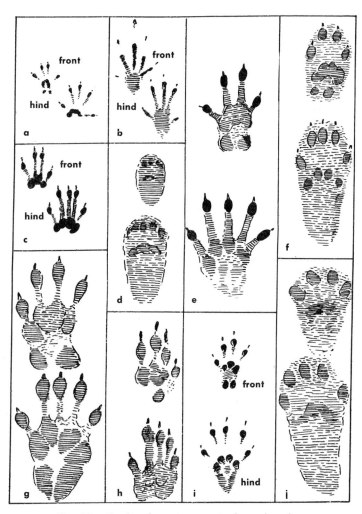

Fig. 63.   Tracks of marmots, squirrels, and gopher

a. Western chipmunk.   b. Northern pocket gopher (*Thomomys*).
c. Chickaree (*Tamiasciurus douglasi*).   d. Flying squirrel.
e. Fox squirrel.   f. Gray squirrel.   g. Marmot.
h. Prairie dog.   i. Uinta ground squirrel (*Citellus armatus*).
j. Tassel-eared (Kaibab) squirrel.

128

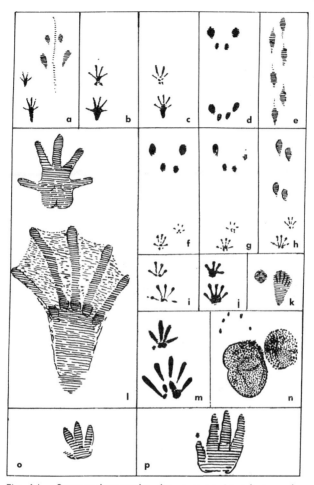

Fig. 64. Some rodent tracks, drawn approximately to scale

a. Jumping mouse, *Zapus*.
b. Cotton rat, *Sigmodon*.
c. Rice rat, *Oryzomys*.
d. Pocket mouse, *Perognathus*.
e. Lemming, *Dicrostonyx*.
f. White-footed mouse, *Peromyscus*.
g. House mouse, *Mus*.
h. Meadow vole, *Microtus*.

i. Norway rat, *Rattus*.
j. Woodrat, *Neotoma*.
k. Kangaroo rat, *Dipodomys*.
l. Beaver, *Castor*.
m. Muskrat, *Ondatra*.
n. Porcupine, *Erethizon*.
o. Agouti, *Dasyprocta*.
p. Paca, *Cuniculus*.

129

were about the same. Note also the similar measurements of the front tracks in *a* and *d*, yellowbelly and woodchuck respectively.

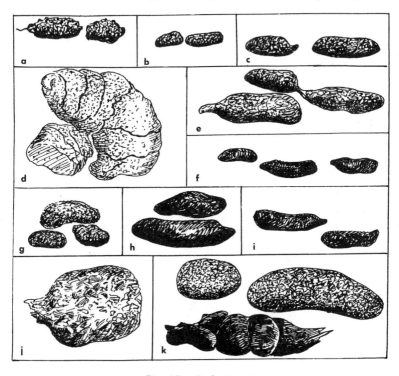

Fig. 65.   Rodent scats

a. Gray squirrel.   e. Prairie dog.   i. Norway rat.
b. Pocket gopher.   f. Woodrat.   j. Beaver.
c. Ground squirrel.   g. Muskrat.   k. Porcupine.
d. Marmots.   h. Aplodontia.

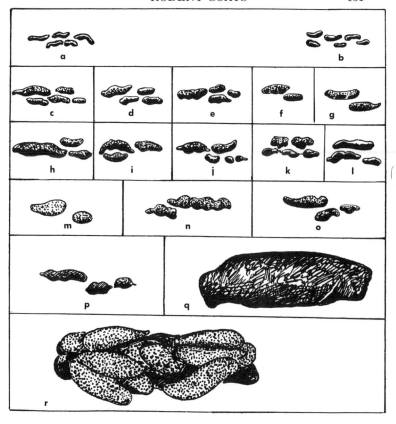

Fig. 66. Rodent scats

a. Redback vole.
b. Pocket mouse.
c. Meadow vole,
   Microtus.
d. Kangaroo rat.
e. Collared lemming.
f. Brown lemming.

g. Grasshopper mouse.
h. Cotton rat.
i. Rice rat.
j. Jumping mouse.
k. White-footed
   mouse
l. House mouse.

m. Tassel-eared
   (Kaibab) squirrel.
n. Red squirrel.
o. Flying squirrel.
p. Chipmunk.
q. Agouti.
r. Paca.

Hoary Marmot

In these walking gaits the hind foot tends to register in the front track more or less, as with so many other mammals. In Figure 67, g, and Figure 68, c, are shown the variations in the running gait of the Wyoming yellowbelly marmot, or rockchuck, which would be similar to those of the eastern woodchuck.

Note that the front foot, rodent-like, has four toes, big enough to show in the track, the hind foot five. Also, the heel of the hind foot very often does not touch the ground, so that in some cases the front track appears longer than the hind track. However, in full plantigrade travel the heel of the hind foot bears down, as shown in some of the figures.

Tracks of the Wyoming yellowbelly marmot on firm mud, as shown in Figure 67, c, illustrate how the front and hind prints sometimes intermingle. The toes of the respective tracks can nevertheless be discerned.

The width of the trail, or straddle, varies from an extreme of 6½ inches down to about 3½ inches.

Under certain circumstances the hind foot tracks of a woodchuck may be momentarily mistaken for those of a small raccoon. But the *front-foot* tracks of the raccoon in the same trail have five toes, the front-foot tracks of the marmot four. The marmots as a whole hibernate, so the tracks may not be expected in winter.

The great variety in marmot droppings, consisting of vegetation, is indicated in Figure 68, b. The inch scale in the figure will indicate roughly the sizes. The bottom sample illustrates the occasional soft type resulting from lush succulent food. The elongated one, too, failed to form the shorter, more normal segments.

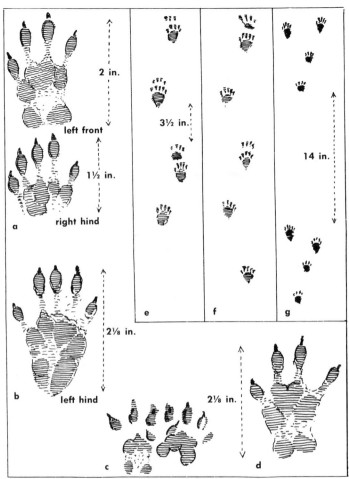

Fig. 67. Tracks of yellowbelly marmot and woodchuck

a. Front and hind tracks of yellowbelly marmot, in sand, heel of hind foot not showing (Yellowstone Natl. Park).
b. Hind track, in mud, showing heel (Wyo.).
c. Intermingled front and hind tracks, on firm mud (Wyo.).
d. Left front track of the eastern woodchuck (Mich.).
e. Walking gait of yellowbelly marmot (Nev.).
f. Walking gait of woodchuck (Minn.).
g. Running gait of yellowbelly marmot (Jackson Hole, Wyo.).

133

Fig. 68.   Yellowbelly marmot (rockchuck)

a. In a favorite habitat, with den in rock cave (Wyo.).
b. Six samples of droppings, showing extremes in variation.
c. Variations in running track patterns (Teton Mts., Wyo.).

134

Eastern Woodchuck in obscure entrance to its burrow

Where do we look for these marmots? Let us consider the familiar eastern woodchuck first. Mostly we find the woodchuck in the woods, but especially at the edges, or in adjacent meadows. In my experience, at least, they have been chiefly in open woods, and are at home among down logs.

Woodchucks dig their own dens. Sometimes you will find the pile of excavated earth just outside the entrance, but other openings may be flush with the ground, with no sign of excavated earth. The woodchuck in the illustration above was peering at me from just such an obscure burrow entrance, on the bank of the Red River in Minnesota. In those same woods we often found woodchucks in a hollow tree, with the opening at ground level, or in hollow logs. Often the woodchuck would be resting on a convenient place on a slanting tree trunk, with a convenient cavity for refuge. And woodchucks do occasionally climb trees.

The woodchuck's voice is somewhat varied. When disturbed or threatened, it will chatter or whistle with a sort of trill and grit its teeth. But it has a more elaborate whistling accomplishment variously described by observers and some interpreters as its song.

Francis H. Allen wrote of this song in the *Bulletin* of the Massachusetts Audubon Society for November 1941:

My notes made in Vermont, June 18, 1895, read: "Heard a woodchuck whistling just above the pine woods. I had never heard the note before and thought at first it was some rare bird unknown to me, but that was when he was some distance off. When heard near at hand the sound was absolutely startling. It begins very abruptly with a loud shrill short whistle followed immediately by another similar whistle not quite so loud and then by a succession of rapidly delivered softer and more liquid notes in a lower key. Quite a pleasing song on the whole. At a distance only the first two notes are heard." Though I am quite sure that I have heard the song several times since then, the only other record I find among my notes is "Sept. 18, 1904. Dover, Mass. Heard a woodchuck whistling in a mellow tone."

In March 1953 I visited the Trailside Museum at the Cook County Forest near Oak Park, Illinois, where there was a pet woodchuck. The young lady in charge called it up to the wires of the enclosure, stroked its face, and said, "Sing!" The woodchuck seized the wire in its teeth and issued a prolonged, piercing whistle in a monotone just as long as the young lady kept her fingers about its muzzle.

The so-called rockchuck of the western states is well named, for it inhabits the high mountains, among the rock slides and cliffs, as well as some of the valleys, and in lava beds. Its favorite retreat is among the rocks, though I have found its den also in the ground, much like that of the eastern woodchuck. I have never heard it "sing" like the woodchuck. The familiar call, undoubtedly an alarm call, is a short sharp whistle, a sound that carries a long distance.

The hoary marmot has also sought the high mountains, and its habits are much like those of the yellowbelly. However, its alarm call is distinctive, being a more prolonged clear whistle, quite different from the brief, abrupt call of the "rockchuck." Another call has been reported, a series of rapid whistled notes. No doubt there will be found a more varied repertoire when the animal is more intimately studied.

Woodchuck

Prairie Dog

The prairie dogs of the western plains region, *Cynomys,* ranged from the Dakotas south through Oklahoma and western Texas to northernmost Mexico, and westward to the Rocky Mountain region. The prairie dog has been poisoned off most of its original home, but may still be found in some national parks and refuges, and occasionally on public domain. A few of the places where these animals may still be observed, according to reports, are the Theodore Roosevelt National Memorial Park in North Dakota, Wind Cave National Park in South Dakota, the Black Hills region of South Dakota and Wyoming, and the Wichita Mountains National Wildlife Refuge in Oklahoma. Small colonies are still scattered here and there in other western localities.

This is a sociable animal preferring to live in colonies or "towns," which are easily recognized by the many burrows, each encircled by a raised earthen rim, in the form of a small crater.

There are several species of prairie dogs, but their tracks and other sign do not differ significantly. The tracks and gaits shown in Figure 69 apply to the group as a whole; the droppings in *d*, *e*, and *f* show the variations. Notice that, as in the case of the marmot and some other rodents, with certain kinds of feed scats are produced in which the pellets tend to be connected, like a string of beads. In such instances the diameter or general size of the pellets is small. *E* and *f* of Figure 69 show the more common types.

Supposedly the prairie dog got its name from the so-called bark, or cry of alarm, as it stands sentinel-like at its burrow. It flips its tail with each call. Then there is the peculiar performance when it rises up and throws its hands in the air, so to speak, as it produces a high-pitched, smooth note. It is next to impossible to

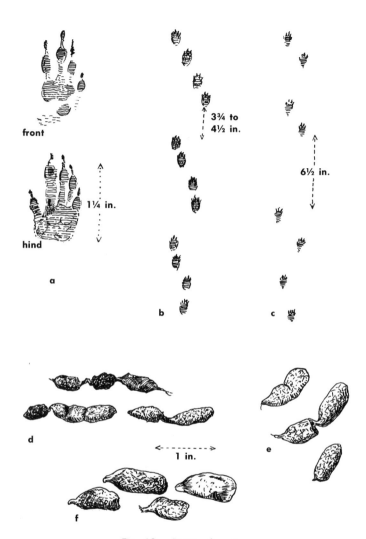

front

hind

1¼ in.

a

3¾ to
4½ in.

b

6½ in.

c

d

e

f

1 in.

Fig. 69.   Prairie dog sign

a. Tracks of blacktail prairie dog (No. Dak.).
b and c. Running track patterns (No. Dak.).
d and e. Blacktail prairie dog scats, one showing less common type in
   which pellets are connected (d, No. Dak.; e, Wichita Mts., Okla.).
f. Whitetail prairie dog scats (southern Wyo.).

138

describe such notes so that they can be recognized. In addition, there are various high-pitched chattering sounds.

Prairie dogs apparently do not hibernate as thoroughly as other ground squirrels. Though they remain inactive in their burrows for long periods in winter, they may be seen occasionally during those cold months.

Arctic Ground Squirrel and Golden-mantled Squirrel

Ground Squirrels

Ground squirrels are terrestrial members of the squirrel family, included in the genus *Citellus*. They are mostly western in distribution, and occupy the country from Michigan, Ohio, Indiana, Missouri, Oklahoma, Texas, and northern Mexico, west to the Pacific Coast, and northward through the western half of Canada and Alaska.

Ground squirrels vary greatly, and some of them are very striking. They live on vegetation but ordinarily are also carnivorous to a considerable extent and will eat birds' eggs and birds if they can catch them. They feed readily on carrion, even the bodies of their own kind. Generally they have a whistle of some kind, which varies with the species. A few major types will be considered briefly.

The golden-mantled squirrel, *Citellus lateralis,* has a stripe suggesting the pattern of the chipmunk, though this ground squirrel is much larger and chunkier. The subgenus *Callospermophilus* live in the Rocky Mountains and other mountain regions of the West, and inhabit rock slides and similar rocky places. The subgenus *Ammospermophilus,* known as the antelope squirrels, live in the desert areas of the Southwest. They are much paler but also have a single light stripe on each side. Other ground squirrels have a

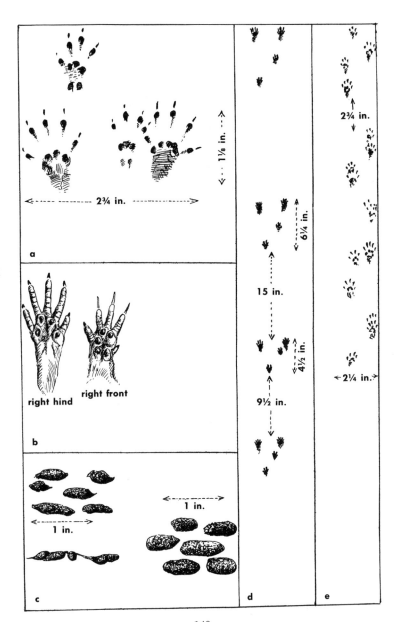

finely speckled coat, lines of spots, or plain gray or brownish hair. There is great variety in color pattern and size in this group, but the track pattern is similar throughout.

The thirteen-lined ground squirrel, *Citellus tridecemlineatus,* of the central part of the continent is the very slender one, adorned spectacularly with long rows of spots. In Minnesota I found that many of its burrows, about 2 inches in diameter and usually without an earth mound at the entrance, were so shallow I was able to excavate them with my hands to find the animal within.

The voice of this animal is musical, as such voices go, for it has a variety of birdlike whistles. Commonly one hears the single sharp alarm note, and the chattering series of notes when it has taken refuge in the den.

Most of the ground squirrel species fall into the large group that may be referred to as gray and are often mottled or finely spotted in various ways, ranging in size from the smaller ones, such as those of the *Citellus spilosoma* species, to the large rock squirrels of the Southwest and Pacific Coast and the relatively large ones of Alaska. Their dens are 3 inches in diameter or more.

These many kinds of ground squirrels have some form of sharp whistle and trills. Those of Alaska, the Arctic ground squirrels, have a sharp double note, from which the Eskimos have given them the name "Sik-sik." In one charming little Eskimo story and song, the ground squirrel dashes into its burrow to escape the raven, and calls sharply, "Sit-it!"

There is one group often mistaken for chipmunks. These are the golden-mantled squirrels, *Citellus lateralis,* richly colored, and with a broad light stripe on each side bordered with black. They live in the Rocky Mountain, Cascade, and Sierra regions of the West, extending up into the mountains of British Columbia and Alberta. They prefer the rock slides, where they find convenient shelter among the many crevices, and are found in various other rocky places, or among logs in open woods. I have not discovered any striking call notes or whistling among this group.

There is another little two-striped ground squirrel, the whitetail antelope squirrel, *Ammospermophilus leucurus;* it and related species are generally known as antelope squirrels. They are mostly gray in over-all color, which is suitable to their desert environment

Fig. 70 (opposite).   Ground squirrels

a. Track of Uinta ground squirrel, *Citellus armatus* (Wyo.).
b. Foot structure of Franklin ground squirrel, *Citellus franklini* (Ontario).
c. Droppings of Uinta ground squirrel at left (lower: a less common form, from more succulent food) and the larger rock squirrel, *Citellus variegatus,* at right.
d. Running pattern in snow, Uinta ground squirrel.
e. Walking pattern on mud, Uinta ground squirrel.

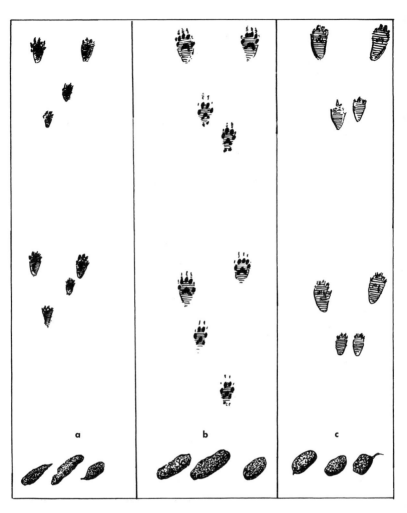

Fig. 71. Tracks and droppings of ground squirrels and gray squirrel;
droppings about ⅔ natural size

a. Uinta ground squirrel, *Citellus armatus*, tracks in snow, and droppings.
b. Rock squirrel, *Citellus variegatus*, tracks in mud, and droppings.
c. Eastern gray squirrel, *Sciurus carolinensis*, tracks in snow, and
droppings.

in the arid regions of the Southwest and northern Mexico. They have the habit of scurrying along with their short tail curled up tight over their backs and, since in most species the underside of the tail is pure white, it flashes bright like the white rump patch of an antelope.

Ground squirrel tracks have some characteristics that help to distinguish them from those of the tree squirrels. First, except in the more southern parts of the country, ground squirrels go into hibernation. So if in snowy country in winter you come upon tracks, they will not be those of ground squirrels. However, you may see their tracks in unusually early snowfalls in autumn, especially in the Far North; and the ground squirrels come out of hibernation early in spring while snowdrifts are still lingering.

Second, tree squirrels are found in woodlands; and whereas ground squirrels may also be found near trees in many places, they generally occupy plains, desert areas, and open country where there are no tree squirrels. Furthermore, in the Atlantic Coast states and as far west as western Ohio, Indiana, Missouri, eastern Oklahoma, and eastern Texas there are no ground squirrels.

Third, ground squirrel claws are longer and straighter than those of tree squirrels, a fact which may or may not be evident in the tracks that you find. Also, the track patterns are on the average different. In the tracks of the tree-climbing squirrels, the pattern tends to be more square, with the two front tracks usually parallel; the pattern of the ground squirrel tracks tends to be elongated, with the forefeet tracks more in line, one behind the other. Refer to Figure 71 and note the position of the front feet, more or less one behind the other, of the ground squirrel tracks in *a* and *b*, and the more parallel position in the tracks of the gray squirrel in *c*.

As we find in so many cases, however, these distinctions are general and do not always hold true. Very often you will find red squirrel tracks elongated in their pattern much like that of the ground squirrel.

In the samples so far collected, it appears that the droppings of the gray squirrel (and even more so those of the tassel-eared squirrels) are shorter than those of the ground squirrels (see Fig. 71).

The many kinds of ground squirrels vary in size, and of course there are minor differences in their tracks. Only two are shown here, the larger ones of the large ground squirrel of southern California, *Citellus variegatus,* and the smaller one of the Uinta ground squirrel, *Citellus armatus,* of Wyoming. These are shown for comparison in Figures 70 and 71. Note the usual variations in track pattern that we find in most mammals. The straddle is about 2¾ inches in the trail of the smaller ground squirrels, and over 4 inches in that of the larger ones (see Fig. 71, b).

Chipmunk

Chipmunks are familiar to most people. The larger chipmunk, *Tamias,* with several subspecies, is found in the eastern half of the United States (except the southeastern corner), from Louisiana, Iowa, Minnesota east and north into southeastern Canada and to the Atlantic Coast. To the west of this range are all the diverse species, large and small, dark and pale, of the genus *Eutamias,* occupying mountains, forests, and deserts. But wherever found, of whatever species, the chipmunk acts the same and is the same pert favorite with those who take note of such things.

These sprightly members of the squirrel family are mostly terrestrial, though they will readily climb trees. Their tracks may be found in mud, dust, sand, or snow. Snow tracks, however, will be seen only in the fall or early spring, for in snow country these animals have stored up food and are not abroad in winter.

Figure 72, a, shows the tracks of a western chipmunk in mud, in which the animal ran mostly on the toes. *B* shows tracks in dust in the same locality, in which the hind heels were put down. These track patterns vary in width from 1⅞ to 2½ inches, depend-

Fig. 72 (opposite)

a. Tracks in firm, wet mud (Wyo.).
b. Tracks in dust, heel of hind foot showing (Wyo.).
c. Scats of three species of chipmunk (top down: *Eutamias alpinus luteiventris,* Wyo.; *Tamias striatus lysteri,* N.Y.; *Eutamias dorsalis,* Ariz.).
d. Tracks in wet snow (Wyo.).   e. Tracks in new snow (Wyo.).

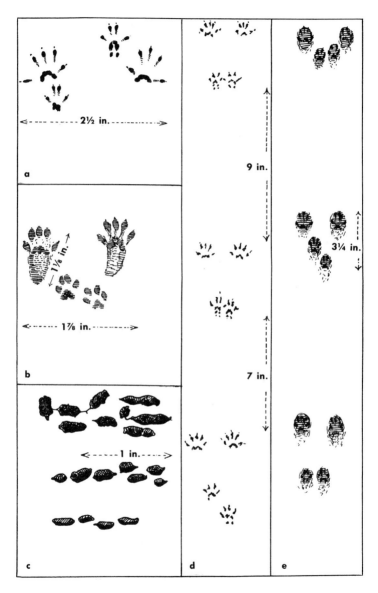

Fig. 72. Chipmunk tracks and scats

145

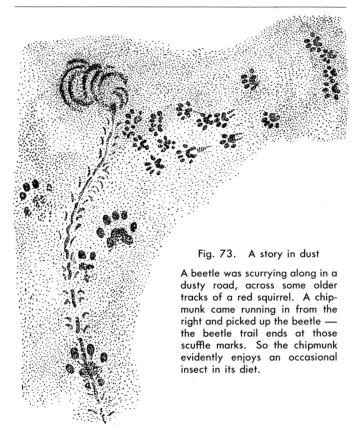

Fig. 73.   A story in dust

A beetle was scurrying along in a
dusty road, across some older
tracks of a red squirrel. A chipmunk came running in from the
right and picked up the beetle —
the beetle trail ends at those
scuffle marks. So the chipmunk
evidently enjoys an occasional
insect in its diet.

ing on the spread of the hind toes. The length of the track pattern,
from rear of hind tracks to toes of front tracks, varies from about
1¾ to 3½ inches. The leaps may be from 7 to about 15 inches.
Figure 72, d, most nearly expresses the pert, neat, and agile movements of the chipmunk.

Again it should be noted that in the leaping gait the hind feet
fall in front of the forefeet tracks, and in the case of the chipmunk
the two pairs of tracks, hind and front pairs, are parallel with each
other in most instances, though sometimes the two forefeet tracks
are one behind the other, as with the ground squirrel.

The tracks of the large eastern chipmunk, which are not illustrated here, should be somewhat larger than those shown.

The droppings are to be found in Figure 72, c. These particular samples show considerable differences in size and form. Much of this difference can very well be due to the type of food used and its quantity. They are not correlated with the size of the three species of chipmunks here represented.

All the chipmunk burrows that I have seen have had simple, unobtrusive openings in the ground, without an evident earth dump at the entrance. The diameter is approximately 2 inches.

The chipmunk's diet is extremely varied, but mostly consists of nuts, berries, and seeds of various kinds. The eastern chipmunk feeds on a diversity of nuts and grains, such fruits as wild cherries and raspberries, mushrooms, insects, and occasionally a bit of carrion. In Minnesota we used to find quantities of dry shells of the basswood nuts, opened on one side. We saw chipmunks pack several white oak acorns into their cheek pouches, and marveled at their capacity. Chipmunks took advantage of hollow trees and logs, and brush heaps.

In the West I have found the chipmunks feeding on grass seeds, and especially the dandelion heads, just when the calyx has closed after blooming. On a log, or stump or rock, or on the ground, you may find remains of such feasts — a little pile of dismembered grass-seed heads, several opened dandelion heads, or remains of other favorite plants. These are sure chipmunk signs.

The chipmunk has a call, but I have not found great variety in its repertoire. Usually the call has been represented as *chock, chock, chock* repeated to various lengths. It may be only two or three "chocks," or these may be repeated for a considerable length of time.

Red Squirrel and Chickaree or Pine Squirrel

The red squirrel, also called chickaree and pine squirrel in its western forms, with a number of subspecies in the genus *Tamiasciurus,* occupies much of the forested area of North America. The familiar red squirrel, *Tamiasciurus hudsonicus,* occupies the transcontinental coniferous forests from Alaska and Canada southward; in the eastern half of the United States to South Carolina and in the western states southward in the Rocky Mountains to Arizona and New Mexico. There is another species, the colorful chickaree or pine squirrel, *Tamiasciurus douglasi,* on the Pacific Coast from British Columbia down into California. It has orange underparts instead of white or whitish.

Tracks of these squirrels, leading from tree to tree, are common enough in winter snow, often appearing as a group of trails where the squirrel has run back and forth repeatedly. The squirrel's

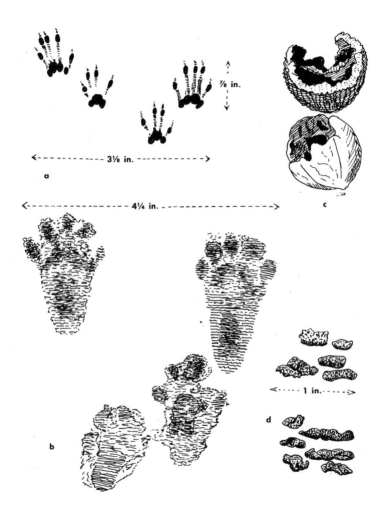

Fig. 74.　Red squirrel sign

Red Squirrel

home range is small; therefore you will find its trails localized within the radius of a small group of trees. Whatever the species, or whether you call it the red squirrel, chickaree, or pine squirrel, the tracks are practically the same, and the same vivacious spirit activates the animal.

Figure 74, a, shows the tracks of the chickaree of the Olympic Mountains, clearly defined in mud. In this case the heels did not touch the ground. In *b* are shown the tracks of a red squirrel, in snow, with the heel marks of the hind feet showing. These two illustrate how much larger are snow tracks than mud tracks.

Figure 75 illustrates the appearance of the running track pattern in various depths of snow and reveals the diversity of shape. Note the variations in the position of hind and front feet — sometimes one foot forward sometimes the other, though generally the hind feet are in front. One could almost say that in the red squirrel track pattern, being made by a tree-climbing rodent, the front feet are parallel, forming a "square-sided" group pattern, in contrast with the elongated pattern of the ground squirrel, which generally puts one forefoot in front of the other when running. But you

Fig. 74 (opposite)

a. Tracks of chickaree, in mud; about ⅔ natural size Olympic Mts., Wash.).
b. Tracks of red squirrel in snow, about ⅔ natural size (Wyo.).
c. Black walnut and hickory nuts opened by a Wyoming red squirrel that found this unaccustomed food in a cellar.
d. Droppings (upper, from Wyoming; lower, from Minnesota).

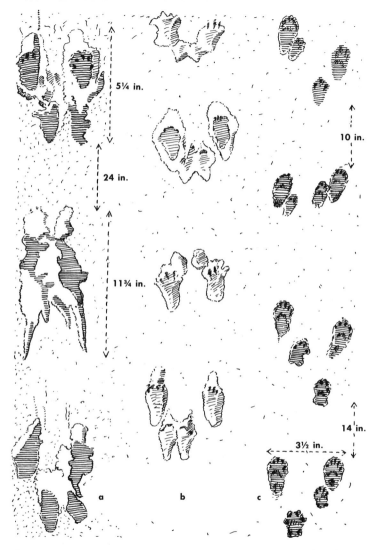

Fig. 75. Chickaree trails in snow, showing variations in squirrel tracks

will notice in the trails pictured here that many times the red squirrel also puts one forefoot in front of the other. We can only say that the red squirrel *tends* to keep the forefeet parallel when running, and one should glance at the trail as a whole to catch this tendency.

Where toe marks show, it should be remembered that there are five toes on the hind feet, four toes on the front feet. And the leaps vary from about 8 to 30 inches. The width of the track group, or straddle, varies from 3 to 4½ inches, even appearing a little more in very loose snow.

The red squirrel makes two kinds of nests — the outside nest, as shown in Figure 76, a, and the one in a hollow tree, such as the one from Minnesota in *b*. The outside nest, about a foot in diameter, is more common in coniferous forest, where hollow trees are less available. They are roughly globular, with entrance in the side, and may be built of grass, fine twigs, and lined with shredded bark. I found one built almost entirely of caribou hair, held together with a mixture of grass and twigs. Sometimes two or three of these nests are built in one tree. One winter a red squirrel built a nest in a box inside our cellar house. A weasel built a nest on a shelf in the same house, and the two spent the winter under that same roof.

The hollow tree dens (often in old flicker holes) are more common in deciduous forest, where such cavities are more available. In the eastern states I have found the squirrel taking advantage of the cavity that has rotted out where a limb has broken off.

Red squirrels also have holes in the ground, especially in the mass of cone scales, or middens, where cones are stored. They will tunnel into the snow to reach the stored food.

Once in a heavy coniferous forest of Oregon I heard a loud thump as if someone had struck a log with a club. Again and again I heard the sound, and at times, when several blows seemed to come in rapid succession, it suggested the clashing of deer antlers and I began to look for the deer. When I traced the sounds to a large sugar pine, the mystery was solved. A huge cone came hurtling down from the top, whacking limbs here and there, finally landing on the ground with a great thump. Up near the top was a squirrel, busy cutting loose one cone after another for its nut harvest.

The autumn is the harvest time for squirrels, east, west, and north. East or west, you may find them carrying mushrooms into the trees, placing them on limbs to dry. They store up acorns and other nuts. Cones of spruce or pine are cut loose and gathered on the ground, to be tucked away in odd corners for future use, especially in the midden heaps of old cone scales, under logs, or in tree hollows. In Alaska certain berries, such as those of the viburnum, are stored. In the Middle West and eastern states these squirrels are fond of the seeds of basswood and box elder.

Fig. 76.   Red squirrel nests

a. Outside nest in spruce tree (Alaska).
b. Hollow tree den (Minn.).

When spruce and lodgepole pine cones are severed, the twigs containing the cones are cut off, and in such places you will find the ground underneath strewn with spruce or pine twigs. The porcupine will do the same, but if it is porcupine work you will generally find scattered porcupine droppings on the ground.

Red squirrels will sometimes nip off the buds of young spruce trees, and gnaw the bark of some trees, and twigs. John Pearce, of the U.S. Fish and Wildlife Service, pointed out that red squirrels will gnaw fresh blister-rust cankers on white pine. Some of these gnawings resemble those of the porcupine. However, if tooth marks show, those made by the red squirrel are about as fine as mouse work, compared with the coarse marks left by porcupine.

The squirrel midden, sometimes covering several square yards of ground and consisting of a great accumulation of cone scales over a period of years, marks the squirrel's home ground. There is the place where cones have been stored and eaten. Also, you will find little piles of scales on a log or stump or hillock where the squirrel has feasted on cones.

Cottonwood leaf galls opened by a Red Squirrel

A Wyoming red squirrel found our store of Christmas nuts, black walnut and hickory nuts, sent to us by Eastern friends. These nuts were of course unfamiliar to this individual squirrel, but it recognized the value of the nuts and gnawed them open, at the end, as shown in Figure 74, c. Contrast this operation with the opening of such nuts by gray squirrels and flying squirrels, illustrated in Figures 77 and 82.

One day in the Snake River bottomlands in Wyoming, I noticed many green leaves on the ground under a large cottonwood. While I puzzled over this, several more leaves came fluttering down. Then I spied a chickaree high in the tree, nibbling loose some more. The answer became clear. At the base of each leaf was a large insect gall. The squirrel was busy opening the galls for the larvae inside and, from evidence of the number of leaves on the ground, a considerable percentage of the insect larvae were eaten.

The voice of the chickaree, or western pine squirrel, is distinctive. One cannot mistake the scolding notes and the varied calls of this most dynamic little creature. There may be the prolonged chatter, then higher-pitched notes, in great variety and often quite explosive in effect. It may be a *tsik, tsik, tsik, chrrrrrrrr — siew, siew, siew, siew,* if one may presume to put into human syllables one version of red squirrel language. Actually, the tirade may be a series of coughs and hiccups and high-pitched notes in a combination impossible to write, but they are easily recognized once they become familiar.

Gray, Fox, and Tassel-eared Squirrels

The tracks and other signs of these three squirrels, all of the genus *Sciurus,* are similar enough to be discussed as a group. The eastern gray squirrel, *Sciurus carolinensis,* is found in the eastern half of the United States, and as far west as the eastern Dakotas, central Kansas, and Texas. The western gray squirrel, *Sciurus griseus,* inhabits Washington, Oregon, and California. And there is the Arizona gray squirrel, *Sciurus arizonensis,* of Arizona.

The eastern fox squirrel, *Sciurus niger,* so much like the gray in size and general appearance, extends just a little farther west, and its western representative — the Apache fox squirrel, *Sciurus apache* — is to be found in the Chiricahua Mountains of Arizona and in northern Mexico.

The beautiful tassel-eared squirrel, *Sciurus aberti,* is found only in northern Arizona, western New Mexico, southwestern Colorado, and northern Mexico. In the Grand Canyon country, it is known as the Kaibab or Abert Squirrel, and by some authorities considered a separate species.

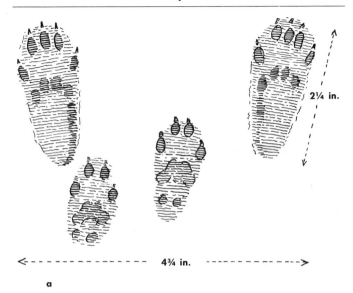

2¼ in.

<----------------------- 4¾ in. ----------------->

a

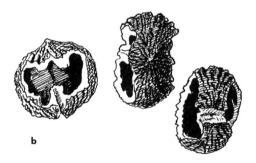

b

Fig. 77.   Gray squirrel sign

a. Tracks in ½ in. of wet snow, about ⅔ natural size (Washington, D.C.).
b. Black walnuts opened by gray squirrel (N.Y.).

Gray Squirrel and
Tassel-eared Squirrel

The tracks and track patterns of this group of squirrels are
similar to those of the red squirrel, on a larger scale. Figure 79,
a, shows Michigan fox squirrel tracks in mud; b shows Oklahoma
fox squirrel tracks in deeper mud, apparently with the toes in a
more cramped position. Note that the heel of the hind foot does
not necessarily leave a mark. In snow, however, the mark of the
entire foot is more likely to be made, as shown by the tassel-eared
(Kaibab) and gray squirrel tracks in Figures 78, a, and 77, a. In
these figures there are variations in track patterns that actually
are common to all species of these larger squirrels. It is important
to avoid ascribing to any one species the particular pattern that
happens to be illustrated for it here.

The width of trail, or straddle, varies from about 4¼ to almost
5 inches, and the leaps may be as much as 36 inches at least.

The droppings of this group of squirrels appear to be propor-
tionately shorter than those of the red squirrel, and this is particularly true of those at hand from the tassel-eared squirrel.

All of these squirrels have a varied diet of nuts, seeds, berries,
mushrooms, buds, and bark. They are fond of the fruit of the
elm, and corn; and they open apples for the seeds. The storage

Fig. 78 (opposite).   Tracks and scats of tasseled-eared
and gray squirrels

a. Tracks of the tassel-eared (Kaibab) squirrel, in snow.
b. Track pattern of running gray squirrel (Washington, D.C.).
c. Track pattern of leaping tassel-eared (Kaibab) squirrel, in snow.
d. Droppings of tassel-eared (Abert) squirrel, about natural size.
e. Droppings of gray squirrel, about natural size (Washington, D.C.).

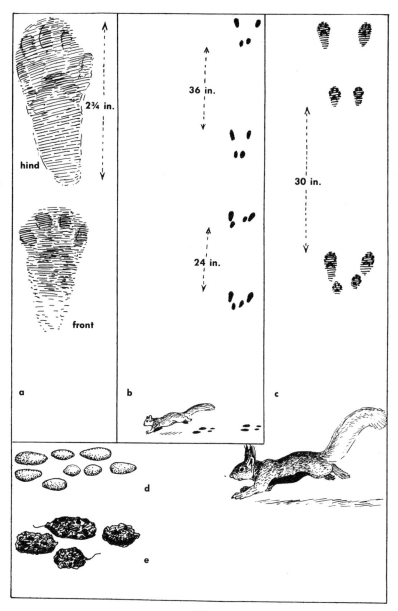

a

hind

2¾ in.

front

b

36 in.

24 in.

c

30 in.

d

e

157

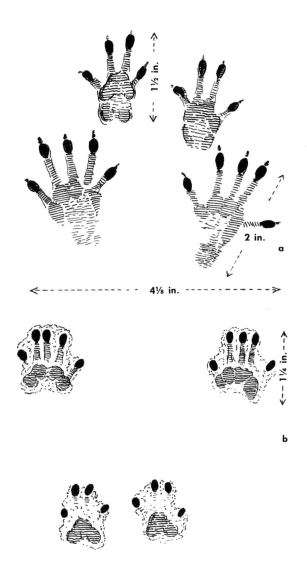

Fig. 79. Fox squirrel tracks

a. Tracks in mud, about ⅔ natural size (Mich.).
b. Tracks in deeper mud, about ⅔ natural size (Okla.).

158

habits of the gray and fox squirrels differ from those of the red squirrel in that their food is not hoarded in one place but buried singly here and there in the ground. They nip the buds of various trees, such as maple, elm, basswood, willow, and oak, and take the terminal tips of conifer seedlings. Like the red squirrel, they eat the bark of various trees and often girdle young trees, sometimes down at the root line. Apparently they seek the sap and the cambium layer right under the bark.

In the eastern states, as well as on the Pacific Coast, gray squirrels or fox squirrels will eat the bark of young conifers, often girdling the stems. Such gnawings on tree trunks or limbs are frequently prominent. Again, it would be difficult to distinguish this work from that of the red squirrel, or even the porcupine. The porcupine tooth marks, if they show, are larger, and if the work is recent there should be some porcupine droppings on the ground beneath the tree.

The tassel-eared squirrel also has a penchant for the bark of twigs of conifers, notably that of yellow pine. It will also gnaw bones and antlers, as several other rodents do. The voice of these large squirrels is quite different from that of the red squirrel, being deeper in tone and, in my experience, not as diversified. It is usually expressed in words as *qua-qua-qua-qua,* with some variations.

The gray, fox, and tassel-eared squirrels all have nests in hollow trees, as well as outside nests, just as the red squirrel does, but they are much more prone to use leaves and twigs rather than the grass and shredded bark used by the red squirrel. There may be several nests in a tree, some of them dummies without a cavity. Compare Figures 80 and 76.

Fig. 80.   Fox squirrel
with tree nest

Flying Squirrel

A flying animal may be expected to leave rather sketchy trails, but so does the red squirrel, since its trails are largely from tree to tree. In fact, often one must look sharp to distinguish between the tracks of the two. Generally speaking, the feet of the flying squirrel are smaller than those of the red squirrel; but snow tracks vary so much in size, depending on the condition of the snow, that positive identification is often difficult. Moreover, in deep snow the red squirrel may show drag marks of the feet somewhat like those of the flying squirrel, *Glaucomys*.

When you find a "sitzmark," or landing spot, in an open area from which tracks lead off, you know that the flying squirrel "set himself down" there. See Figures 81, a and c, and 82, b. In 82, b, the drag marks extended for some 50 inches (including the tail mark). In such landings the body leaves a definite gouge in the snow.

Figure 81, e, f, and g, shows droppings from Wyoming, Washington, D.C., and New York. There is probably much variation in

Fig. 81 (opposite)

a. A landing mark, in snow, with trail leading off in leaps of 14, 21, and 20 in. (tracks in *a*, *b*, *c*, and *d* from Wyoming).
b. Snow trail with leaps of 29, 21, and 11 in. In one spot the squirrel slid.
c. Another landing mark, 9½ in. long, with irregular track pattern.
d. More flying squirrel tracks, in slow hop.
e, f, g. Scats, about natural size (from Wyoming, Washington, D.C., and New York, respectively).

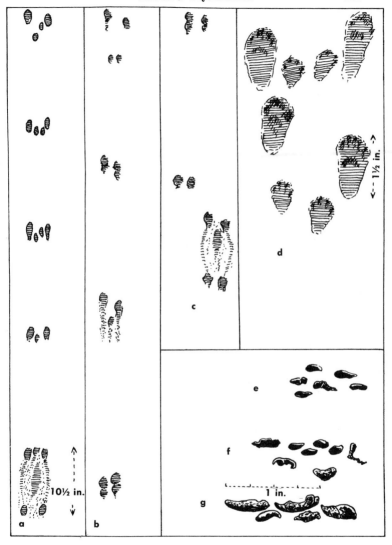

Fig. 81. Tracks and scats of the flying squirrel

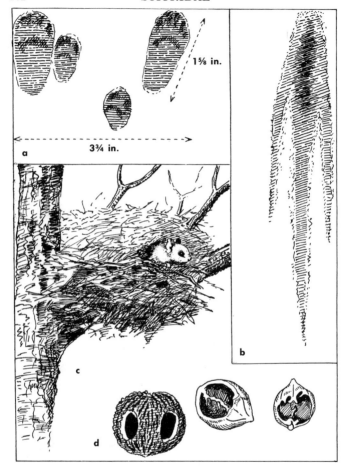

Fig. 82.   Flying squirrel sign

a. Tracks in snow (Wyo.).
b. Landing mark in snow, length 50 in., where the animal slid on the surface.
c. A renovated bird's nest (Wyo.).
d. Black walnut, opened in four places by flying squirrel; hickory nuts, opened generally only on one side (N.Y.).

size, depending on food, but on the whole the scats are smaller than those of the red squirrel. Figure 82, d, represents a black walnut and two hickory nuts opened by a flying squirrel, with the openings on the side.

Hollows in trees and outside nests are used. On the bank of the Red River in Minnesota I came upon a mother flying squirrel with a family of young in a hollow in the side of a tree, less than five feet from the ground. Other nests are in woodpecker holes or similar cavities high in the trees.

One early spring day in Jackson Hole, Wyoming, I climbed a fir tree to examine an old bird's nest, possibly built by Steller's jays. As I came within a couple of feet of the nest and had just noticed that it was domed over with added material, it seemed to explode when several flying squirrels burst out of it and sailed away in different directions. I watched one plane far down the mountain slope. It pays to examine old birds' nests. Flying squirrels will also use other squirrels' nests, and attics of houses.

One moonlit night in Minnesota when two friends and I were camping out, tentless, we noticed shadowy figures sailing above us from tree to tree. Then we heard the quiet *tick* as the animals, which proved to be flying squirrels, landed on the trunks of trees. Next we heard the rustlings and gnawing as they gathered the seeds of the ash trees. Faint sounds up in the trees at night may call your attention to the aerial activities of these nocturnal squirrels.

Pocket Gopher

Once when I was out on a mountainside with a troop of Boy Scouts to help them interpret what they saw, we stopped at a fresh mound of earth.

"What has happened here, boys? Who did that?"

"Mole," someone declared. "Mole, mole," was repeated by one after another.

So I had to explain, "There isn't a mole in this part of the Rocky Mountains. Ever hear about the pocket gopher?"

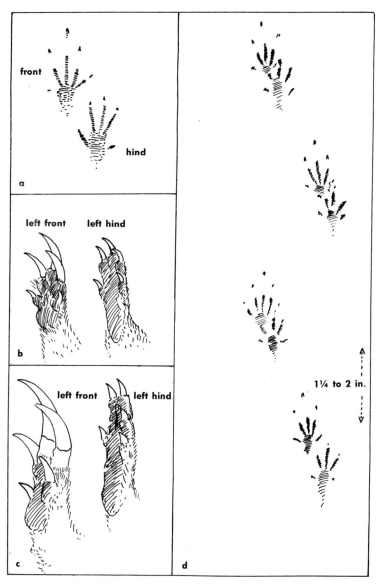

front

hind

left front   left hind

left front   left hind

1¼ to 2 in.

a

b

c

d

Fig. 83.   Pocket gopher

164

Northern Pocket Gophers

The boys reflected the confusion prevalent everywhere about these two unrelated animals. We examined the mound of earth. "See that little hollow there, with the earth plug in it? That's where the animal finished digging. When he wanted to dig a new burrow here he pushed out the dirt, and as the pile grew, he came out and pushed it over pretty much to one side. Then, when he finished his excavating down there, he pushed up enough dirt to plug the entrance. That's the little dirt cap you see there at one side of the mound. If that had been a mole, he would simply have pushed that earth upward from below, without shoving it to one side, and there would be no earth cap like the one we see here." (See Fig. 84.)

We walked on a little and stopped again. "Now, can you explain that?"

No, they couldn't. There were some heavy ropes of earth lying on the ground, earth cores exposed when the snow had thawed away in spring. Pocket gophers continue their digging in winter, too, and shove the earth into snow tunnels. These ropes of earth were the mud casts of snow tunnels, about 2 inches in diameter, of the northern pocket gophers.

You will not often find pocket gopher tracks. Figure 83, a and d, illustrates the tracks in mud. Note that there are five toes in both front and hind tracks, when they all show, and that the

Fig. 83 (opposite)

a. Tracks of northern pocket gopher, *Thomomys talpoides*, in mud; natural size.
b. Left feet of *Thomomys talpoides*, natural size.
c. Left feet of the much larger *Geomys bursarius*, from Minnesota, natural size. Note long front claws used for digging.
d. Walking track pattern of *Thomomys talpoides*, of Wyoming, in mud. About ⅔ natural size; straddle 1½ to 2 in.

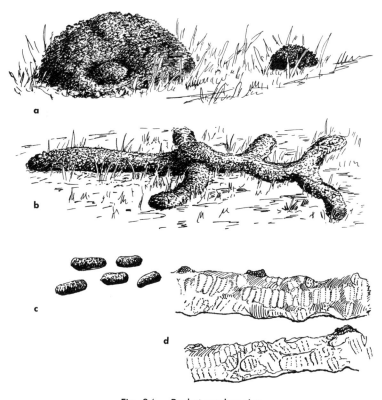

Fig. 84. Pocket gopher sign

a. A large mound, showing earth plug near one edge, and a small mound that itself constitutes the plug.
b. Earth cores that had been pushed into snow tunnels in winter.
c. Pocket gopher droppings (Wyo.).
d. Aspen limbs gnawed by northern pocket gophers, individual tooth marks about 1/16 in. wide.

front claw marks are far out in front. Note also the much greater size of the feet of the pocket gopher of the prairie, *Geomys,* shown in Figure 83, c, than that of *Thomomys* in *b*. Its tracks would be far larger than those shown here.

One spring day in Yellowstone Park I followed the tracks of a grizzly on intermittent patches of snow and found an excavation he had made in an open meadow. The story was plain. His keen nose had located a pocket gopher cache of roots a few inches underground and he had feasted with satisfaction. Some of the roots, half a dozen kinds, lay scattered about. I was studying the bears at the time and so took the roots. Since I did not know what plants they came from, I took them into my camp and planted them. When the plants grew I could list them as the food of pocket gophers for the long winter under the snow, as well as of the robber grizzly.

Under the winter snow the pocket gophers still forage over the ground with snow tunnels, and when the snow thaws in the spring you will find fallen limbs and bases of small trees and bushes gnawed by these rodents. There will be mud cores nearby, and the limbs will show that the teeth have gouged deeply into the wood, leaving a very ragged surface. The individual tooth marks are about 1/16 inch wide, a little wider than those of mice.

It should be explained that there are three genera of pocket gophers: *Thomomys,* with its multitude of forms, large and small, occupies the western states and Canada, and part of Mexico; *Geomys* is the one in the Great Plains region and southeastern states; *Papogeomys* is found in the Southwest and Mexico.

Pocket Mouse

The pocket mice of the genus *Perognathus* are distributed over the western half of the United States and Mexico, usually in the more arid plains sections. The one pictured here is *Perognathus parvus*. Other species have a variety of hair structures, and they vary in size.

Their tracks are similar in pattern to those of the white-footed mice, but are smaller, the outside spread being about 1⅛ inches

Fig. 85.   Pocket mouse sign

a. Tracks of pocket mouse in dust.
b. Droppings of spiny pocket mouse, about
   natural size.

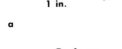

1 in.

a

b

for those I had opportunity to measure in Nevada (see Fig. 85, a). Their bounds varied from ¾ to 4⅝ inches. It has been reported that tail marks may show. However, this may occasionally be true also of white-footed mice in snow. The droppings are tiny, black, and seedlike in appearance (see Fig. 85, b).

Although it is difficult in many cases to identify burrows, the pocket mouse burrows generally have near the entrances a mound of fine soil, much like that made by the pocket gopher, but usually smaller. Like the pocket gopher, too, they may plug branch burrows with loose soil. The mounds, unlike those of the pocket gopher, are not made in spring or early summer, except by some species. The burrow itself, a little less than an inch in diameter and a little smaller than that of *Peromyscus,* goes to a depth of several feet, with the nest far underground. Seed caches may be made closer to the surface.

Pocket mice apparently may be dormant during a cold part of the winter.

Kangaroo Rat and Kangaroo Mouse

The kangaroo rat, an interesting rodent included in the genus *Dipodomys,* inhabits the plains and deserts of the West.

As one would expect of such a "kangaroo" structure, travel is performed by hops, with the hind legs only, and when traveling at any appreciable speed the animal runs on its hind toes (Fig. 86, c). When shuffling along slowly for feeding purposes, all four feet are down, including the heels of the hind feet, as in Figure 86, a. At such times, too, the tail drags in the sand.

Kangaroo Rat

Built on the same lines, but smaller, is the so-called kangaroo mouse, well named *Microdipodops*. It is relatively rare, or at least little known. It looks much like its larger relative but has no brush at the end of its tail. It leaps in the same kangaroo manner, leaving the twin tracks shown in Figure 86, d.

Both of these, when traveling slowly, will put down the front feet, and then more of the hind foot may show as the animal lands on it more solidly. In leaps, the hind heel apparently is off the ground and tail marks do not show.

Comparative measurements are about as follows: outside width of straddle in the trail — for kangaroo rat, 1¼ to 2 inches; for kangaroo mouse, about 1⅛ inches. A kangaroo rat will leap from as little as 5 or 6 inches up to 15 inches or more, and some of the larger species are reported to leap upward of 30 inches or more. The full hind-foot track will measure 1½ to 1¾ inches at least; with the heel, as in running, it varies from ⅞ to well over 1 inch. According to the few kangaroo mouse tracks I have been able to measure, it will leap at least 3¾ to 4½ inches, probably farther. The running tracks are about ½ inch long.

The scats of *Dipodomys* are from about ⅛ to ¼ inch long, and may be dark green or brown in color. Those of the kangaroo mouse are similar but smaller, from about ⅛ to ⅙ inch. Droppings may be found in the den tunnels, or on the ground near the burrows.

It should be remembered that the kangaroo rat as a group is differentiated into a large number of species and subspecies diversified a great deal in size. Therefore the tracks will vary. Moreover, some have four toes, others have five. But all have the same track pattern.

A characteristic feature of desert areas consists of the mounds of sand or fine soil thrown up by kangaroo rats. Those of the largest species may be over 3 feet high and over 12 feet in diameter. These have a number of burrow entrances, 4 or 5 inches in diameter. Smaller species have smaller mounds and burrows, and some do not throw out conspicuous mounds. Usually you will find some of the burrow entrances plugged with loose earth or sand.

You will find trails leading from one mound to another, or radiating to feeding places. It should be kept in mind that the

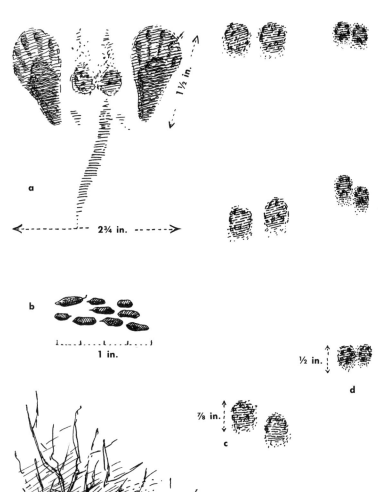

a

1½ in.

← - - - - - - - 2¾ in. - - - - - →

b

├ - - ┴ - - - ┴ - - - ┴ - - - ┤
1 in.

½ in.

d

⅞ in.

c

e

170

pocket mice also may throw out a small mound. Kangaroo rats enjoy a dust bath, so you will find little dusting spots, which are occasionally scooped out slightly.

There is another indication of the presence of this rodent. If you scrape or tap at the entrance to an occupied burrow, you may hear within a light thumping sound, which has been referred to as "drumming." The woodrat will thump with its feet, and so does the skunk. The kangaroo rat shares this habit.

Around the burrows and along the paths leading from them you may find fragments of grass or other plants that have been cut.

Beaver

The familiar *Castor canadensis,* which has contributed to the fur supply so importantly, is pretty well distributed over North America, wherever it has been able to find its food among forest products. It is the rodent that most obviously affects the landscape, and its works are the easiest to discover, even if you never see the footprints.

The most obvious beaver sign is the dam and the lodge. These (suggested in Fig. 87, e) are so obvious that for recognition purposes they need no further comment here. It should be remembered, however, that the beaver also digs burrows in banks of ponds, lakes, and rivers, with underground entrance. Thus "bank beavers" may have built no lodge, depending entirely on the burrows. What the beaver is after is deep enough water for winter. This is present in streams of large enough size. Ponds are built by damming the smaller streams, for the same purpose.

Beaver cuttings, too, are prominent. Fallen trees and stumps will show the characteristic gnawing techniques that felled the trees — simply an encircling cut in a deepening groove, until the tree falls. The tooth marks and the chips reveal the workman. On the bank, or in the water, you will find peeled logs and twigs, smooth and gleaming white when fresh. These are the remains of the feast on bark. Aspen, cottonwood, birch, and willow are

Fig. 86 (opposite).   Kangaroo rat and kangaroo mouse sign

a. Tracks of kangaroo rat, in sand, on a slow short hop (Nev.).
b. Droppings of a Nevada kangaroo rat, about natural size.
c. Tracks of kangaroo rat in sand, only the toes touching (Black Rock Desert, Nev.).
d. Tracks of kangaroo mouse, *Microdipodops,* in sand (Black Rock Desert).
e. Burrow mound of kangaroo rat.

Beaver

some of the favorite food trees, though a beaver will occasionally gnaw some of the bark of a standing pine, and conifers are sometimes felled.

The tooth marks of beaver are relatively broad, usually from ⅛ to ¼ inch in width, more commonly ⅛ inch. See Figures 87 and 191.

The scent mound is a pile of mud scraped together, or a pile of mud, grass, and sticks, on which the beaver leaves its scent from the glands developed for that purpose (Fig. 87, e). This is similar in function to the "sign posts" of some of the carnivores. Along the shore you will often see little dabs of mud with stems of sedges, apparently perfunctory efforts to establish scent piles. The more elaborate ones may be over 3 feet in diameter and upward of a foot in height.

Droppings are not often found, since they are deposited in water. They consist of oval pellets of coarse "sawdust." Occasionally several pellets may be temporarily connected, like beads, but being in the water, such material soon disintegrates.

Scats may be 1 to 1¼ inches long, and about ¾ inch in diameter, and of course will vary in size and shape (see Fig. 87, d).

Perfect beaver tracks are hard to find, for the tail may drag and obscure them. Nevertheless, they are distinctive, because of the

Fig. 87 (opposite)

a. Tracks in mud. Hind track, 6 to 6½ in. by 4¾ to 5¼ in.; front, about 3 in. long (Wyo.).
b. Trail, with track intervals of about 3 to 5½ in.
c. Tooth marks, natural size. See also Fig. 191, e, f, g.
d. Scats, natural size.
e. Beaver dam, pond, and lodge, with beaver leaving scent mound in foreground.

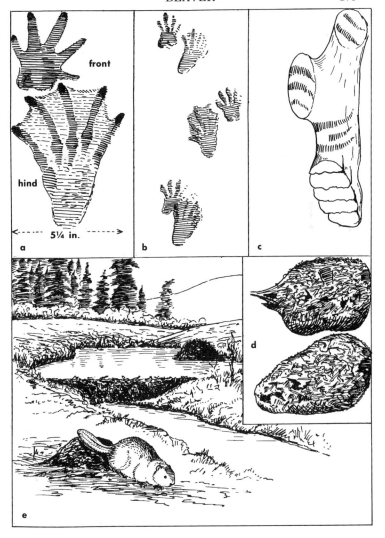

Fig. 87. Beaver sign

large webbed hind feet, and even if only part of them shows. Rarely do you find all five toes of the front tracks. More often they appear as three- or four-toed tracks, and not always does the full number appear even in the large hind track.

There are well-beaten trails across dams from one pond to another, or overland between two bodies of water. You will find drag marks on the ground where beavers have dragged limbs or lengths of small logs to the water, and you may find the telltale chips where the wood was cut. In connection with beaver ponds, too, there may be long canals, sometimes several hundred feet long, dug by the animals for the purpose of floating in logs.

In snow country, when the beaver climbs out of the water for foraging in the woods, it leaves a trough that at first may be mistaken for that of the porcupine or otter, especially at a distance. However, search for even a fragment of a footprint should identify it.

Sometimes you find beaver cuttings or patches of bark eaten from a tree trunk at such an astonishing height above the ground as to suggest a true "giant" beaver. The mystery is solved if one is mindful of the fact that these cuttings were made from the top surface of deep winter snow, which may have held the beaver several feet above the ground.

Occasionally you will come to an area, perhaps an old pond or marshy place that used to be a pond, surrounded by ancient dead trees. You may find the remnants of a beaver dam built long ago. This is what happened. The beavers built a dam that permanently flooded the surrounding trees. These eventually died. As the pond, in the evolution of such landscape, becomes a meadow, trees will once more cover the area.

The beaver's voice is not conspicuous, but he does make noise. When excited, or alarmed, he dives and slaps the water with his flat tail, causing a loud resounding splash. Whether intentionally or not, no doubt this serves as a signal to fellow beavers.

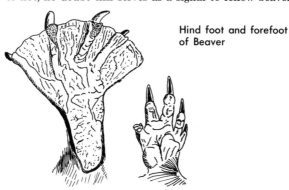

Hind foot and forefoot
of Beaver

Muskrat

The muskrat, *Ondatra zibethica,* is so widespread over the continent that only the more desertlike regions and the true Arctic are outside its range.

Muskrat tracks are, of course, found mostly near water, though occasionally the animals will make fairly long overland journeys. Both feet have five toes, though the inner toe of the front foot is so small that it rarely shows. See the minute imprint in Figure 88, a. In the track pattern the front foot very often precedes the hind foot. At other times the hind foot is foremost, or may cover the front track. Examples are shown in Figure 88. Very often, too, the drag mark of the tail is shown, but not always. The width of trail, or straddle, is about 3½ inches.

One winter day at a sluggish stream I watched a muskrat running hurriedly across a sheet of ice covered with a little snow. The tail moved about, sometimes swinging high aloft. The trail in this hasty gait was very irregular, with only an occasional tail mark, and with front and hind feet in many arrangements, as shown in Figure 88, e.

Muskrat droppings are elongated, varying above and below ⅝ of an inch in length. They may be found in clusters on logs in the water, beaver dams, rocks, or favorite resting places on the bank (see Fig. 88, d).

There are other signs of muskrat. Prominent among these is the muskrat house, built of matted vegetation, on the shore at the water's edge, or in shallow water. It consists of marsh grasses and sedges, sometimes heaped up to as much as 4 feet in height. Then there is the food shelter, or eating house, which may be built over a "plunge hole" in a marsh, or on the ice in winter. In areas where the winter is cold enough, the muskrat will push up through a hole in the ice various types of debris, forming a mass in which a cavity large enough for one animal is formed. This becomes covered with snow, with enough insulation to keep the

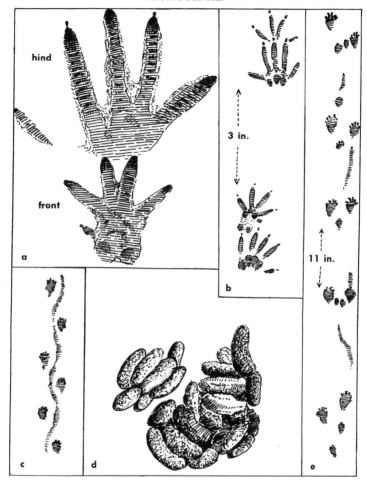

Fig. 88.   Muskrat tracks and scats

a. Tracks, right side, in mud, natural size.
b. Walking tracks in mud.
c. Track diagram, showing tail mark in snow.
d. Droppings, about natural size.
e. Tracks in light snow on ice, running gait.

Fig. 89. Diagrammatic section-view of muskrat burrow
and feeding platform, all under a layer of snow

a. Feeding station on the ice, with chamber and plunge hole down
   through the ice.
b. Simple burrow, with underwater entrance and nest chamber, c, at
   the end above water level.
d. Pile of vegetation covering an accidental hole (?) or ventilation hole
   that leads down to the burrow.

plunge hole in the ice open. Figure 89 shows such a hut on the
ice, together with a bank burrow, all in cross section.

In waters used by muskrats you will see floating blades of sedges
or other food remnants left by these animals. It may be a collection
of cattail stalks, apparently cut into convenient lengths for handling, much as you may find lengths of grass stems in field mouse
runways. Or there may be a floating raft of cut stems of various
kinds, on which the muskrat rests to feed. In dense masses of marsh
vegetation, too, you will find holes where muskrats have dug for
roots. They often go ashore on favorite spots to feed, where you
will find fragments of stems and blades.

The muskrat is not entirely vegetarian, and you may find heaps
of clamshells on a bank or in shallow water, on favorite feeding
spots, where the animals have opened the mollusks and fed on
them.

The muskrat often builds bank burrows, with underwater entrance. The home burrow may be complicated, with various
passages, and a nest chamber. There is also a simpler type used
for a refuge, or retreat — in fact, it may be simply a shallow cavity
under a bank where the animal can rest and feed. In some instances
I have found an opening covered with vegetation leading up from
the tunnel to the open air on the bank. Was this an accidental
hole that had to be covered over, or was it intentional? The
diagram in Figure 89 illustrates such a one found on the Koyukuk
River, Alaska, in 1924.

There is still another sign that should be mentioned. On the
bank near the water you may come upon a little platform, or mat,
of cut sedge leaves or similar fragments, sometimes mixed with a

little mud. This is a scent post, for the muskrat also has scent glands and leaves an odor record for other muskrat passers-by. I have never found them large or elaborate, such as those made by beavers. It may be simply a handful of stems and a little mud. Occasionally I have found a little mat of stems without mud, which may or may not have been a scent post.

The muskrat voice seems to be mostly a squeaking, which I have rarely heard.

It is worth mentioning, too, that although muskrats are especially partial to swamps and marshes and certain streams and lake shores, they are prone to seek the beaver ponds as ready-made habitat for their homes. They appear to associate regularly with beavers in this way.

Water Rat at nest

Florida Water Rat

Neofiber alleni, the Florida water rat, or "round-tailed muskrat," is found only in the Okefenokee Swamp of southeastern Georgia and in Florida. It looks like a young muskrat, or a huge field mouse, but, unlike the muskrat, it has a round tail.

The most likely evidences of its presence are probably the houses, 1 or 2 feet in diameter, sometimes larger, built of vegetation,

Fig. 90 (opposite)

a. Tracks in mud. Right, about natural size; left front track enlarged; and side view of hind foot.
b. Walking trail in mud, showing tail drag as often found; front and hind tracks often overlap as shown.
c. Droppings vary in size and shape; about natural size.

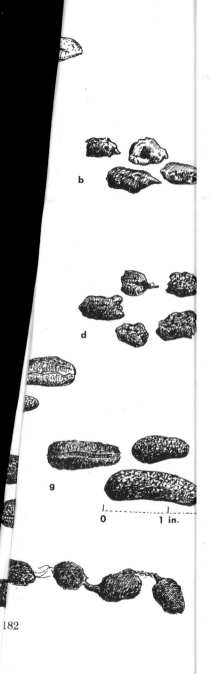

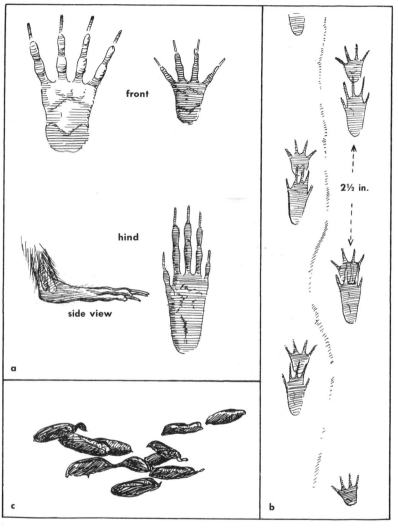

Fig. 90.   Florida water rat sign, from Withlacoochee Swamp, Florida
(drawn by Carroll B. Colby)

but without the mud used by muskrats. These houses are said to have two entrances, on opposite sides. Some of these houses may be in shallow water, but often they are on boggy or peaty ground. The illustration on page 178 shows a simple house in very shallow water which I noted by a roadside in Florida.

The water rat resembles the muskrat in that it uses floating platforms for feeding, constituted of a mass of vegetation augmented by food remains. As with the muskrat, you may find cut stems on the surface of the water.

The paths, or runways, made by water rats are similar to those of the field mice, but are about 3 inches in diameter. There are also tunnels underground.

Apparently these water rats, reminiscent of Kenneth Grahame's *Wind in the Willows,* are not nearly as aquatic as the muskrat. They are at home, nevertheless, both in the water and on land. In this respect they resemble the large field mouse (Richardson vole) of the West, *Microtus richardsoni.*

To distinguish the sign of this animal from that of the muskrat, it is helpful to keep in mind that the water rat inhabits only Florida and southern Georgia, where the muskrat normally does not occur. Tracks and scat are shown in Figure 90.

Porcupine

The porcupine is found in the coniferous forests of Canada and Alaska, and down through the timbered areas of the West, as far east as the western part of the Dakotas and northwestern Texas. It is also in the north woods of the eastern states, around the Great Lakes, and as far south as West Virginia.

Officially known as *Erethizon dorsatum,* the porcupine plays the role among rodents that the skunk has among weasels. Both have developed such a strong defense that they require neither speed nor agility. The skunk when disturbed can spray a vile-smelling liquid. The porcupine can curl up and bristle like a live pincushion. When it is touched or approached closely, the heavily armed tail flips up, and the exceedingly sharp quills readily come loose from the skin. The quills cannot be thrown, as some people imagine.

Fig. 91 (opposite).   Porcupine tracks

   a. Footprints in mud, natural size.
   b. Trail in snow, showing drag marks of feet.
   c. Trail in dust, showing brush marks of tail.

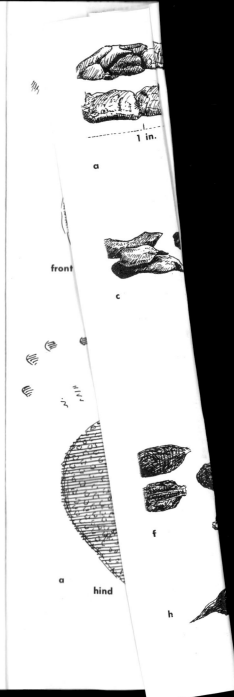

Porcupine

The waddling gait of this animal reveals a great deal. One day a group and I were walking up a well-worn trail in the Teton mountains of Wyoming. In the dust we saw at frequent intervals little brush marks, as if someone had gone that way with a whisk broom. It was clear that a porcupine had passed by. The heavy stiff tail swings back and forth with the clumsy gait, and the wiry hair on the underside lightly brushes the ground, producing those zigzag whiskbroom marks in the dust. They are not always prominent, and sometimes, on ground where the footprints themselves do not show, they are very faint. See Figure 91.

When you find the tracks in wet snow or mud, or heavy dust, several things are revealed. You see the short toed-in steps, somewhat in the style of the badger. These prints are 5 or 6 inches apart. Also, there are marks far ahead of the print, denoting the long claws. Finally, the pebbled appearance of the print itself, the "fingerprint" pattern of the heavy calloused soles of the feet (Fig. 91, a and c). In snow there are drag marks of the feet, sometimes connecting one print with the next, and in deep snow a wallowed trough is formed. Usually I have found the hind track in front of the front track, although sometimes, as in Figure 91, a,

Fig. 92 (opposite).   Porcupine droppings, about ⅔ natural size

A and c are the soft summer droppings (Wyo.). The others are various types of fall and winter scats: b and e from Jackson Hole, Wyoming; d from North Dakota; f and g from Alaska; h, from Wyoming, illustrates how pellets are sometimes connected when the food is semi-soft.

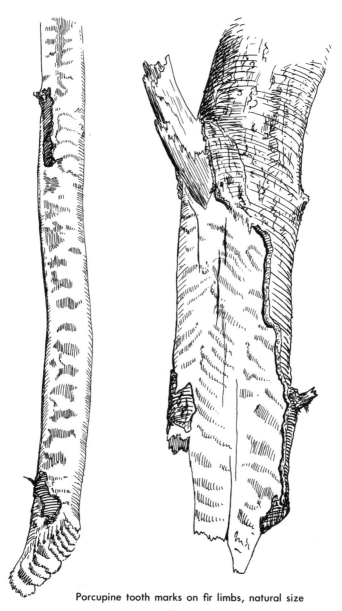

Porcupine tooth marks on fir limbs, natural size

the front print is ahead. In snow the hind track usually registers in the front one. The width of trail pattern, or straddle, is 8 to 9 inches.

Porcupine droppings are variable, and looked at carelessly could be mistaken for those of deer. But note the characteristics shown in Figure 92. The winter scats, of the pellet type, tend to be rough on the surface, and somewhat irregular. Occasionally they are perfectly smooth, as in *e* and *g*. A series is sometimes connected with strands of vegetation (*h*), as in the case of the marmot and some other rodents. The longer types tend to be curved slightly, and often on the inner curve there is a slight groove (*e* and *g*), which also appears on some of the rounder types (*f*). In summer, from succulent feed the pellets become elongated and soft and tend to cling together in a mass (*a* and *c*). In *b* we have an intermediate stage — the short pellet, rather soft and irregular in shape.

During the winter porcupines tend to spend considerable time in a single feed tree and often one finds a large number of scats at the base. They are also found at and in caves in the rocks where the animals find refuge.

One evening when making camp I found a great quantity of pine twigs around the base of a tree, enough to make a comfortable bed on which to spread my sleeping bag. Around the tree were many porcupine droppings, and some barked areas on the trunk. The porcupine often nips off twigs, which can be found strewn on the ground below. However, be careful not to confuse these with twigs dropped by squirrels. The latter nip off cone-bearing twigs and then pick off the cones on the ground. The porcupine scats on the ground will tell the story.

The twigs thus dropped by porcupines are presumably to be eaten later, at leisure, but frequently they don't get around to it. Deer and elk often find these and other fallen limbs and accept them as food.

In winter porcupines eat the bark of twigs and gnaw large patches of bark off the tree trunk. These have neatly gnawed edges, irregular in shape. Often a tree will be spotted with these gnawed patches, all the way up the trunk and on many of the limbs. They are distinguished from elk or moose barking by the neatly gnawed edges, irregular outline, and numerous small tooth marks; and of course if high from the ground, there can be no doubt who has been at work.

Porcupines are generally thought of as living in the forest, but sometimes they occupy treeless areas, such as the Alaska Peninsula, where they find willows and alder brush for winter forage; and in summer they may be found out on the open high mesa, in mountain country — where they find refuge in rock crevices. I have found porcupines occupying caves in rocks, when these are available. In such places, at least those in the West, you may find a mixed accumulation of dung of the woodrat, marmot, and porcupine. They also seek cavities in the ground. I have found them using for shelter the dry portions of caved-in beaver burrows, near streams. And they may use a hollow tree.

These rodents will feed on the buds and catkins of willows — but I do not know how to distinguish such bud evidence from that of ptarmigan or other grouse.

The porcupine generally appears silent, but actually it can be quite vocal. One time I thought I heard the bleating of a moose calf, traced the sound to its source, and found two porcupines, one of them up in a hawthorn bush. Elsewhere I have described the calls in Alaska as "a combination snort and bark, an unexpected and startling sound heard on two occasions when the animal was approached suddenly; and a moaning sound, heard once, which my companion at first attributed to a cub bear." Others have described "screams" and crying like a baby's. At any rate, you may expect to trace such sounds to the porcupine.

Porcupine tree, with characteristic bark gnawing

Aplodontia
cutting twigs

Aplodontia

In the Pacific Coast mountains, particularly in the rain forest environment, from the redwoods of northwestern California to southern British Columbia, lives an interesting rodent, *Aplodontia rufa,* the aplodontia, often called the mountain beaver. It is not closely related to the beaver, but is a chunky, virtually tailless animal almost as large as a muskrat.

As you travel a coastal forest trail, or particularly in logged-off areas, you may come upon little piles of vegetation — ferns and other plants — apparently laid out to dry. They may be on the ground, but are often on logs. These represent the haymaking of the aplodontia, generally thought to be for nest material as well as for food storage, and suggest the hay storage of the cony. But remember that the cony piles will be in rock slides, or similar rocky habitat, and not in the rockless forests.

Furthermore, near these plant piles you will find the aplodontia burrows, in diameter about 4 to 8 inches. They form an irregular network, with several openings. There may also be a "dump pile" of earth thrown out from burrows. In the Olympic Mountains I have come across these burrows along the trails, sometimes caved in, apparently wet and soggy in the rain-soaked woods. The animals have their well-constructed nest within, so they do not mind water.

Nearby you may find limbs nipped off bushes or small saplings. It is reported that they may even cut down a small sapling. They

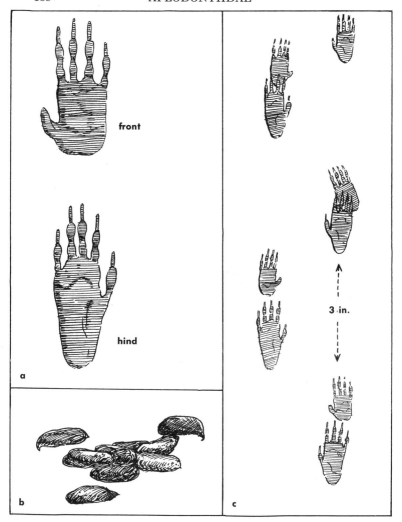

front

hind

3 in.

a

b

c

Fig. 93. Aplodontia (*Aplodontia rufa*) tracks and droppings (drawn by Carroll B. Colby from specimens in The American Museum of Natural History, New York City)

will climb among the limbs to nip off higher ones (see illustration).

In winter, like some other rodents, the aplodontia will move about under deep snow. In spring the earth cores are revealed, consisting of the excavated dirt pushed into snow tunnels after the manner of the pocket gopher. These cores are much larger, however, being 6 inches or more in diameter, corresponding with the burrow size.

I have never heard the aplodontia utter a sound, and it has always seemed to be a silent dweller of the wet burrows of the dark forest. A few observers have described it as producing a series of whistles, a fact that seems to be corroborated by the testimony of early Indians. Since it is active at dusk and during the night, that is the time one might expect to see and hear this animal.

Agouti

The agouti, of the genus *Dasyprocta*, is one of those large-sized rodents of South America that have pushed through Central America into Mexico. It has a humpbacked appearance, is tailless, and in attitude reminds one of a large rabbit (without the big ears).

Fig. 93 (opposite)

a. Above, impression of right front paw (note horny "thumb" without claw); below, left hind foot. Both natural size.
b. Scat, about natural size. Structure of droppings depends upon size of animal and diet; color dark green to black if fresh, turning gray green to tan with age.
c. Walking track. Span depends upon size and age of animal, that shown made by normal-sized mature animal. Tracks rarely found in sequence. Those shown based upon individual tracks and observed gait of animal.

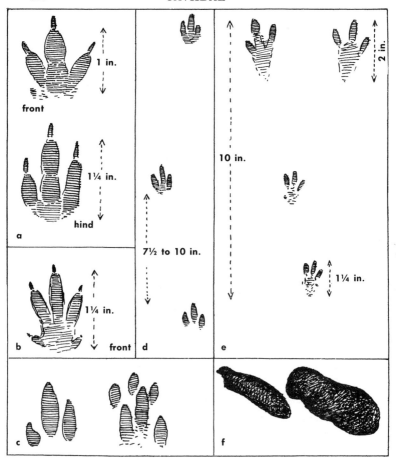

Fig. 94.   Agouti tracks and scats

a, b, c. Tracks in mud (Panama Canal Zone, 1952). C shows the
   fragmentary toe marks that one often finds.
d. Walking pattern.   e. Leaping pattern.
 f. Scats, about ⅔ natural size.

Once from a jungle trail on Barro Colorado Island in the Canal Zone, I saw one of these animals running off across the forest floor into a thicket — the first I had seen in its native home. On the muddy banks of a small stream I found tracks where one had crossed. I saw the little three-toed prints in the muddy trail after a rain. Only in similar locations are you likely to find the footprints, for the jungle floor elsewhere is so littered with debris that such small animals are not apt to leave a trail there.

Strictly speaking, the front feet have five toes, the two outside ones very small, but the tracks you find commonly will appear three-toed (see Fig. 94).

Paca

The paca, *Cuniculus paca,* is one of those stodgy tropical rodents, gaily adorned with stripes and spots, that seem so incongruous with our notions of a rodent when we see them on display in the zoo. They live in the heavy vegetation of the jungle of tropical America, coming as far north as parts of Mexico.

When seen individually the front track shows four toes, the hind track three, but when the hind track is superimposed on the front one, as you will generally find them, you get an impression of a long-toed, three- or four-toed track (see Fig. 95).

The scats are in the form of consolidated pellets, as in Figure 95, e, and sometimes in pellet form.

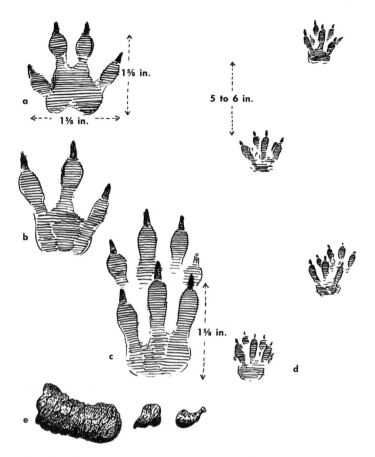

Fig. 95.   Paca sign, about ⅔ natural size, the tracks in soft mud
(Canal Zone, Sept. 12, 1952)

a and b. Front and hind track, respectively.
c. Hind track partly covering front.
d. Track pattern.   e. Droppings.

Norway Rat

The Norway rat, *Rattus norvegicus,* is one of the exotic rodents that has made itself at home over the North American continent, chiefly at human habitations.

Apparently this common creature, so parasitic on man's food supplies, has not been an attractive subject for study by naturalists. However, R. G. Pisano and Tracy I. Storer made such a study and recorded a description of the burrows and other evidence of their presence. The burrows were 2 to 2½ inches in diameter. It was also found that burrow entrances would sometimes be plugged with earth, much as a pocket gopher would do it.

Like other rodents, rats will make runways through the vegetation. On Atka and Rat Islands in the Aleutian chain of Alaska, rats have adapted themselves to a natural habitat. There you will find their burrows and runways with little piles of cut grass segments in the manner of our native meadow voles. On Rat Island, where vegetation is rather scarce, the rats have found refuge in the boulder beaches. Some have had the audacity to dig their burrows into the foundations of the cliff nests of the bald eagle! Perhaps they are clever enough to pilfer food scraps from the nest itself. Tracks and scats are shown in Figure 96.

House Mouse

Mus musculus, an immigrant from the Old World, is a sophisticated creature that has learned to thrive in the homes of men, in the cupboards, the barns, the dump ground, among the cages at the zoo — wherever man has left his food or refuse. Although this mouse does at times venture into the woodlands, it is primarily commensal with man.

Consequently, you will not commonly find the tracks in the woods. If you do, they will be quite similar to those of the white-

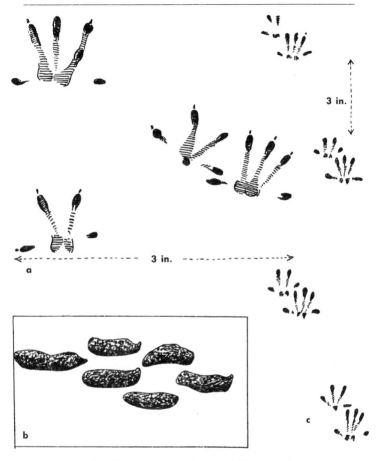

3 in.

3 in.

a

b

c

Fig. 96.   Tracks and scats of Norway rat

a. Tracks, in leaping pattern, on mud surface, about natural size.
   Distance between jumps, 7½ in. The heels of the five-toed hind
   feet did not show.
b. Droppings, natural size.
c. Walking track pattern. Note the four-toed front, and five-toed hind
   feet.

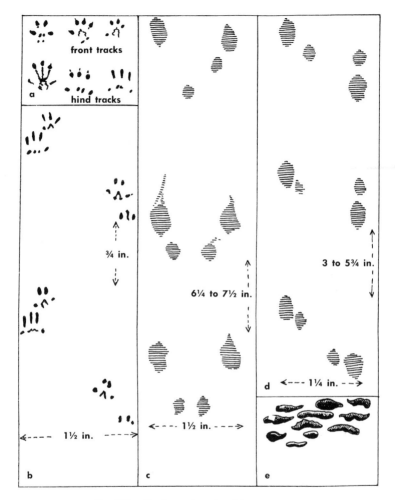

Fig. 97.   Tracks and scats of house mouse

a. Sample tracks in mud, natural size. With such prints the sole of
   the foot is scarcely indicated.
b. A "scurrying" gait — a slow run — in mud, natural size; somewhat
   similar in pattern to the run in snow as shown in d.
c and d. Running gaits, in snow, the more typical of the fast leap being
   that shown in c.
e. Droppings, about natural size.

195

House Mouse

footed mouse, as you see by the accompanying sketches. Note the similarity of patterns in mud of the slow run, or scurrying, shown in Figure 97, b, for the house mouse and in Figure 101, e, for the white-footed mouse. There is a difference in the position of the hind and front tracks in the two, but this could easily be a variation that occurs with either mouse. Note that in each case the hind track is recognized by the three forward-pointing toes and the two at the sides — five toes — while the front track has four, two forward and two lateral. Note also the similarity in the bounding gaits of the two in snow (Fig. 97, c and d, and Fig. 101, c and d).

It is interesting that the common house mouse, so much despised as a pest, occasionally gives voice to a birdlike trilling song. This has been described by observers from many parts of the world. However, the song is very rarely heard, and only at a distance of a few feet.

Jumping Mouse

The jumping mouse is not well known to the public, yet it is distributed over most of the United States, and northward into Canada and Alaska, in some regions as far as the Arctic Circle, southward in the West into California and Nevada and in the

Fig. 98 (opposite)

a. Tracks in mud, natural size.
b. Right front and hind feet, underside. Slightly over natural size.
c. Tracks in mud, where the hind heel did not touch the ground; natural size.
d. Droppings, natural size. These are all from the same individual.
e. Tracks in mud, on slow hopping gait, tail drag continuous. About ⅔ natural size.

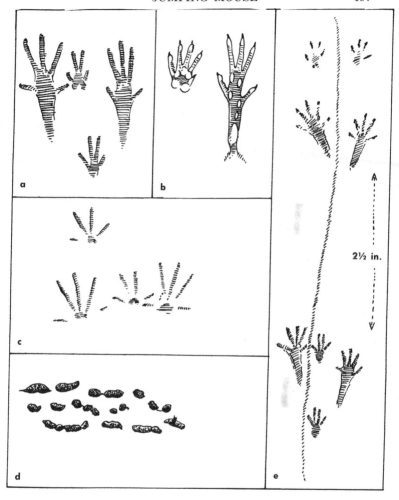

Fig. 98. Tracks and scats of jumping mouse

Jumping
Mouse

East to North Carolina. There are two genera: the more widely
distributed *Zapus,* with many forms, and the larger *Napaeozapus,*
confined to eastern Canada and the eastern states.

The common jumping mouse is frequently found in meadows
and grassy mountain slopes, though it lives in woodlands as well.
Generally you are aware of its presence by seeing a small creature
leap away from you with half a dozen froglike jumps, then suddenly stop and apparently vanish. Many times in such instances
I have crept up carefully to where I last saw it and spied it
crouching there in the thick grass or border of a bush. Then, when
in range, I have pounced on it with cupped hand to look it over
before releasing it.

In Ungava I have seen the large *Napaeozapus* leap into the water
and dive when frightened. It appears to frequent streambanks
quite commonly.

These mice make long leaps, some leaps recorded to be from 6
to 12 feet, or more. I have never seen them leap more than an
estimated 4 or 5 feet; sometimes they only make a hop of 2 feet
or less.

You will not find the tracks of this mouse in the winter snows,
for they spend the winter in hibernation. Nor have I found their
tracks in summer, since they occupy grassy and brushy areas where
tracks are not readily left on the ground. However, a pet jumping
mouse left the tracks in mud which are shown in Figure 98. The
long legs suggest those of the kangaroo rat of the desert, but the
jumping mouse appears to land on all four feet when it jumps,
not on the hind feet only as does the kangaroo rat.

Although the jumping mice do not make runways in the grass,
you will find the little piles of grass stems where they have been
feeding, similar to those left by meadow mice but usually longer.
Also, they build a globular nest on the ground, or at the end of
a short burrow.

Woodrat

Woodrats, or packrats, as they are sometimes called, which include a great many forms within the genus *Neotoma,* are pretty well distributed over western North America, from the southern border of Yukon Territory south into Mexico. They occur more sparingly in the eastern states. Woodrats live in a great variety of places, some species choosing a home among the cacti of the deserts, others preferring cliffs or slide rocks, still others the forest floor.

The woodrat feet have fairly stubby toes with short claws. This is reflected in their tracks, as shown in Figure 99.

These animals are most easily discovered by their bulky nests. It may be a pile of sticks and miscellaneous debris of moderate size in a bush, or back in a crevice of a cliff or cave, or a huge pile of sticks rising to a height of 4 or 5 feet or higher in a thicket or up against a tree. Some are built in trees, up as high as 20 feet or more. In the desert a nest is often built into a clump of cactus or mesquite. These houses, whatever their location, usually include in the material a collection of odd objects — an old spoon, several bones, horse dung, tin can, almost anything that catches the fancy of this unusual architect. In fact, some of these structures look more like a pile of junk hoarded by a collector of heterogeneous curios than a domicile. And that may be what some of them are. Generally there is a pile of rubbish in a corner of an old cabin, the nest may lie snugly on top of the collection, in the open. Woodrats also have their burrows in the ground.

The scats (Fig. 99, f) are fairly large, varying somewhat in size with the species. It has been reported that there is a slight size difference between the scats of the sexes. They are generally plentiful in the vicinity of the house or cliff abode, often accumu-

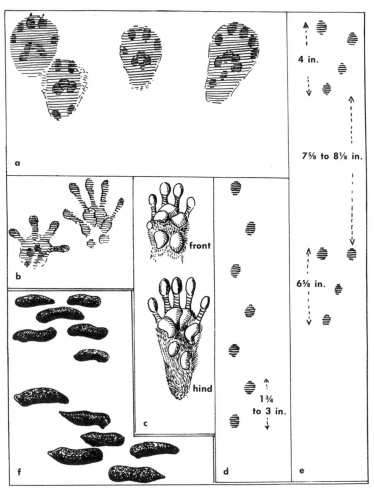

Fig. 99.　Woodrat

a. Tracks in mud of *Neotoma albigula*, natural size.
b. Front and hind tracks in mud, toes more spread; natural size.
c. Feet of a woodrat from British Columbia, *Neotoma cinerea*; natural size.
d. Walking track pattern.　　　e. Galloping pattern (Nev.).
f. Scats, natural size (upper, from Chisos Mts., Tex.; lower, Jackson Hole, Wyo.).

200

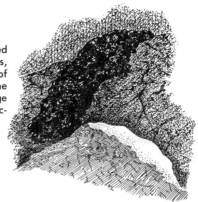

Fig. 100

Black tarlike material deposited on rock ledges by woodrats, apparently an accumulation of a soft type of droppings. The white stain on the rock edge appears to be caused by accumulated urine.

lated in heaps. In many areas, especially on cliffs near the home crevice, there is an accumulation of dung that has a homogeneous, tarlike consistency, black in color — a mass that may be 6 inches or more in diameter. In some instances this black deposit drips over the edge of the rock and extends down the face as a somewhat sticky overflow for a distance of a foot or more (see Fig. 100). In the same areas are white spots or streaks that appear to be the residue of urine. On little rock edges smeared with this whitewash type of stain, you will find little honey-colored drops, or streaks, along the ridge. So prominent are these stains that in some western states it is possible occasionally to see the white woodrat spottings on certain cliffs while driving by on the highway. They may be distinguished from the familiar whitewash stains left on rocks by ravens and some hawks and owls in this way: stains left by birds tend to be vertical streaks and heavily concentrated below a nest site or favorite perch; those left by woodrats tend to be shorter, may be vertical, diagonal, or horizontal, thus presenting an irregular pattern on a cliff face.

Often, if you find woodrat at home in his rubbish domicile, he will respond to a disturbance by drumming or thumping with the hind feet, both coming down together. You may hear this if you are in a house or cabin that has been invaded by a woodrat. Or he will drum by pounding his tail. This has been referred to as a clatter or drumming. This and thumping with the feet appear to be nervous reactions to disturbances, though they may have a more specific meaning in woodrat communications.

The woodrat personality — native American, antique collector, at home in the cactus desert and the northern forest, as well as on the steepest cliffs and in rocky caves — is well worth cultivating. The traces he leaves are the means toward acquaintance.

White-Footed Mouse or Deer Mouse

White-footed mice, known also as deer mice and included in the genus *Peromyscus* with numerous species and subspecies, are abundant and well known. Certain species make their homes in arid regions of the Southwest, others have adapted themselves to all habitats, from the plains to the mountaintops and from Central America into much of Canada.

The usual sign is the four-print pattern in the snow, as shown in Figure 101, c and d. This leaping pattern may be confused with that of the house mouse, and also resembles that of the shrew. However, the deer mouse track-straddle is larger than that of the shrew, being from 1½ to 1¾ inches. Sometimes the tail drags, as in Figure 101, b, and in this type the front and hind feet make one elongated print in the snow on each side, suggesting certain arrangements of weasel tracks. The front-foot tracks show only four toes, the hind tracks five. There are numerous kinds of white-footed mice, varying in size, but the track pattern is similar among all of them.

White-footed mice are primarily seedeaters and you may find as much as a quart of seeds stored for winter use in any convenient hole or hollow or cranny. They open large fruit pits, such as the wild cherry pits shown in Figure 102, d, for the kernels inside. The hazelnut pictured in *c* was one that the mice found in the cupboard, uncommon food for the mice of northern Wyoming. In eastern forests the mice open the basswood seeds, and you will find many of the shells with a hole in them.

These mice do not cut runways through the grass, as do the field mice, but live among logs and stumps. They will climb up on tree trunks and into bushes; they live in holes in plowed furrows, among rocks, and on ocean beaches. In fact, the white-footed mouse as a genus is extremely adaptable and finds a congenial home almost anywhere, though many of its species have chosen special habitats.

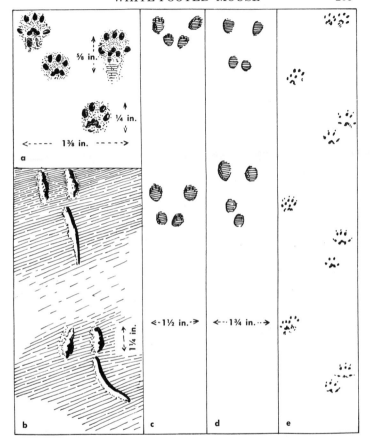

Fig. 101.   White-footed mouse tracks, from Wyoming

a. Running tracks in dust, about natural size. Front track (four-toed) ¼ in. long and wide.

b. In light snow, with tail marks. Hind and front feet make one elongated print, about 1¼ in. long. Leaps measured 3 to 9 in.

c. On very light layer of snow. Leaps 5 to 8 in.

d. On firm snow. Leaps 2 to 3 in.

e. Slow run in wet mud. Individual tracks about ⁵⁄₁₆ in. wide.

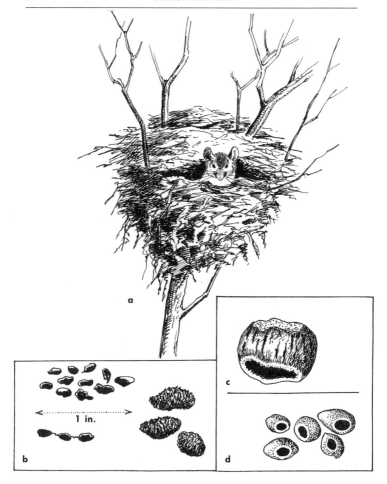

Fig. 102.   White-footed mouse sign

a. Old bird nest roofed over by *Peromyscus*.
b. Droppings, natural size; at right, three samples much enlarged (Wyo.).
c. Hazelnut opened by white-footed mouse (in kitchen cupboard). This Wyoming mouse would not find wild hazelnuts.
d. Wild cherry pits opened by white-footed mouse (N.Y.).

The nests vary in size from a few inches to nearly a foot in diameter, and their location varies greatly — burrows, logs, holes in trees, even bushes. Often a white-footed mouse will roof over an abandoned bird's nest and live in it (Fig. 102, a). It is sometimes difficult to distinguish signs of harvest mice from those of *Peromyscus.*

Mr. R. DeWitt Ivey has given us a published account of the habits of three species of white-footed mice on the east coast of Florida. He found that the so-called golden mouse, *Peromyscus nuttalli aureolus,* lives in loose communities of three or four nests. These nests are at heights up to 15 feet, usually 4 to 6 feet above ground, placed in Spanish moss, vines, or other vegetation. They are globular, 3 to 6 inches in diameter, with an opening about 1 inch in diameter.

The cotton mouse, *Peromyscus gossypinus gossypinus,* also makes globular nests in hollow logs and stumps and on the ground.

The interesting whitish beach (or Oldfield) mouse, *Peromyscus polionotus phasma,* builds its nests within ground burrows. Mr. Ivey warns us, however, that "burrows are not reliable as evidence of the presence of beach mice except when excavated, since they may be readily confused with the burrows of the sand crabs."

Everywhere you go you will find this little mouse, adapted in color and habits to its special surroundings. We find it abundantly among the forests and the fields of New England and all the eastern and midwestern states; other species adapted to the mountains and plains of the West; the pale-colored ones in the desert, the big, dark-colored ones in the Pacific Coast rain forests, the little white ones on the Florida beaches. But everywhere, from the subtropics to the high western mountains, the little foursquare track pattern reveals it.

Generally speaking, all mice squeak in the manner familiar to us. Some mice sing and, according to some opinions, both the house mouse and the white-footed mouse may have a song too high in pitch for the human ear, but descending in pitch on rare occasions to become audible. The series of notes, when heard, are described as a birdlike trill that can be heard only at a distance of a few feet.

I recall a number of times when I lay in my sleeping bag in the woods and could hear the tiny patter of mice across my bed. When a mouse came very close to my ear I could hear little vocal sounds, a rapid series almost like a chatter, but very faint and less forceful than that term implies.

Grasshopper Mouse

This mouse, of the genus *Onychomys* and largely insectivorous and carnivorous, is found in the western United States and adjacent parts of Canada and Mexico.

The tracks of the grasshopper mouse have seldom been observed or recorded, or at least positively identified in the field. The tracks

Fig. 103. Tracks and scats of grasshopper mouse

a. Tracks of captive mouse (drawn from a photograph by Vernon Bailey, courtesy of the U.S. Fish and Wildlife Service).
b. Droppings, about natural size; upper ones dried, lower ones still moist.

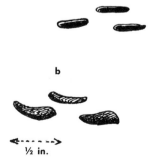

b

◄····· 1¼ in. ·····►

◄----►
½ in.

in Figure 103 were roughly sketched from a photograph of tracks of a captive animal. The scats also shown here are from a captive animal. Note the difference in size between the moist fresh ones and the older dried ones.

Harvest Mouse
at nest

Harvest Mouse

Harvest mice, *Reithrodontomys,* are inconspicuous creatures seldom seen. They are found in certain areas throughout the United States, particularly in grassy plains or deserts, and range into Central America.

The most conspicuous evidence of the presence of these mice is the globular nest they build, approximately 3 inches in diameter, either on the ground or in bushes.

On one occasion in a canyon in northern Nevada I found a bird's nest in a large sage bush filled and domed over with the feathers of a flicker (see illustration). Snug inside this adapted structure was a harvest mouse.

There were little platforms of sage twigs with leaves lodged in forks of the branches of tall sagebrush. These bushes, it was determined, were climbed by both the harvest mice and the white-footed mice. Which one had built the leafy platforms?

The harvest mouse is another animal for which "sign" cannot

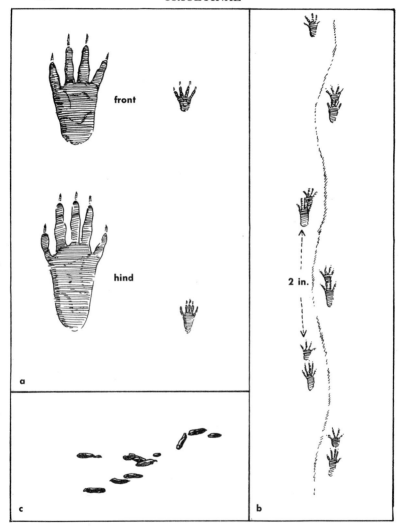

Fig. 104.   Harvest mouse tracks and droppings (drawn by Carroll B. Colby from specimens in The American Museum of Natural History, New York City)

be adequately presented here. I have never seen its tracks or identified its scats. Mr. Carroll B. Colby has provided a drawing of tracks and scats reconstructed from specimens in the American Museum of Natural History (see Fig. 104).

This dainty little mouse also has a song, which Ruth Svihla has described as "a tiny, clear, high-pitched bugling sound, very ventriloquistic in character." It would be interesting to know more about the accomplishments of these obscure animals that we so seldom see.

Cotton Rat

Rice and Cotton Rats

The rice rat, *Oryzomys,* is found in the eastern United States, from eastern Kansas and Oklahoma onward and from New Jersey south to Florida and Central America. The cotton rat, *Sigmodon,* is found "in greatest abundance from Mexico to Peru," but is also plentiful throughout our southern states.

The tracks of these two rat groups are quite similar, as suggested by Figure 105. Both make runways in the vegetation that are

Fig. 104 (opposite)

a. At left, enlarged imprint of front and hind feet; at right, about natural-size imprints, as they might appear in dust or soft mud. Perfect prints are difficult to find because of habitat of harvest mouse — grass, leaves, etc.

b. Reconstructed track of a harvest mouse, showing walking gait and drag marks of tail.

c. Droppings are of typical mouse characteristics: small, dark, and scanty in number for each deposit; vary with size of animal.

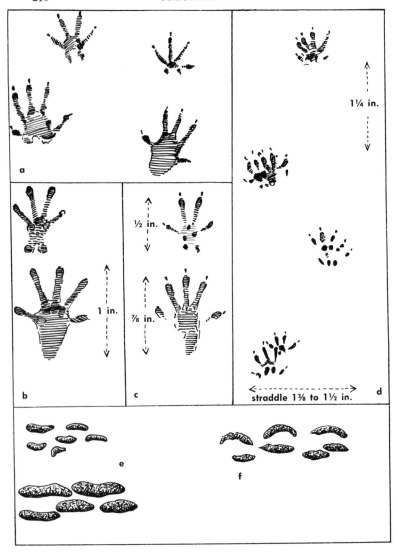

Fig. 105. Tracks and droppings of cotton rat and rice rat

hardly distinguishable. Both also make nests of grass or leaves, above or below ground.

In cases like this, one must keep in mind geographic distribution of animals. When you find small rodent tracks in Montana or Maine or Canada, you can rule out both the cotton rat and rice rat. In the more southern states, where meadow voles are also present, one must rely on size of track for identification, since the vole is a much smaller animal. Here, again, one may see the sign of a *young* cotton rat.

It is interesting to note, also, the difference in size between the scats of a captive cotton rat in the zoo and those of wild rats from Texas, as shown in Figure 105, e.

Meadow Vole or Field Mouse

How can one properly characterize a group of mice made up of nearly a hundred species and subspecies, many of them specialized in habits, and varying in over-all length from about 5 inches in the smaller forms to 10 inches in the so-called big-footed meadow mouse and its related varieties? We can surely say that the meadow vole, of the genus *Microtus,* is more widespread over America, from Mexico to the Arctic, than any other mouse group. Also, in general appearance the numerous species and subspecies have a similar appearance — chunky build and ears more or less snuggled into the fur, which is rather long. Those illustrated here are suggestive of the group.

Meadow voles and white-footed mice together furnish most of the tracks one finds in winter snow. But in heavy snow country the meadow voles tend to remain beneath the surface, where they travel in snowy tunnels and have their snug nests.

In their typical patterns the tracks of the vole differ from those of the white-footed mouse. The white-footed mouse ordinarily

Fig. 105 (opposite)

a. Cotton rat track pattern, when at rest; natural size (Chisos Mts., Tex.).
b. Cotton rat tracks in mud, showing heel of hind foot; natural size (Natl. Zoological Park, Washington, D.C.).
c. Rice rat tracks, in mud; natural size (Natl. Zoological Park).
d. Walking gait of cotton rat, in mud.
e. Cotton rat scats, natural size (upper ones from zoo animals; lower ones from Chisos Mts., Tex.).
f. Rice rat scats, from zoo animals; natural size.

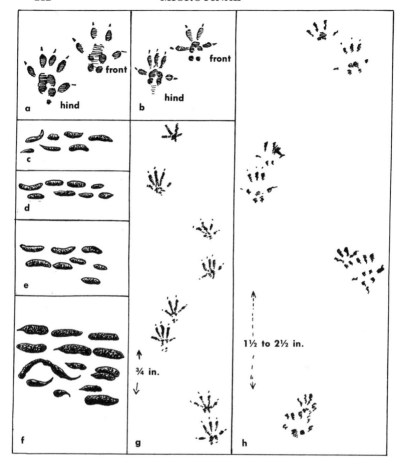

Fig. 106. Meadow vole sign

a. Tracks in mud of the big Richardson vole, *Microtus richardsoni*, natural size (Wyo.).
b. Tracks in mud of *M. montanus*, natural size (Wyo.).
c to f. Droppings, natural size: c, *M. operarius* (Alaska); d, *M. montanus* (Wyo.); e, *M. miurus* (Alaska); f, *M. richardsoni* (Wyo.).
g. Trail pattern of *M. montanus* walking in mud; straddle, 1¼ in.
h. Trail pattern of *M. richardsoni* walking in mud; straddle, 2 in.

Alaska Vole
("Hay Mouse")

leaves a leaping four-print pattern (see Fig. 101, c), whereas the leaping vole generally leaves a double-print type of trail (Fig. 107, g), similar to that of weasels in diminutive form. This is the form generally given in instructions on tracking mice. But the vole leaves a variety of track patterns, depending on depth of snow, character of mud, sand, dust, gait, and speed. Look at some of the patterns in Figures 106, 107, and 108.

The form of the footprint itself is shown in Figure 106, a and b, in mud, and in Figure 107, a, in the leaping pattern in light snow. Note the four toes of the front foot and five toes on the hind. In Figure 107, c and d, walking pattern in thin film of snow, the hind foot registers in the front track, though in c sometimes one print is left beside the other. The same tendency is shown in f, where the animal was traveling in snow and the hind foot left a print a little behind the front track. Here the snow shows toe drag marks and front and hind tracks tend to connect. When we speak of a mouse walking we must not visualize the slow stepping of a raccoon or deer; even in slow speed mice seem rather to be scurrying. But when they leap, or bound, they leave a track pattern such as in e or g, in which the bounds may measure 2 to 6 inches ordinarily and in the case of a large mouse, as much as 19 inches at extreme speed. These tracks are those of an average-sized mountain vole, *Microtus montanus,* in Wyoming. The tracks of the large Richardson vole, *Microtus richardsoni,* the adults of which suggest a young muskrat in size, are shown in Figure 106, a and h.

I am afraid that in many cases the droppings are not distinctive, for they vary somewhat with the food. Scats of several species

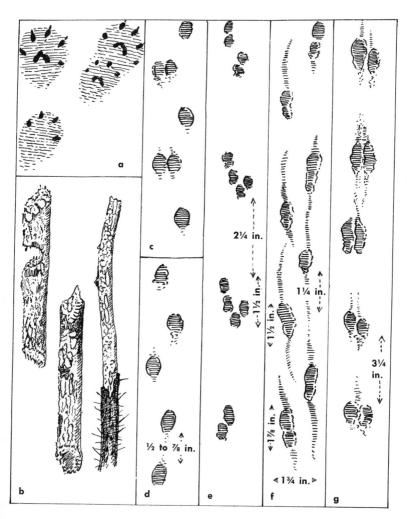

Fig. 107. Tracks of meadow vole

a. Tracks of *Microtus montanus* in light snow, natural size (Wyo.).
b. Wild rose twigs gnawed by *M. montanus*, natural size (Wyo.).
c and d. Tracks of *M. montanus*, walking in light snow.
e. Running in snow.   f. Fast walk, in snow.
g. Running in snow, a common track pattern.

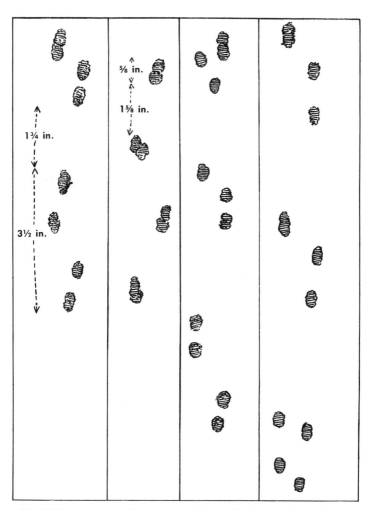

Fig. 108. Some sample segments of the trail of a meadow vole that had scrambled across the frosty surface of hard snow. These samples were taken from a section of the trail about 20 feet in length. In this short distance in the travel of the same individual meadow vole were found all possible variations, from the two-two pattern to the four-print pattern shown at the end. The outside width, or straddle, was from 1 1/16 to 1 3/8 in. The jumps were from 1 3/4 to 4 1/4 in. (March 5, 1953).

are shown in Figure 106, c through f. Those of the big *Microtus richardsoni* are enough larger so that they may be fairly well identified in the field.

An important feature in the life of the meadow vole is the runway in the grass. Part the heavy grass cover where these mice are living and you will find these little pathways cut through the grass, radiating from a burrow, leading from one bush to another, or otherwise furnishing the traffic lanes to where the little grasseaters want to go. In these runways, too, you will find little piles of cut grass stems where they have been feeding — a good sign of the vole. In the winter the vole will gnaw the bark of bushes. Figure 107, b, shows the gnawed twig of wild rose. Mouse tooth marks are much finer than those of the rabbit, beaver, and other gnawing animals, but, as shown in the rose twigs illustrated here, very often the bark or wood is chipped out without leaving clean-cut tooth marks. One must judge the work by the generally fine-marked appearance.

In snow country the vole lives below the snow surface, coming out only occasionally, and for such a life builds a nest on the surface of the ground. When the snow thaws in spring you will find these globular surface nests constructed of dry grass, with an entrance at one side.

Sometimes too you will find rope-like cores of dirt and grass cuttings mixed together which are the material that had been shoved into snow tunnels in winter (Fig. 109), similar to dirt cores left by pocket gophers.

In spring the mice move to underground nests in a subterranean burrow network. Some species will build their globular summer nests in tangled stems of reeds or cattails over the surface of water, and swim readily to and from the nest. If you are wandering over a flower-studded meadow in some of the western mountains, look closely along some of the small winding meadow streams. You may see a sizable mouse dash along the edge of the water into a bank burrow, or even into the water. This is the home of the large vole, *richardsoni,* mentioned previously. Some entrances to the burrow are under water, for these mice are quite aquatic in their habits.

Then again you may be traveling across a sage flat in the Rocky Mountain region, or on the high short-grass mesa above timberline. Here you may find the network of tunnels and burrow entrances of the small dwarf mouse, *Microtus nanus,* which often seeks the dry short-grass areas of sage or mesa. Sometimes you will find them occupying old, abandoned pocket gopher tunnels.

In some of the arid sagelands of the Southwest you may find a green oasis where a small spring oozes out. Look about in the green grass and you *may* find vole runways there.

A number of species are known to store up food for winter,

especially roots of plants. In North Dakota this habit was so noticeable that a variety of meadow vole, *Microtus pennsylvanicus,* became known as the bean mouse, because of its underground storage of the beans of *Falcata comosa* and the tubers of a wild sunflower. My brother found a store of 706 tubers of bistort gathered by *Microtus nanus* and a cache of dandelion and other roots stored by *Microtus montanus.*

Not long ago, when we were traveling over the open tundra slopes of Mt. McKinley National Park in Alaska, my brother showed me the workings of one of the most remarkable voles, described as *Microtus miurus oreas,* whose life history he had been studying. We examined elaborate root caches stored away under

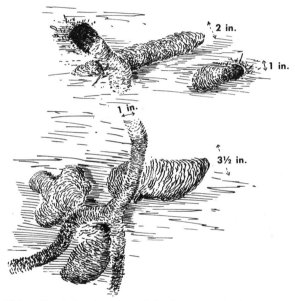

Fig. 109. Meadow vole cores of dead grass and other debris that had been pushed into snow tunnels in winter. This material is scraped out of shallow grooves in the ground, and small pits where the mice have been digging. Sometimes these cores consist of grass, sticks, and dirt; they are from 1 to 3½ in. in diameter. Often in spring the thawing snow will reveal these runways and cores radiating from an abandoned winter nest. Sometimes the cores of the meadow vole will be intermingled with the larger ones of the pocket gopher.

the moss. There were, in addition, heaped-up stores of dried plants, some of them nearly a bushel in volume. So extensive is this haymaking that we have been calling this Alaska vole the "hay mouse" ever since. Dried material included grass as well as the stems and leaves of many other plants. As we fought our way through willow patches, we found many willow tips nipped off, and found the dried leafy twigs in the miniature haystacks nearby. The mice had climbed up among the willow stems to harvest the twigs. These haystacks were similar to those of another haymaker, the pika, but the pika lives up in the rockslides. The hay mouse piles his around the base of a willow, or the roots of a spruce tree (see below). Furthermore, if you excavate its burrow, you may find that it consists of a series of larger sections connected by narrower passages.

This can be but a brief introduction to the myriad mouse population of the continent which we know as voles, or meadow mice.

Fig. 110. Alaska vole, *Microtus miurus oreas*

a. Hay mouse, munching a root.
b. A haystack in the base of a willow, stored by the hay mouse.
c. Underground burrow, showing the narrow passages between the larger portions.

Pine Vole, Sagebrush Vole,
Bog Lemming, and Redback Vole

These four members of the vole family are in form so similar to the common meadow vole that their tracks probably cannot be distinguished.

The pine vole or mouse, *Pitymys pinetorum,* is by no means confined to pine woods. In Oklahoma I found them in oak woods and open grasslands. This animal is really a meadow vole somewhat specialized for subterranean existence, for it lives pretty much in underground burrows a few inches below the surface. It makes underground storage of roots and tubers, and is very prone to gnaw the roots and bark of small trees and shrubs. Examination of plaster casts of their tracks reveals no practical difference from the individual tracks of *Microtus* shown in Figure 106, g.

The sagebrush vole, *Lagurus curtatus,* is a mouse of the western dry lands whose individual tracks I have not seen. They have runways and burrows, and leave cut grass stems just as do the common meadow voles.

The bog lemming, *Synaptomys,* is a short-tailed vole of the northern and eastern part of our continent. I have not found its tracks so as to be sure of their identification, but they could not differ materially from those of the common meadow vole. They are known to use the same runways with *Microtus* at times. Their droppings are rather small, but not distinctive.

The redback vole or mouse, *Clethrionomys,* is still another member of the vole tribe that has the general form of *Microtus.* It is common in the northern forests of the continent, as well as in the western and eastern mountains farther south. You are likely to find them among stumps and logs and forest litter, or in the mossy muskeg country of the North. I have not found this vole building elaborate runways in the vegetation to the extent that the meadow vole does. It runs about more freely, like the white-footed mouse. I may unknowingly have seen its tracks, for they would surely be in the familiar meadow vole pattern; the droppings (Fig. 111) are smaller than those of *Microtus* but otherwise not distinctive. Figure 112 shows boreal redback vole sign drawn by Carroll B. Colby.

Fig. 111
Droppings of
redback vole.

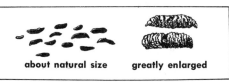

about natural size   greatly enlarged

219

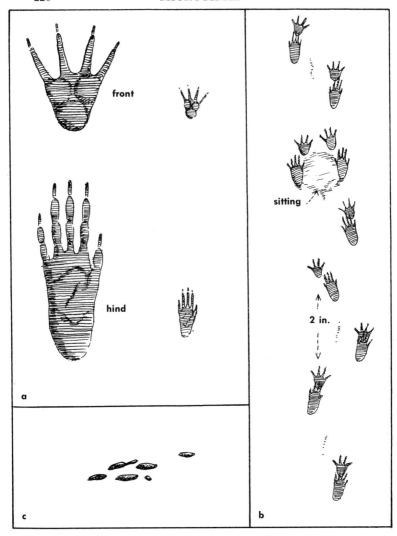

Fig. 112.   Boreal redback vole tracks and droppings (drawn by Carroll
    B. Colby from specimens in The American Museum of Natural History,
    New York City)

Tree Phenacomys
and its nest

Tree and Mountain Phenacomys

One day many years ago, in the heavy woods near Forest Grove, Oregon, I climbed a fir tree to look at a nest some twenty feet from the ground. It was an old nest, possibly built by a hawk. But I was puzzled to find it filled completely by shredded fir needles. It was not until a year later that I learned that I had obviously come on the nest of the tree phenacomys, or red tree mouse, *Phenacomys longicaudus.* The everyday, common meadow vole, *Microtus pennsylvanicus,* which we have discussed already, lives on and in the ground. Here is a mouse of a related genus of voles that has fol-

Fig. 112 (opposite)

a. Tracks of *Clethrionomys gapperi* as they would appear in mud, shown enlarged at left, and about natural size at right.
b. Trail as it would appear in dust about den, or in soft mud. Tail impression rarely shows; length of span would vary with speed and size of animal.
c. Droppings are tiny, resembling those of common house mouse. They vary with diet and size of animal. Natural size.

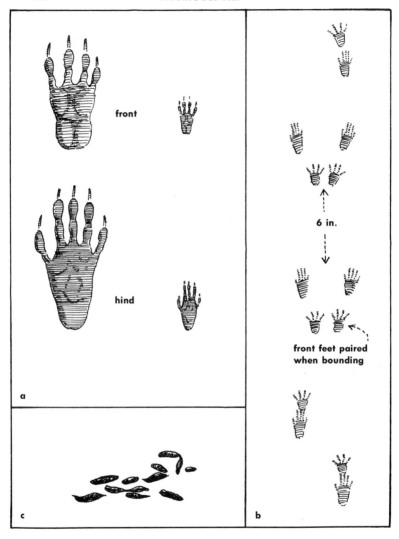

Fig. 113.   Tree phenacomys sign (drawn by Carroll B. Colby from specimens in The American Museum of Natural History, New York City)

lowed the example of the harvest mouse, but has gone much farther, and builds a nest high in the trees. Not only that, it has specialized its diet chiefly to needles of fir, spruce, and hemlock and eats only the central strip of the needle, leaving the two edges for building a nest. Like the porcupine, and probably other animals, it prefers the young terminal needles, and eats the whole needle in this case. Nests may be original structures built by the phenacomys, close to the trunk of small trees or out on big heavy limbs of large trees, or this vole-like creature might build its structure into an old bird's nest, abandoned squirrel nest, or woodrat nest. It is roughly globular, with entrance in the side. It varies in size from a few inches in diameter to a large mass two feet or more in diameter with several entrances. The nests built from scratch by the mice are made on a ground structure of fine twigs and possibly lichens, filled out with split conifer needles. They may be placed from ten to nearly a hundred feet above the ground.

This mouse is restricted to the humid forests of Oregon and northwestern California. Figure 113, b, shows the tracks of the tree phenacomys with the parallel placing of the front feet characteristic of animals that habitually live in trees, like the gray squirrel (Fig. 78, b). Animals like the mountain phenacomys (Fig. 114, b) and the ground squirrels of the genus *Citellus* (Fig. 70, d and e), which have their nests on the ground and spend most of the time there, generally place their forefeet in a diagonal pattern. The same principle applies to the track pattern of birds: game birds that frequent the ground place their feet alternately and songbirds that spend most of their time in trees hop with both feet together.

The claws of animals living on the ground are commonly less curved and less sharp than the claws of tree animals.

There are other mice of this genus that live on the ground like the meadow voles. The Pacific phenacomys, *Phenacomys albipes,* is a rare species of which we know little except that it lives along streams in the coastal forests of northern California and Oregon.

The mountain phenacomys, or heather vole, and its related forms are found in the Rockies, Cascades, and Sierras, and through

Fig. 113 (opposite)

a. Front- and hind-foot prints: shown enlarged, at left; about natural size, at right.
b. Reconstruction of walking and bounding trail. Spacing of bounds depends upon size and speed of animal.
c. Droppings are small and dark in color and vary with size and diet of individual animal, but generally resemble those of common house mouse. Natural size.

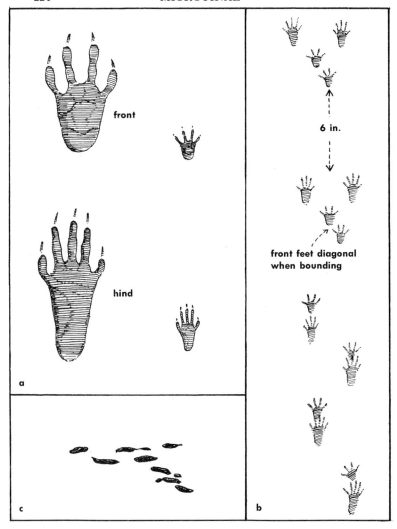

Fig. 114.   Mountain phenacomys sign (drawn by Carroll B. Colby from
    specimens in The American Museum of Natural History, New York
    City).

the boreal forests from Labrador to British Columbia. In the Rockies, after the snow has disappeared from the timberline, I have found the winter nests, quite similar to those of the meadow voles (*Microtus*), with quantities of droppings nearby.

The mountain phenacomys prefers the picturesque high meadows near or above timberline, though of course it is found in other locations, too, down through the mountain forests. These are fascinating animals, but so far as their actual footprints are concerned I know of no way to distinguish them from those of *Microtus* (Figs. 106, 107, 108). Nor am I sure that we can say that the droppings differ materially in comparable seasons.

Collared and Brown Lemmings

One winter evening near the Brooks Range in Alaska, my brother and I were talking with a group of Eskimos. They told us about Kilyungmituk, "the little one who came down from the sky." It seems that there was a bear up in the land of the sky, but it began falling, and the closer to earth it fell the smaller it became, until it plopped into the snow in the form of the lemming. "We know this," Pooto declared, "because his tracks are like small bear tracks." Selawik Sam spoke up and gravely told us that he, himself, had seen the holes in the snow where the lemmings had landed.

Here, then, is an instance where a mouse track has woven itself into human legends. In Figure 115, d, are shown the front feet of the collared lemming, *Dicrostonyx*, with the peculiar claws that no doubt produce an interesting footprint if the details show. I can only show the trail patterns, however, adapted from photographs kindly lent by Charles O. Handley, Jr., who obtained them in the Canadian Arctic, and from photographs and drawings by Dr. Robert Rausch, of Alaska. The detailed footprint in mud is not available. It will be noticed that these lemming trails (Figs. 115 and 116) do not fit in with the usual pattern of the common meadow vole, as shown in Figures 107 and 108.

Finding lemmings is fairly easy where they are plentiful, for

Fig. 114 (opposite)

a. Enlarged impressions of front and hind feet of *Phenacomys intermedius* at left. At right, feet shown about natural size.
b. Usual trail as it would appear in dust or soft mud.
c. Droppings resemble those of majority of voles and mice; natural size.

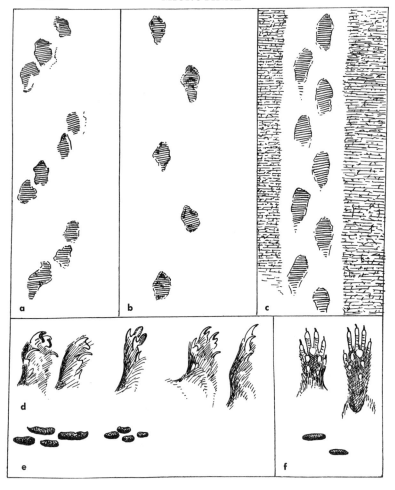

Fig. 115. Collared lemming and brown lemming

Collared
  Lemming

they have their burrows in the mossy tundra, but I had a particularly frustrating experience on Unalaska Island in the Aleutians, where specimens of the little-known lemming of that island were particularly desired for scientific studies. I searched diligently and trapped in likely places for several days without getting a single specimen. During the same period I was also collecting red fox scats for analysis, to determine the fox diet. It was exasperating to find lemming remains in many of the fox scats. Evidently a keen fox nose and training in nature from puppyhood can outdo the efforts of the field biologist.

The collared lemming, found across the Arctic, turns white in winter. However, the species that have developed in the southward extension along the Bering Sea in the Aleutian chain do not turn white.

This is one of the most interesting animals of the Far North. Periodically hordes of these northern lemmings move over the lowlands toward the sea, into which they finally plunge and drown. The journeys seem to occur when the lemming population has become too great for its natural habitat.

The brown lemming, *Lemmus trimucronatus,* is found in the tundra and the boreal forests. It does not change to a white coat in winter as the collared lemming does, nor does it grow the peculiar "double" claws in winter. You will find it pretty much in the

Fig. 115 (opposite)

a, b, c. Track patterns of the collared lemming, *Dicrostonyx,* in snow, from the Canadian Arctic. In c the tracks are in a snowy trough formed by the body.

d. The front feet of collared lemming: at left, showing the "double" middle claws developed in winter; at right, the summer claws, from which the under part has been shed.

e. Scats of *Dicrostonyx groenlandicus,* showing variations. Natural size.

f. Feet of the brown lemming, *Lemmus trimucronatus,* which do not produce the enlarged claws in winter. Below are typical scats, natural size.

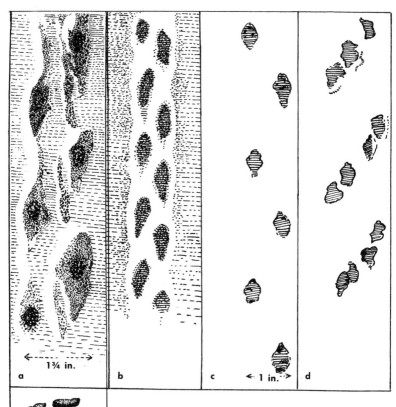

Fig. 116.   Collared lemming sign

a. Trail in snow, from Alaska. Individual footprints,
⅜ in. wide by about ½ in. long. Width of the
trail pattern, 1¾ in.
b. A similar trail in snow (Canadian Arctic).
c. Tracks in snow with 1⅜ in. between footprints,
and slightly over 1-in. straddle (Alaska).
d. A different gait.   e. Scats.

Fig. 117 (opposite)

a and c. Trails in light loose snow, showing irregular pattern, about
⅔ natural size.
b. Droppings, about natural size.

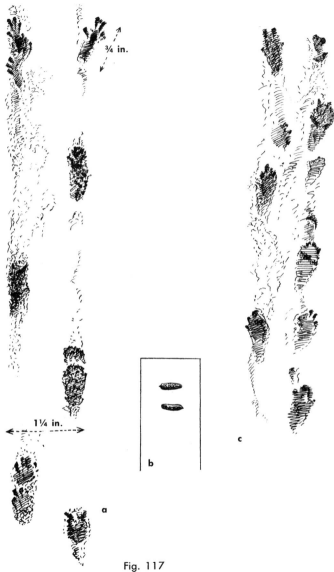

¾ in.

1¼ in.

a

b

c

Fig. 117

Brown lemming tracks and droppings

same habitat as that of some northern voles of the genus *Microtus*.

In northern Alaska I was told of certain mass migrations of "reddish mice," similar to the migrations of the collared lemmings. These reports may have referred to the brown lemming. In the Yukon delta region I have seen the brown lemmings in spring among the stranded ice blocks along the coast, but did not see them actually take to the water.

In Figure 117 are shown some brown lemming tracks in light snow, with rather irregular pattern, suggesting similar patterns of the meadow vole.

Fig. 118. Rabbits and pika

a. Arctic hare.   b. Whitetail jackrabbit.   c. Blacktail jackrabbit.
d. Snowshoe hares. The Washington hare, at the left, does not turn
   white in winter as do the other snowshoe hares.
e. Pygmy rabbit.   f. Cottontail.   g. Pika.

Rabbit and Pika Families:
Leporidae and Ochotonidae

EVERYONE is familiar with rabbits, even if through nothing more
than the Easter rabbit and Bugs Bunny. But the rabbit of the
wilds is something more than the generalized Peter Rabbit of
delightful stories. If you go forth as a naturalist, amateur, or professional, you will find before you a story with great significance.
A glance at Figure 118 reveals a gallery of distinct rabbit person-

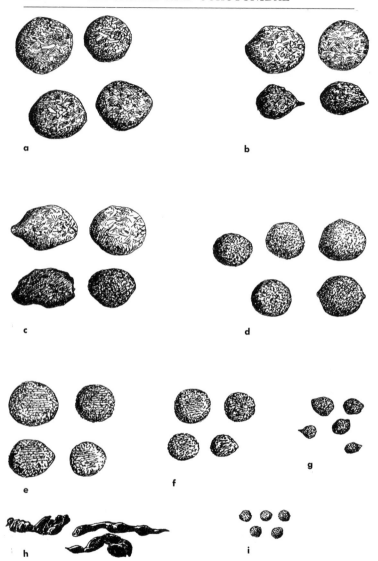

Fig. 119. Rabbit and pika scats, natural size

alities. You will find these linked to distinct territories in which, through the many centuries, each type of rabbit has "sunk to its roots," so to speak, and become an intimate part of the particular environment. I hope the following accounts will help to reveal this story of adaptation. In this group is included the diminutive mountaineer, the pika, or cony, a relative of the rabbit clan.

The rabbit track is distinctive as a track type, varying in size with the many kinds. The dropping also is very distinctive and varies in form less than in other animal species. Normally it is somewhat flattened and circular; we might call it a thick disk. Even the pika scats approach this form, except when the diet has been soft food. Figure 119 presents the rabbit type, as well as the differences in size characteristic of the several species. You will also note that there are some variations in each case.

Since the rabbit track is of a distinctive pattern, and the tracks of the different kinds vary chiefly in size, they are not presented at this point.

In the following individual accounts an attempt is made to show not only the characteristics of each group but also, collectively, variations that are more or less common to all.

Arctic Hare or Tundra Hare

The Arctic hare has become specialized for living in the high North, from Greenland to Alaska. Chiefly it inhabits tundra, or open country, but on the shores of the southern Bering Sea you are likely to find *Lepus arcticus* in the alder brush. One variety lives as far south as Newfoundland. Like our familiar whitetail jackrabbit, which it resembles in many ways, the Arctic hare turns to white in winter. In northern Greenland and on Ellesmere Island and adjacent parts of the Arctic Archipelago the hares don't even bother to turn gray for the short summer they have, but remain white the year round.

These Alaskan hares weigh 9 or 10 pounds, and some even

Fig. 119 (opposite)

a. Arctic hare (Bristol Bay, Alaska).
b. Whitetail jackrabbit (Jackson Hole, Wyo.).
c. European hare (New Zealand).
d. Blacktail jackrabbit (Nev.).
e. Snowshoe hare (upper, Minn.; lower, Wyo.).
f. Cottontail (upper, Nev.; lower, No. Dak.). g. Pygmy rabbit (Nev.).
h. Pika. Soft type from succulent feed (Alaska).
 i. Pika. Hard type, on dry feed of fall and winter (Alaska).

Arctic Hare

heavier weights have been reported, so this animal is in many respects quite comparable to our whitetail jackrabbit of the open plains. In general form the tracks are similar to those of the whitetail jackrabbit shown in Figure 120. I was unable to obtain any tracks for illustration here; droppings are shown in Figure 119, a.

The Arctic hare has a remarkable habit that produces tracks very different from the usual rabbit type. Occasionally it will hop along on the hind feet only, kangaroo style, for some distance before dropping back to all fours. Travelers who have witnessed this say it is a striking spectacle to see a sizable group of these animals take off all together on their hind toes. Colonel John K. Howard, who photographed these animals in Greenland many years ago, kindly made available some movie film, on the basis of which the accompanying sketch was made.

Arctic Hares hopping on their hind toes

Whitetail Jackrabbit

This big rabbit of the plains, *Lepus townsendi,* is found from the prairies of the middle-western states and southern Canada, west through the sagelands to the high mountain slopes of the Rockies, Cascades, and Sierras. It is almost as big as the Arctic hare, weighing 7 or 8 pounds, and more. Here is an animal that looks much like the Arctic hare, but it has found the northern plains and high western slopes more to its liking than the wastes of polar regions.

The whitetail jackrabbit is a good subject with which to illustrate some of the difficulties in tracking. Figure 122, a, b, d, and e, shows well-known tracks and some track patterns in snow. In my experience the leaps vary from 1 or 2 feet in slow hopping up to 9 feet or more at high speed. Others have reported as much as 12 and 20 feet at extreme speeds.

You do not always find perfect tracks. As boys in Minnesota, my brother and I used to hunt jackrabbits by tracking. Sometimes in bad weather we would lose the trail when the rabbit had crossed an area of hard crusted snow where the wind was sweeping away all loose material. There would be no indications of the long hind foot, but the typical pattern of a few claw marks on the crust still spelled rabbit and we could recognize the speeding pattern of Figure 122, e, or the slowing pattern of *a.*

Figure 122, c, by itself would suggest coyote. But remember that snow conditions play tricks with footprints. Examine the pattern closely and its size will tell you the true story. It is important not to expect perfect tracks, or to rely on one set of known characters. We have seen that even in good mud tracks of the

beaver you rarely find all five toe prints of the front foot, although
you know that is the number he really has. And so you learn to
add previous knowledge and judgment to what you find recorded
in mud or snow. For instance, any rabbit track in Greenland or
the polar region *beyond the limit of trees,* would mean Arctic hare
and not jackrabbit. If you find a certain type of dropping in the
trail of a forest where it is known that there are no bobcats, you
may conclude that a coyote has passed that way, but if bobcats
also live in the forest, you are not so sure. A store of dried grass
and leaves heaped up at the base of a willow in the tundra area
of the Alaska Range means the Alaska vole, the little "hay

Fig. 120

The zigzags in the trail spoke of an attack, and a snowy owl
nearby suggested the foe (Moorhead, *Minn.,* Jan. 20, 1918)

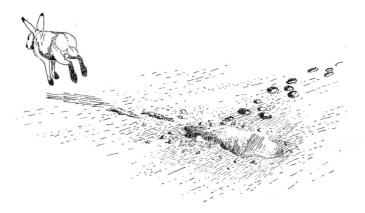

Fig. 121. Whitetail jackrabbit speeding away
from its form in the snow

mouse" that puts up winter supplies. A similar pile of hay up in
the rocks more likely means pika, or cony, and certainly would
in the Rocky Mountains.

It is this sorting of facts and previous experience, combined with
the imperfect evidence in the snow or mud before you, that makes
success in reading nature's print, and makes of such reading an
exhilarating experience.

One winter day in Minnesota I was following a jackrabbit track
across the snowy fields. Presently I came on some peculiar maneuvers. The trail suddenly broke in several zigzag turns. There
were no other tracks there on the snow. Had the rabbit been seized
by a giddy playful mood, or a nightmare? The trail straightened
out as I followed along, puzzled, and very soon I came to a
haystack. There sat a snowy owl, one of those winter visitors from
the far north. The story then became clear. The owl had made
several swoops at the running rabbit, the rabbit had nimbly dodged
each attack, and for some reason the owl gave up and went over
to perch on the haystack (see Fig. 120). A flying bird leaves no
track, but it can create a mystery in the snow!

The whitetail jackrabbit digs no burrow, but rests in the traditional "form" — a hollow in the snow or in the grass, at the base
of a bush or tree, beside a rock, or the entrance to a badger hole
(see above). In cultivated areas this rabbit often snuggles down
beside a clod in a plowed field. If the snow is deep enough, it may
dig a shallow hole in the snow where it can crawl in out of the
weather.

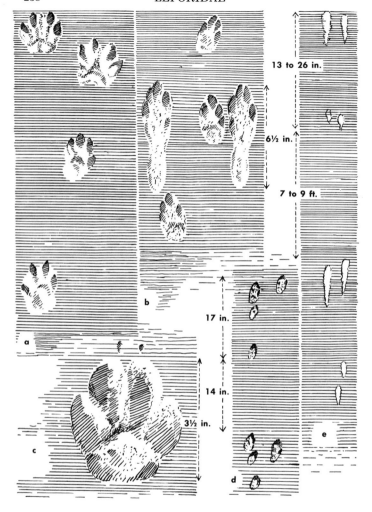

13 to 26 in.

6½ in.

7 to 9 ft.

17 in.

14 in.

3½ in.

Fig. 122. Whitetail jackrabbit tracks in snow (northwestern Wyo.)

Blacktail Jackrabbit
walking (Ariz.)

Blacktail and Antelope Jackrabbits

The blacktail jackrabbit, *Lepus californicus,* is primarily the rabbit of the western sage and cactus country, though it has occupied grassy plains as well — from Nebraska, Kansas, and Oklahoma west to the Pacific and from Washington south into Mexico. The related antelope jackrabbit, *Lepus alleni,* ranges up from Mexico into New Mexico and Arizona. Neither of these turns white in winter.

In parts of the western range both blacktail and whitetail occupy the same areas, hence their tracks could be confused. However, in general the tracks of the blacktail jackrabbit are somewhat smaller than those of the whitetail.

You will notice that the rabbit track patterns are similar in all the species, the hind feet coming ahead of the front feet in the normal gaits. The reason is that the rabbits are primarily *hoppers,* even when moving slowly. One day my son and my brother and I,

Fig. 122 (opposite)

a. Typical running track pattern, only the toes of hind feet touching. Length of pattern 19½ in.; length of hind print (in front) about 3½ in.; length of front prints (in rear of pattern) 3 in.
b. Sitting track pattern, hind heels down, the front tracks of last leap showing between the hind tracks. Greatest width of this pattern, or straddle, is 8 in.
c. Hind-foot tracks without heel mark, showing general resemblance to coyote track.
d. Pattern in moderate speed.   e. Speeding.

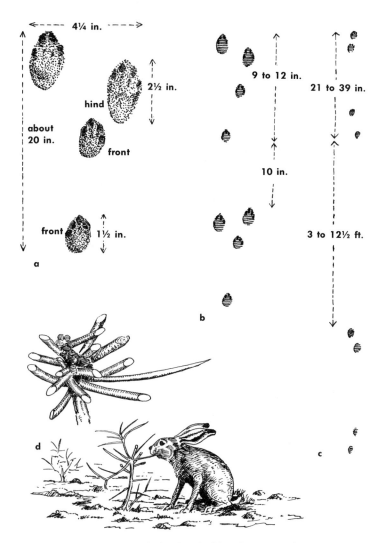

Fig. 123. Blacktail jackrabbit, from Nevada

a and b. Typical tracks in sand, at slow speed. Width, or straddle,
    4¼ in.   c. Speeding, in snow.
d. Feeding on "crown of thorns" (*Koeberlinia spinosa tennispina*) in
    the Texas desert. Cut twigs are shown above.

240

traveling through Arizona, came on a blacktail jackrabbit at close range. My brother took a series of motion pictures. To our surprise the rabbit began *walking* away, quite unrabbitlike. Had he become stiff lying in his form? Later he hopped away vigorously enough, but he did walk, and the illustration on page 239 is a sketch taken from the motion picture. It is interesting to refer to Figure 127, in the marsh rabbit section, and the drawing of Arctic hares hopping, shown on page 234.

I have not seen the tail mark in the snow described by Seton, though sometimes there are drag marks of the toes, similar to those of the snowshoe hare in Figure 125, b.

Note the slight differences in size of droppings, in descending order, of the Arctic hare and whitetail and blacktail jackrabbits (Fig. 119).

As with some of the other rabbits, this species occupies forms rather than burrows. You will find these slightly hollowed resting places under bushes, in a grassy place, by a rock, or any handy spot that gives a little protection.

The blacktail jack feeds on a variety of desert shrubs and cacti. You will find prickly pear cactus gnawed by these as well as other animals. Note the slant cut characteristic of rodent work in the upper part of *d*, Figure 123. A deer would leave a "pinched-off" effect.

European Hare

This European immigrant, *Lepus europaeus,* about the size of the whitetail jackrabbit, has been introduced in some of the northeastern states, from New Jersey and eastern Pennsylvania and New York to Vermont and Ontario. My own experience with this hare was not in America, but in the Southern Alps of New

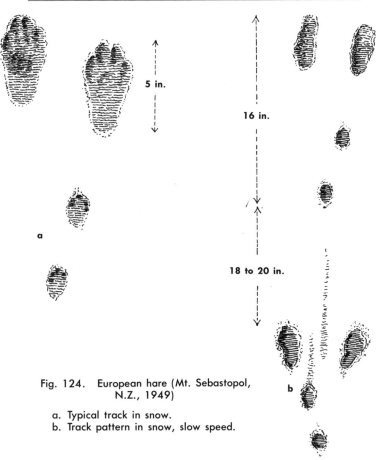

Fig. 124.   European hare (Mt. Sebastopol,
N.Z., 1949)

a. Typical track in snow.
b. Track pattern in snow, slow speed.

Zealand. There, on the slopes of Mt. Sebastopol after a recent snow,
I found the tracks of this animal — an emigrant from Europe. It
was living on a high open mountain slope, where it had been
trimming the lower portions of native shrubs, while the introduced
chamois and tahr had been cropping the higher twigs. The hare
cuttings were diagonal, like those shown in Figure 123, d.

In Figure 124 are shown the tracks, only slightly smaller than
those of the whitetail jackrabbit. The droppings (see Fig.
119, c) seem fairly comparable in size to those of the whitetail.

Snowshoe Hare

Lepus americanus and the related species and subspecies have occupied a tremendous area — the entire transcontinental coniferous forest, including Canada, Alaska, the northern states, and the Rocky Mountains and Pacific Coast forests as well. This hare has found the temperate climate best, but has gone as far north as it can find forest. It is well named, for its hind toes spread to form a broad "snowshoe" surface on the snow (see illustration). In Figure 125 note the wide shape of the tracks that is a result of this feature. Around the cabin in Wyoming where I am writing these lines the patterns *a* and *b* are everywhere on the surface of the snow (which is 4 feet deep). These animals are foraging for twigs — and the vegetable peelings we throw out for them. One that had been frightened by a coyote went off in great bounds, as in *c*. The tracks of the Washington hare (also a snowshoe rabbit), *Lepus washingtoni,* from the Olympic Mountains, do not differ essentially (compare *a* and *d* with *b* and *c*). Both species produce the variations shown here.

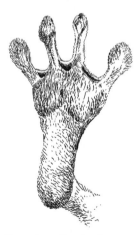

Snowshoe Hare's "snowshoe." Spread toes of the right hind foot (Hudson Bay, 1914)

In the north woods, when these rabbits become numerous, they form well-established trails in the snow. During a big rabbit year in the Hudson Bay country, 1915, the Indians snared great numbers of them in these trails. Since several goshawks and barred owls were snared in the same region, this indi-

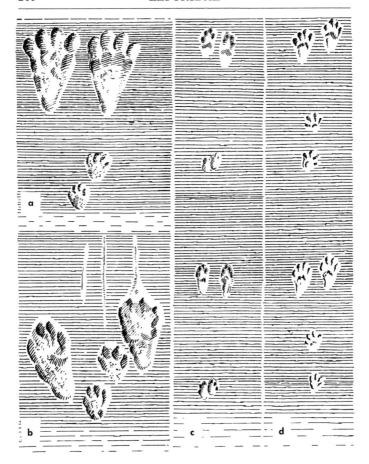

Fig. 125.   Tracks of snowshoe hare in snow

a. Track of Washington hare, *Lepus washingtoni*, slow hopping, in snow. Length of track pattern, about 11 in.; hops, about 14 in. (Olympic Mts., Wash.).
b. Snowshoe hare of Rocky Mts., slow hopping. Length of track pattern about 10 in.; hops, about 10 in. (Wyo.).
c. Rocky Mt. snowshoe hare speeding. Track patterns about 24 in.; leaps, 38 to 67 in. (Wyo.).
d. Washington hare speeding. Track patterns 20 to 22 in.; leap, 66 in. (Olympic Mts.).

cated that they too recognized good rabbit-hunting grounds, and apparently at times actually used the trail for the chase.

Sometimes you will find twig cuttings left by the snowshoe. A lodgepole pine beside my cabin in Wyoming was blown over in a high wind and during the winter these rabbits trimmed all the twigs within reach.

Once on a gravelbar of the Snake River in Wyoming I found some lupine plants that had been nibbled. What rodent had cut these? The slant cuts on the eaten stems meant rodent work, of course. I thought of setting a live trap to find out. But I went back for another look and this time noticed the telltale round scats of the snowshoe hare. There were several beside each plant that had been cropped.

Lupine cropped by
Snowshoe Hare

Usually the snowshoe will rest at the base of a tree or bush, but often takes shelter under a log or brushy place. In winter, when the snow is deep, some excellent tunnels form under logs and limb tangles, sheltered above by a great load of snow, and the hare finds refuge there, far out of sight. Like the cottontail it will also find refuge under a log cabin.

Cottontail

Cottontail, *Sylvilagus floridanus,* is probably the best known of the rabbit family. In one form or another, the cottontail is native to nearly all of the United States and Mexico and extends into Central America.

The familiar tracks of this rabbit may be found equally in sagebrush deserts and the eastern woodlands, though of course in different species. You will even find the tracks in the outskirts of cities. In fact the tracks shown in Figure 126 were drawn in Washington, D.C. You will note that they follow the usual rabbit pattern, in a special size and edition.

Cottontails will gnaw twigs in winter and occasionally will eat the bark on orchard trees. It is not always easy to distinguish their tooth marks from those of other rodents, but the marks are larger than those of mice. The twig shown in Figure 126, d, is

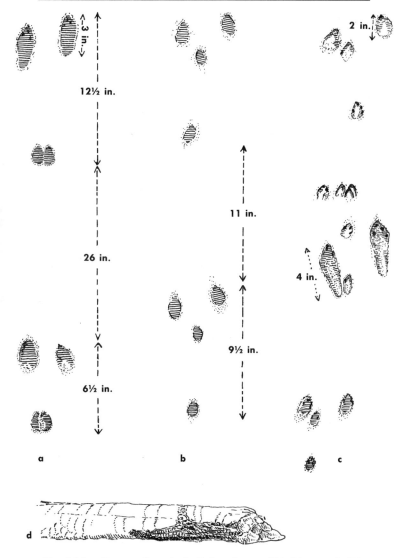

Fig. 126.   Cottontail tracks in ½ in. of snow (Washington, D.C.)

Cottontail

from Wisconsin. The end of the twig shows the effect of repeated bites, different from the clean cut on the small twigs eaten by the blacktail jackrabbit (Fig. 123, d), or plants eaten by the snowshoe hare (see page 245).

Cottontails will often rest in the usual "form," under a sage bush or similar shelter in the West, or some other bush or tangle of vines or a brush heap in the East. They will hide in hollow logs, stumps, burrows in the ground, or a crevice in a rock.

Ordinarily these rabbits are not found in the same places as the snowshoe hare, so their tracks and droppings are not likely to be confused. Reference to Figure 119 will show that cottontail droppings are much smaller than those of jackrabbits, whose territory they often share.

Marsh and Swamp Rabbits

The marsh rabbit, *Sylvilagus palustris,* with two subspecies, inhabits marsh country from Virginia to Florida. The somewhat larger swamp rabbit, *Sylvilagus aquaticus,* occupies wooded swamps, marshes, and river bottoms from western Kentucky and Georgia westward into Texas. Related species occur in Mexico and Central and South America.

Although these specialized rabbits are at home in water and choose wet lands to live in, and sometimes readily plunge into water to escape pursuit, they really have many habits in common with the cottontail. For example, they rest in forms in brier patches,

Fig. 126 (opposite)

a. Hops in shallow snow.   b. Shorter leaps.
c. Cottontail coming to a stop, then hopping on. The hops were from 6 to 4½ in.
d. Twig gnawed by cottontail, about natural size.

thickets, and similar shelter, and enter burrows of the gopher tortoise — hollow logs and stumps and hollow trees. When danger approaches, they will climb up some distance inside these trees, as I have found cottontails doing in Minnesota. In short, all of these rabbits seek some kind of cover for concealment, using whatever is available in their chosen habitat. The marsh rabbit finds shelter in tall grass and cattails. It will also venture into floating vegetation, as one would expect from such a water-loving animal. Marsh rabbits have definite runways in the vegetation, and also on old mossy logs, I am told.

The droppings are similar to those of the cottontail. I doubt if

Fig. 127.   Tracks and scats of marsh rabbit

a. Close-up of tracks of walking marsh rabbit.
b. Walking track pattern of marsh rabbit.
c. Droppings of marsh rabbit, natural size (Everglades Natl. Park).

Marsh Rabbit

they could be distinguished consistently. However, if you find them on logs, along runways, or on floating material in water of the swamp areas, you may conclude the marsh rabbit or swamp rabbit has been there. The final decision depends on the territory. The cottontail normally seeks higher ground.

One investigator, Ivan R. Tomkins, discovered that *walking,* with alternate steps, is one gait of the marsh rabbit — a significant departure from the almost universal hopping of the rabbits. Figure 127 is adapted from photographs kindly furnished by Mr. Tomkins. It is interesting to refer to the illustration on page 239, which shows that the blacktail jackrabbit of the arid plains also knows how to walk, though it probably does so very seldom.

Pygmy Rabbit

This pygmy of the rabbit clan, *Sylvilagus idahoensis,* is a Westerner of restricted range. It has chosen the dry sagelands in an area including parts of Idaho, Oregon, northern California, and Nevada. And within this area it seeks out the tall sage growth. In northwestern Nevada, where so much of the sage is the low sparse kind, I would come to one of the thick patches of tall sage, *Artemisia tridentata,* looming up like a miniature forest on the flatland. There I would find the pygmy, which measures 8½ to 11 inches in length. I was able to approach close, and when the little gray rabbit fled it scuttled away among the heavy bushes and soon

Pygmy Rabbit

disappeared. It regularly seeks shelter in underground dens. For track patterns, see Figure 128.

The droppings of this rabbit are so small that they approach a spherical form, rather than the disk (see Fig. 119).

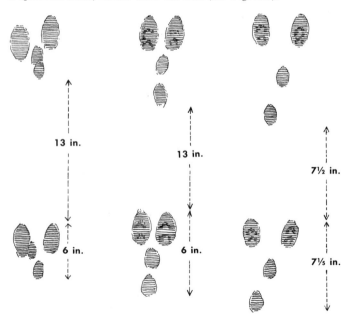

Fig. 128.   Several track patterns of the pygmy rabbit, at slow speed (northwestern Nev., Jan. 1942)

Pika or Cony

The pika, of the genus *Ochotona,* is 6 to 8 inches long and is found in the Rocky Mountain regions of the western states, southern British Columbia and Alberta, the Cascades and Sierra Nevada, and the mountains of interior Alaska and the Yukon. This distribution reveals the way of life of this diminutive relative of the rabbits which has chosen to spend its time among the jumbled blocks of a rock slide, or in some other rocky habitat.

The pika, or cony, is hairy-footed like the rabbits, but has short round ears and shows no tail. You will not commonly find pika tracks, though you may see them in late, lingering snowdrifts or early fall snow, or in the mud at the edge of the water near their rock refuge. Figure 129 shows track patterns in somewhat fragmentary form. Note that the front feet have five toes, though often all do not appear in the track. The hind feet have only four toes, like the rabbit.

One obvious sign of the pika is the distinctive call. If you are following a trail through rough rock and from somewhere nearby comes a small voice, a sharp little bleat crying *Enk!,* look around carefully and you may spy a small furry lump sitting still, or a little gray form running smoothly over the rock surface to disappear in a crevice. It will be the pika.

In the winter of 1921 I was driving a dog team up the Toklat River in the Alaska Range. I had not come to the higher mountain slopes, but was passing a tall bluff of the riverbank when I heard a familiar sound. I listened and heard it again, and recognized the pika's voice. It came from within that mass of snow. From its retreat inside, the animal had heard us passing out there in the Alaskan winter and, true to its nature, had given voice to curiosity or excitement.

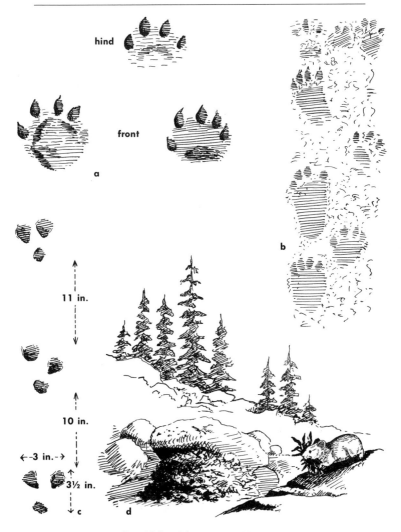

Fig. 129.   Pika sign, in Wyoming

a. Tracks in mud at margin of stream.
b. Fragmentary trail, shuffling gait, in rough snow.
c. Running gait.   d. Pika putting up hay for winter.

The incident illustrates another important part of pika economy. It can spend the entire winter under the snow, for it has put by stores for that purpose. In the late summer you will find a pile of dried plants and twigs under an overhanging rock or beside a large boulder, often with fresh green food on top of the pile. There may be little bundles of plants nearby, left there for one reason or another and not yet added to the winter store. And if you look around, you may see the old matted vegetation of former haystacks.

The droppings lie among the rocks and look like round pellets of black tapioca. If the animals have had succulent feed the droppings will be elongated. Compare Figure 119, h and i.

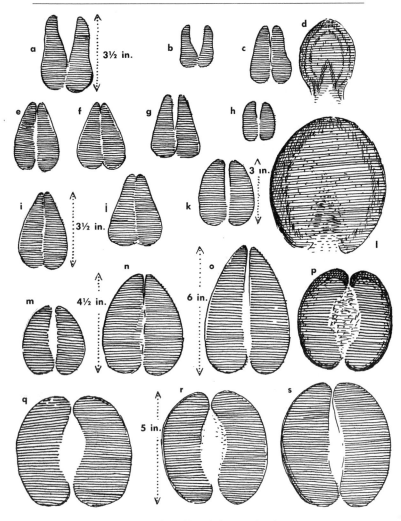

Fig. 130.   Tracks of hoofed animals, drawn to
scale, roughly ¼ natural size

Hoofed Animals: Ungulata

THE HOOFED ANIMALS leave tracks that are distinctive as a group, but within the group there are confusing similarities (see Fig. 130). I would not try to distinguish the three kinds of deer track, for example. Geographical distribution can often be a help in identification. The whitetail deer inhabits the eastern states, the mule deer the Rocky Mountain region, and the blacktail deer the Pacific Coast. In the Big Bend National Park in Texas you will find the whitetail deer on the high forested areas and the mule deer on the more open desert. However, there are intermediate zones in many places where two of these three deer mingle. It should be noted, too, that, although the track of the pronghorn is very often more blocky and squared off behind than those of deer, you will find some tracks that are indistinguishable.

The following keys to droppings of hoofed animals (Figs. 131 and 132) illustrate the great similarities between the droppings of different species. A series of variations is shown for the pellet types of each animal. There are other variations, however, and it would be difficult to be sure of mule deer pellets in mountain goat, pronghorn, or mountain sheep territory. It is discouraging not to be able to present a more clear-cut key, but that is the way these animals are! So much depends on the kind of food they happen to be eating at a given time, whether dry or succulent or ranging in between.

Figures 131 and 132 give both the pellet type of droppings that characterize the winter feeding or a dry diet and the soft type of

Fig. 130 (opposite)

a. Mountain goat.   b. Domestic goat.
c. Domestic sheep.   d. Burro.
e. Mule deer.   f. Blacktail deer.
g. Mountain sheep.   h. Peccary.
i. Whitetail deer.   j. Pronghorn.
k. Pig.   l. Horse.
m. Domestic calf.   n. Elk.
o. Moose.   p. Caribou.
q. Domestic cow.   r. Muskox.
s. Bison.   t. Baird's tapir (at right)

255

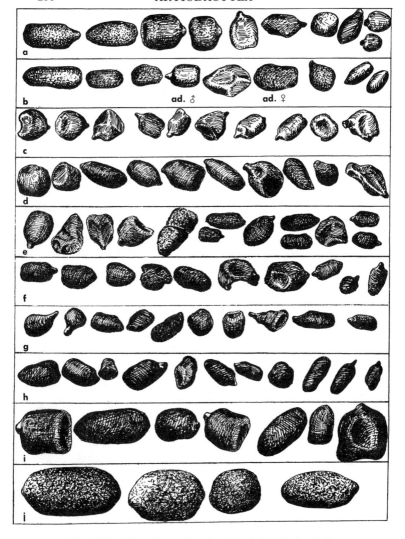

Fig. 131.   Droppings of various hoofed animals. Pellet
type, drawn to scale; about ⅔ natural size.

droppings that result from green or succulent food in summer. Here, too, there are many variations in appearance and size, only a few of which can be given.

For more detailed treatment see the sections devoted to each animal that follow.

Whitetail Deer

When we speak of deer, to most Americans it probably means the whitetail or "flagtail," as it is often called, *Odocoileus virginianus*. This is the common deer of eastern and central North America. Its range extends northward into southern Canada, southward through Mexico and Central America, and westward into the Rocky Mountain region, including parts of Idaho, Wyoming,

Fig. 131 (opposite)

a. Whitetail deer.   b. Mule deer.   c. Caribou.   d. Pronghorn.
e. Mountain sheep (first three samples, from bighorns in Wyoming; next five, desert bighorns; last five, white (Dall) sheep in Alaska).
f. Domestic sheep.   g. Mountain goat.   h. Domestic goat.
i. Elk.   j. Moose.

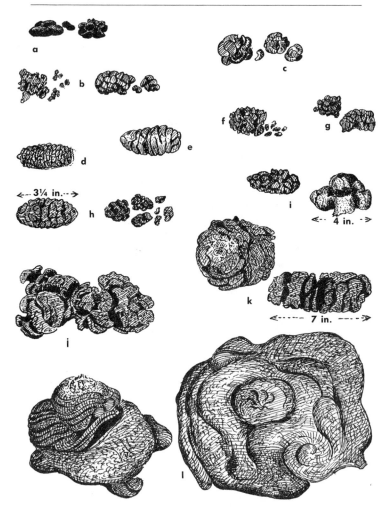

Fig. 132. Droppings of hoofed animals, of the soft, summer type,
drawn to scale. It is important to note that there is great variation
in form for each species. These are only random specimens. In some
cases two samples are illustrated. A few measurements are included
for estimate of size. Note that domestic cattle droppings are similar
to those of buffalo, or bison.

Left front and left
hind feet of male
Whitetail Deer

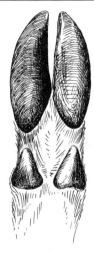
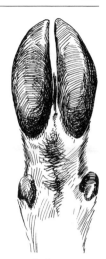

Colorado, New Mexico, and southern Arizona. And there are a few small colonies in Washington, Oregon, and California.

Generally speaking, this is the deer of the forests and brushlands, in contradistinction to the mule deer of the West, *Odocoileus hemionus.* As might be expected over such a wide and varied range, there is much diversity in size, from the large deer of Minnesota and Wisconsin, which weighs several hundred pounds, to the smaller, more trimly built deer of Texas and Mexico. The "Key deer" of certain Florida Keys is the smallest of all. The few survivors of this diminutive species are struggling for existence in the face of an expanding real-estate business. This striking diversity in size among the white-tailed deer is reflected in their tracks and other sign. In Figure 133 are shown tracks from Minnesota, Oklahoma, and Texas. Those of the Key deer are even smaller than those from Texas.

When we come to Figure 134, showing track patterns of this deer, we should note a conspicuous difference between the actions of the whitetail and the mule deer. In galloping, the whitetail uses the "rocking horse" gait so common among large animals, in

Fig. 132 (opposite)

a. Peccary.	g. Domestic goat.
b. Mule deer; 2 samples.	h. Caribou; 2 samples.
c. Whitetail deer.	i. Pronghorn; 2 samples.
d. Mountain sheep.	j. Moose.
e. Domestic sheep.	k. Elk; 2 samples.
f. Mountain goat.	l. Bison; 2 samples.

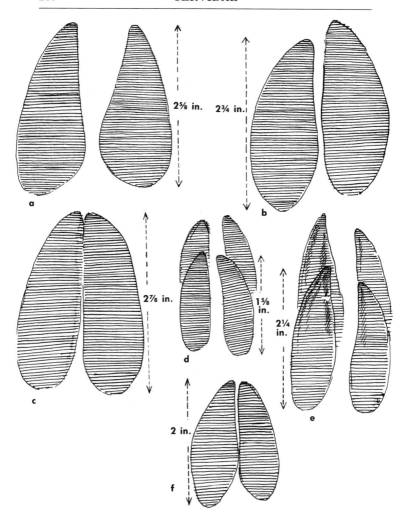

Fig. 133.　Whitetail deer tracks, in mud, about ⅓ natural size

a, b, c. Various tracks from Wichita Mts., Okla.
d. Fawn tracks from Michigan (July 7, 1934).
e. Tracks from northern Minnesota (1924).
f. Track of a small deer in Chisos Mts., Texas (March 1950).

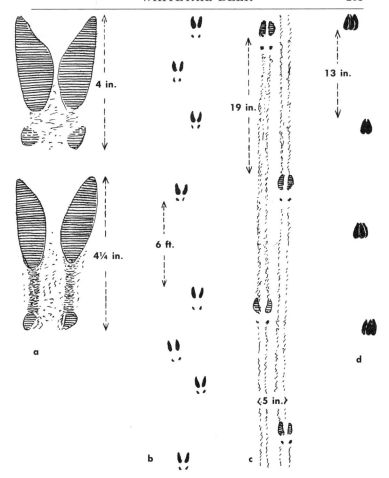

Fig. 134. Track patterns of whitetail deer

a. Leaping tracks, in mud, with dewclaws showing. In front track (upper) dewclaws are close to hoofs. In hind track (lower) dewclaws are farther from hoofs (Okla., 1935).
b. Galloping track pattern, in snow; hind tracks in front (Mich.).
c. Walking pattern in snow, showing drag marks of toes (Mich.).
d. Walking pattern of young deer, on dirt road, showing the traditional heart shape of footprint (Minn.).

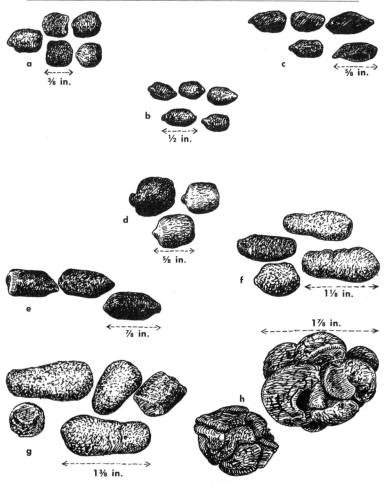

Fig. 135.   Whitetail deer droppings, about ⅔ natural size

a. A smaller type (Minn.).   c. Softer type of pellets (Minn.).
b. Pellets (Chisos Mts., Tex.).   d. Winter droppings (Wisc.).
e and f. Large types (Minn.).
g. Unusually large winter droppings (from a deer yard near Grand
   Marais, Minn.).
h. Soft summer droppings (Minn.).

which the hind feet swing far ahead of the front-foot tracks. This produces the familiar hind print in front of front print pattern so common, from the white-footed mouse and rabbit to the moose and horse in running gaits. The mule deer, on the other hand, generally proceeds in speed with a bounding rubberball action, all four feet coming down together, hind feet behind.

You will notice among the tracks of this and the other deer that you do not always find the neat, well-formed heart-shaped print so often figured. Very frequently the toes are separated. Moreover, I have been unable to distinguish the footprints of the whitetail from those of mule deer. Fortunately, over most of the range only whitetails are present. Don't worry about confusing any animal with mule deer in the Adirondacks, the deer country of Pennsylvania, Minnesota, or indeed over most of the country east of the Rockies, for there are very few mule deer in these parts.

Like the elk, the whitetail buck will occasionally wallow in mud during the rutting season. Such messed-up muddy spots, if made by deer, should contain some identifying hair. However, I have not found this practice nearly as common as among elk.

Should you see a white flashing signal disappear before you at dusk, or in heavy brush, it may have been a fleeing whitetail. For when a whitetail runs, true to its name it holds aloft its large white tail, which becomes a prominent sign that can be seen at considerable distance.

The deer too have a voice. Most commonly heard is a sharp snort, or whistle. This is a somewhat prolonged *whiew-ew-ew,* which carries quite far and is given when the deer is alarmed or curious. There is also a sort of bleat, a sound produced by the vocal cords that is difficult to describe. The low calls between fawn and mother are hardly to be detected at any distance.

Mule Deer

The mule deer of the West, *Odocoileus hemionus,* is larger than the whitetail, has a different antler structure, and has a round "mule tail" tipped with black, in contrast to the large white flagtail of the eastern deer. The mule deer occupies western America from the northwestern tip of Minnesota and southwestern Manitoba, the Dakotas, westernmost Nebraska, Colorado, New Mexico, western Texas, and northern Mexico west through the Rocky Mountain region to eastern British Columbia, eastern Washington, Oregon, and California. It also extends far north in the Canadian provinces.

This deer often ranges into more open country than the habitat

264 CERVIDAE

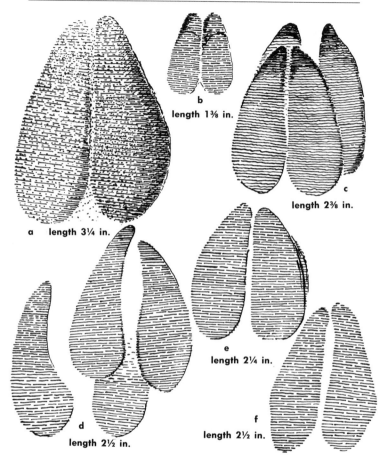

Fig. 136. Mule deer tracks, about ⅔ natural size

a. Adult male, in dust (Grand Teton Natl. Park, Wyo.).
b. Fawn (Yellowstone Natl. Park, July 16, 1929).
c. Adult female, in mud (Grand Teton Natl. Park, Wyo.).
d, e, f. Tracks in dust (northern Nev.).

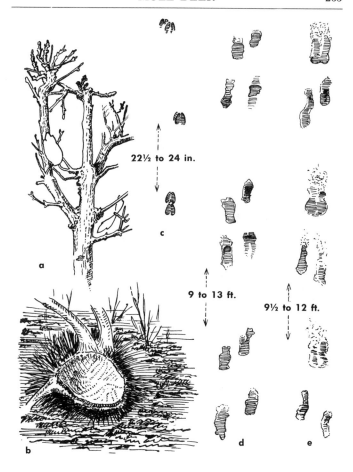

22½ to 24 in.

9 to 13 ft.

9½ to 12 ft.

Fig. 137.   Mule deer sign

a. Shrub severely browsed by mule deer, producing a stubby form.
b. Base of the spiny lechuguilla eaten out by mule deer (Chisos Mts., Tex.).
c. Walking track pattern (Wyo.).
d and e. High-bounding track patterns in deep snow of adult female mule deer. In d the doe was pursued by a coyote. In these patterns the hind feet land behind the front feet.

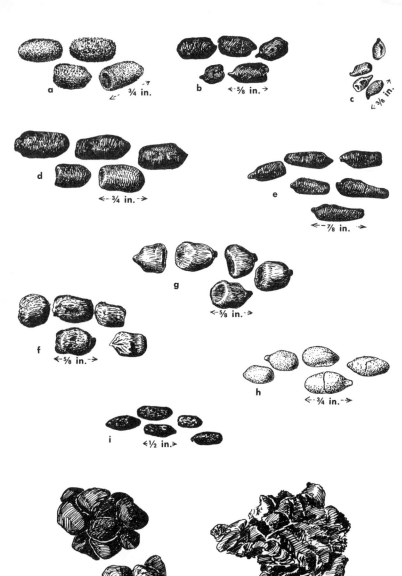

266

Mule Deer

chosen by the whitetail. It is true that mule deer inhabit the western forests, but they are more of a mountain animal than the whitetail, and in many places are found out on the desert plains, in both cactus and sagebrush country.

As described in the whitetail section, the mule deer ha˙ a distinctive bounding gait, in which all four feet virtually come down together, hind feet behind the front feet. This track pattern is shown in Figure 137, d and e. Figure 136 illustrates a variety of footprints.

The shape of the track of the mule deer will vary somewhat with the type of ground on which the animal lives. On soft soil, as in some woodlands, the toes are likely to be relatively more pointed. On hard, rocky ground, found in some areas occupied by these deer, the hoofs are worn enough to produce blunt tips.

Fig. 138 (opposite).   Mule deer droppings, about ⅔ natural size

a. Winter droppings of adult male (Dinosaur Natl. Monument, Utah, 1950).
b. Autumn droppings of adult male (Wyo., Nov. 8, 1938).
c. Fawn droppings (Wyo.).
d. Adult female droppings (Wyo., Jan. 22, 1939).
e. From Wyoming (April 1937).
f. From British Columbia (June 12, 1935).
g. From northern Nevada (Aug. 24, 1939).
h. Droppings of pure clay, resulting from use of mineral lick (Salmon Natl. Forest, Idaho).
i. Scats probably from young animal (Wyo.).
j and k. Summer scats, of the softer type.

As with all deer, the droppings vary in size and shape, as shown in Figure 138. The quantity in a given sample varies from less than ⅛ to ½ pint, and the number of pellets in a series that was studied varied from 68 to 128. Incidentally, I have been unable to distinguish with certainty between some deer pellets and those of the mountain goat.

The mule deer emits a snort, or blowing, sometimes prolonged slightly to produce a whistling effect. This may indicate alarm or surprise, or curiosity. Like other deer species, as well as pronghorn, the mule deer will stamp a front foot. Is this defiance, fear, or excitement? All that we can say is that it denotes some kind of intense feeling.

The mother and fawn, of course, make the low bleating sounds common among such animals. A neighbor of mine who lives on a ranch beside a high hillside extending up to the forest told about hearing the mule deer "talking" among themselves as they fed there on winter nights. They made various sounds, grunts and other expressions, difficult to describe. These deer offer excellent opportunity for study of vocal performance of animals and their meanings.

Blacktail Deer

This animal of the Pacific Coast, once classed as a distinct species but now as a subspecies of the mule deer, has many of its characteristics, with the same antler type, even the same bounding gait, but it has a flat tail much like that of the whitetail deer,

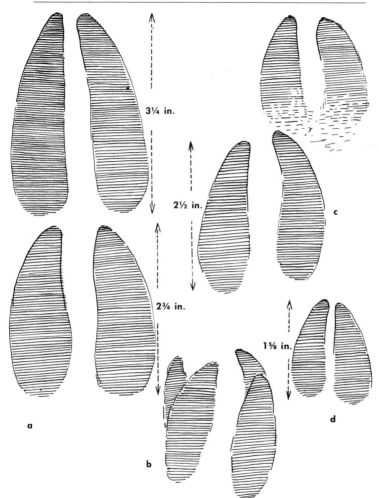

3¼ in.

2½ in.

2¾ in.

1⅝ in.

a

b

c

d

Fig. 139.   Some tracks of coast blacktail deer (*Odocoileus*).
About ⅓ natural size

a. Adult doe, in mud (Olympic Mts., Wash., March 1934).
b. Yearling, accompanying this doe.
c. Adult Sitka deer (Long I., Kodiak, Alaska, Sept. 3, 1936).
d. Young Sitka deer (Long I., Sept. 3, 1936).

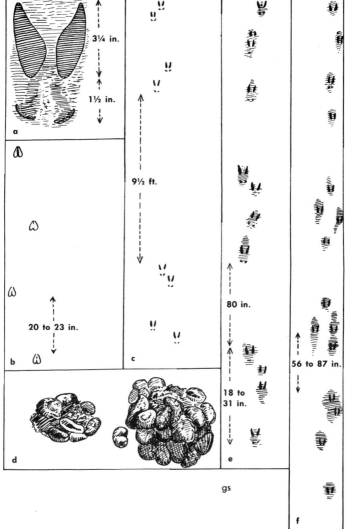

Fig. 140.   Blacktail deer tracks and droppings

yet smaller and black on the upper surface. It is found from the
Sierras and Cascades west to the coast in California, Oregon,
Washington, and northward along the coast of British Columbia
into the southeastern coastal part of Alaska.

Deer sign found in the coastal rain forests will be of this animal,
but in parts of the Cascades and Sierras the ranges of mule deer
and coast blacktail overlap. I must confess that I have found no
way to distinguish the footprints or droppings of our three kinds
of deer. Blacktail sign is shown in Figures 139 and 140. Tracks
will reveal a bounding gait similar to that of mule deer.

From personal experience with the blacktail I am unable to
describe any calls that might differ from those of other deer.
Generally I saw them among the vine maples, or up on the steep
slopes among the hemlocks, moving about silently. Certainly they
appear to be much more silent than the whitetail.

There is one sign more pronounced with elk traveling in large
numbers which also applies to other deer. When the bucks are
rubbing the velvet from their antlers they will scar a sapling, break
some of the limbs, and bruise the bark. Any of the antlered animals
will leave this evidence of the approaching rutting season.

Elk or Wapiti

The elk, *Cervus canadensis,* is now being redistributed into many
parts of the continent where it was once numerous.

Elk tracks are definitely larger and rounder in outline than
those of deer, and there is no difficulty in distinguishing them.
They are rounder and somewhat smaller than those of moose,
though occasionally even these may cause a little confusion. In
localities where elk share the same range with Hereford cattle
there can easily be difficulty. The adult cattle tracks are large
and blocky, and quite distinct. But *young* cattle leave a track

Fig. 140 (opposite)

a. Typical running gait track, in snow (Olympic Mts., Wash.).
b. Walking pattern, with conventional track shape, toes together
   (Olympic Mts.).
c. Bounding track of yearling, toes spread (Olympic Mts., March 24,
   1934).
d. Sitka deer droppings, soft type, about ⅔ natural size. (Hinchinbrook
   I., Alaska).
e. Bounding gait track of female, in shallow snow (Olympic Mts.).
f. Same, in deep snow (Olympic Mts.).

that is often very similar to those of adult elk. In such cases one must look around for more distinctive tracks, and for possible cow chips. Tracks are shown in Figure 141, which include a track of a domestic calf for comparison.

In New Zealand it was noted that wapiti living on moist lowland earth developed exceptionally long and pointed hoofs, while those on the rocky uplands had worn the hoofs relatively blunt. It is well to keep this principle in mind in studying hoofprints.

The elk scats are fairly distinctive, but examination of Figure 143 proves that variability is great. In joint elk-moose country some puzzling samples will be found, for the elk, too, will produce elongated "sawdust" pellets somewhat similar to those of moose, when on a dry, exclusively browse diet. However, the quantity of the scat material is much less in the elk.

In summer the droppings lose the pellet form and are left as flat, elongated or circular chips similar to those of domestic cattle. Elk chips are smaller, usually about 5 or 6 inches in diameter, though they may be longer. The much larger cow chips are at least twice as big. Of course, in either case there may be very small ones.

The sign left by European red deer, *Cervus elaphus,* which have been imported to America, is very similar to that of elk, though the average tracks are smaller.

There are other signs of elk. In winter you will find pits dug in the snow where elk have been pawing through for food, or you may find the beds in the snow, and in summer, the flattened places in the grass where they have rested.

I remember a particularly pleasant day on summer elk range in the Rockies. Over a rise I came upon a depression, a green meadow, in the middle of which was a pond. A band of elk was just then coming in to water. As they came near, some of the eager ones rushed on ahead, jumped into the water, and romped along in the shallows, splashing the water, shaking their heads, and hopping with the same joy that a group of children go splashing

Fig. 141 (opposite)

a. Adult cow elk track, on sandy soil (Wyo.).
b. Adult elk track (Olympic Mts., Wash.).
c. Adult elk track (Wyo.).
d. Domestic Hereford calf track, for comparison (Wyo.).
e. Elk track, showing dewclaws when running (Wyo.).
f. Elk track in New Zealand, showing the long pointed type when animal has been living on soft ground.
g. Elk calf track (Wyo., June 13, 1932).
h. Aspen trunk, with elk tooth mark, and elk barking aspen in a "high-lined" grove.

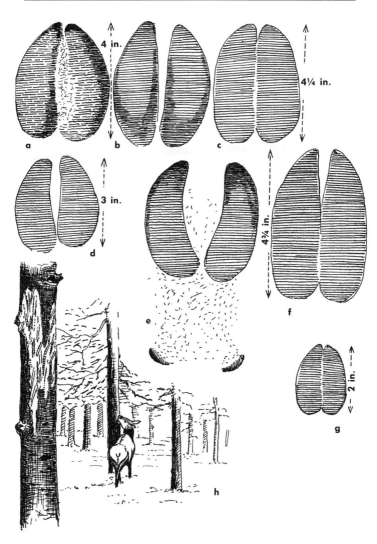

Fig. 141. Elk tracks and browsing

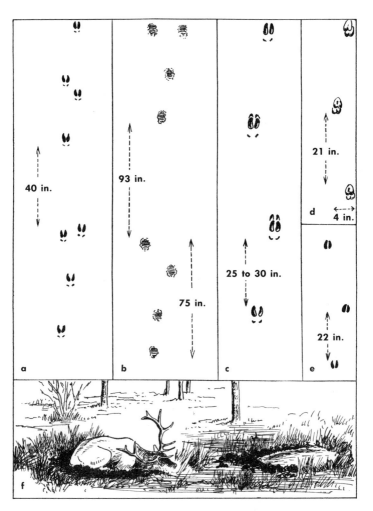

Fig. 142. Elk tracks and wallow

a. Cow elk, gallop, in mud (Wyo.).   b. Elk gallop in snow (Wyo.).
c. Cow elk walking in sand (Olympic Mts., Wash.).
d. Yearling elk, walking. Hind foot slightly forward of front track (April
   9, 1928).
e. Young calf elk, walking (Wyo., June 1, 1929).
f. Bull elk wallowing, during the rut. An old wallow, into which water
   has seeped, shown at right.

274

into the water at a beach. This is one of the rewards of watching the animals in their native home.

If you are in high-mountain elk country and come upon a shallow pond, look for tracks at the muddy borders. If the water is roiled up and milky you may guess that elk have been there to bathe, drink, and frolic not so long ago.

In the autumn during the rutting season, if you don't actually find a bull elk prodding the wet ground with his antlers, pawing the dirt with his hoofs, and wallowing in the mud, you should at least find the muddy pits where the bull elk has cooled his mating fervor. Sometimes you will find a permanent little pool of water, with vegetation around it, which was an elk wallow several years before, into which water has seeped (see Fig. 142, f).

The elk will also thrash about in bushes and small trees with his antlers, to rub off the velvet and polish them. Saplings will have many limbs broken off and the bark torn and bruised. Often the sapling is girdled and dies, and you will find many such dead trees, victims of the ardor of the wapiti rut. On such trees the bark is obviously bruised, torn, and shredded by the rubbing, in contrast to those that have been gnawed.

There is still another tree sign. Elk are fond of the bark of certain trees, particularly the aspen, and you will often find the bark scored by tooth marks, where the animal has gnawed at it with its lower incisor teeth. These grazing animals have no upper incisors. This is done also by moose, and one must guess which it is by knowledge of which animal is known to spend the winter in a given locality. Aspen trunks that have been gnawed year after

Elk

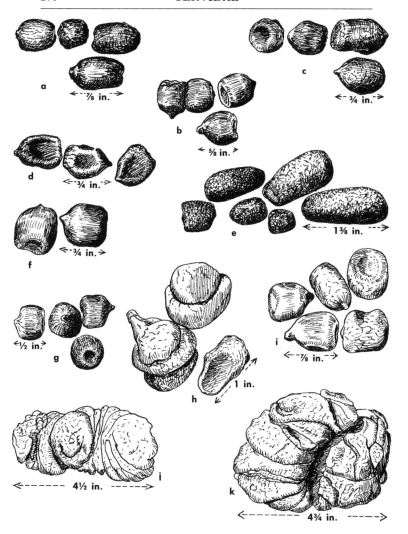

Fig. 143. Red deer and elk droppings;
all except *j* and *k* about ⅔ natural size

year eventually develop a rough, blackened trunk as far up as the elk reached. Such a black-trunked aspen grove denotes a much used elk winter range.

In New Zealand, where wapiti were introduced from America, these animals find a substitute for aspen in the exotic flora, and they regularly eat the bark of the pokaka, *Elaeocarpus hookeria-nus*. In the Fiordland National Park forests you will find these trees stripped of bark, the exposed wood turning red — a sure sign of wapiti or red deer.

The mineral lick is also worth noticing. Here the ground is gouged out by the mud-eating animals — deer, elk, moose, or mountain sheep. The tracks in the mud will tell you which. In the forests of the Olympic Peninsula you will find old hemlock logs gnawed by elk, the lower sides apparently being preferable. I have seen pits gouged out under such a tasty log where the animals had knelt to get at the underside. Sometimes, too, you will find old rotten limbs or small tree trunks, mushy in consistency, eaten into by the elk.

All such indications are revealing of the activities of the elk.

Finally, there is one delightful indication: the bugle call in the autumn months. If you are fortunate enough to be in elk country at that time of year, a moonlight night can be specially enriched by the calling of the bull elk. It rises with a glide to a high-pitched silvery note, then glides down again, to end in some guttural grunts. This is wapiti music.

There are other sounds. The mother and calf will call to each other with a squealing sound, more pleasing to hear than this description implies. When a band has been put to flight by some disturbance, then slows up to reassemble, there may be a babel of voices as the mothers and calves seek each other.

There is also a sharp, loud bark. This explosive sound signifies either alarm or curiosity perhaps a combination of the two. I have

Fig. 143 (opposite)

a and b. Adult red deer stag droppings (southern New Zealand, March 28 and April 5, respectively, 1949).
c. Adult female red deer (southern New Zealand, March 24, 1949).
d. Droppings of elk bull in its fourth year (Wyo., Oct. 25, 1950).
e. Roosevelt elk droppings, a browse diet (Olympic Mts., Wash., March 1935).
f and g. These two samples are from American elk introduced in New Zealand, both large bulls weighing over 550 lbs. (in the same locality, early March 1949).
h. Soft pellet type (Sun River, Mont., July 21, 1934).
 i. Common pellet type (Sun River, Mont., July 21, 1934).
 j and k. Soft coalesced type, from most succulent forage.

heard an elk bark repeatedly for a long time, evidently puzzled
by a lighted tent at night.

All such vocal expressions enliven your experience with the elk
herds in their native surroundings.

Moose

This is our greatest deer, of the genus *Alces,* which inhabits the
boreal forests of North America and the northern part of the Rocky
Mountains. Maine, Michigan, and Minnesota are the eastern and
middle-western states that have moose in their northern parts. In
the Rocky Mountains they are present chiefly in western Montana,
northern Idaho, and western Wyoming. Moose occur all the way
across the wooded portions of Canada, throughout most of Alaska,
and even out on the Alaska Peninsula. Willow appears to be its
staple food, though of course not its only food, and probably the
presence of sufficient willow growth determines moose distribution
over most of its range.

The moose track is nearest to the elk track in size and shape,
though it is larger and more pointed (Figs. 144 and 145). Occasionally a moose with more blunt hoofs will produce an unusually
rounded track. One day when I was out in the mountains, a veteran
skier and mountain climber asked me, "How do you distinguish
moose and elk tracks?"

I explained the difference, stressing the more elongated, sharper-
toed form of the moose track. Shortly afterward he said, "Now
what's that one?" I looked at the track and saw it to be one of the

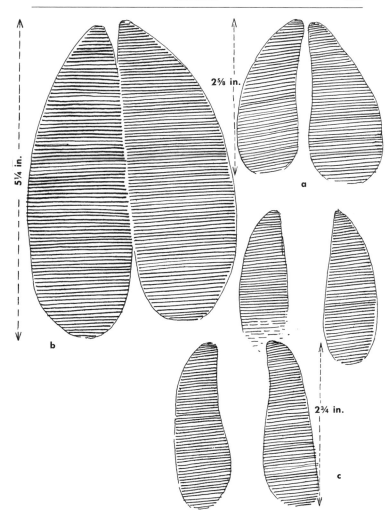

Fig. 144. Moose tracks, about ⅔ natural size

a. Calf track on wet sand (Alaska, June 22, 1922).
b. Adult track in mud (Wyo.).
c. Calf front and hind track in mud (Wyo., June 30, 1951).

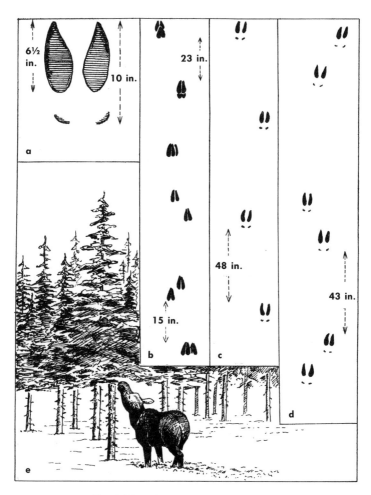

Fig. 145. Moose tracks and browsing

a. Track in running pattern, with dewclaws showing (Alaska).
b. Irregular walking pattern (Brit. Col., 1935).
c. Adult cow moose trotting, on old hard snow (Wyo., 1950). A walking pattern of another cow moose in the same locality was similar, but with steps from 24 to 30 in.
d. Another trotting pattern (Alaska, 1922).
e. A ''high-lined'' grove of fir trees, on which foliage has been eaten as high as the moose can reach (Wyo.).

intermediates. In some confusion I admitted that I wasn't so sure — and he knew I was working at that time on the material for this book!

In partial defense I will cite a cow moose track on hard snow in Alaska that measured 5½ inches in length and 5 inches in width. A yearling made a track 3¾ inches long and 4½ inches wide, in this case wider than long. However, as you generally find them, the moose track will be long and pointed.

Moose droppings in winter are distinctive. Because of the dry browse diet in that season they appear like compressed sawdust, and may be round or elongated, usually smooth. The variations are shown in Figure 146. The quantity of pellets in a sample is greater than that of an elk, as would be expected from such a large animal. In 18 samples of winter droppings measured, the average quantity was one quart, with a minimum of ½ quart and a maximum of 2 quarts. The number of pellets varied from 78 to 192, with an average of 128. One fact to be noted is that a sample found at a moose bedding place, where the animal has been lying a long time, is likely to be large, while the samples along the route of travel, where a moose has been feeding, will be more frequent and less in quantity.

In midsummer the droppings are soft and a sample may be almost formless, resembling certain ones of the domestic cow. In spring and fall, with the shift to and from a succulent diet, the samples are intermediate, retaining the pellet form, but distorted and clinging in a mass. The total mass will be greater than that of an elk.

You will find moose beds in snow or in tall grass where the vegetation has been mashed down. Since there is such a great diversity of size, from the calf and yearling to the large bull, it would be difficult to distinguish a moose bed from an elk bed by size alone in an area occupied by both animals. Nearby tracks and droppings are a clue.

In winter moose will trim the limbs of fir trees, aspens, and other favorites as high as it can reach. Traditionally, the moose is recorded as "riding down" a sapling, by bending it over with its body and straddling it so as to reach the top twigs. I must admit that I have never seen moose do this, but I have seen them reach high up, seize the stem in their teeth, and bend it over until it breaks. Then they will proceed to feed on the drooping tips. I have seen them do this with young cottonwoods and tall willow brush. A much used willow winter range will be characterized by numerous broken tops, dead and slanting across or downward in diverse directions, as shown in Figure 147. Moose, as well as elk, will gnaw the bark of aspen trunks, as shown in Figure 148, a.

In summer moose feed extensively in ponds, where they seek the submerged aquatic vegetation. They have favorite ponds that

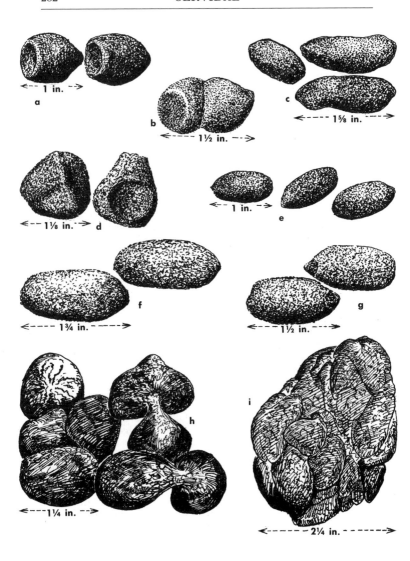

Fig. 146.   Moose droppings, about ⅔ natural size

Fig. 147. Moose browsing on willows in winter, showing willow tops broken over to bring the high twigs within reach (drawing by Grant Hagen)

they visit repeatedly, especially in early morning or in the evening. They do not graze extensively. Their necks are too short for reaching the grass easily, but I have seen them get down on their front knees to do so, and they do have a number of other herbaceous plants in their diet. One day we watched a cow moose busily feeding on the tall vegetation near our home. When the cow had left I examined the place and found that it had been picking out only the tops of fireweed. You will notice that twigs or plants nipped by hoofed animals with their blunt dental equipment do not show the neat, sharp-cut edge left by the chisel teeth of rodents. For example, compare Figures 148, b, and 123, d.

In hunting journals we have read much about moose calling, and the birchbark horns devised for that purpose. There has been much misunderstanding about this. The bull moose in rut produces a low sound, a brief grunt — *Mm-uh!* It is the cow

Fig. 146 (opposite)

a. Pellet form, with concave end (Alaska).
b. Double pellet (Brit. Col.).
c. Long and narrow scats, irregular in shape (Wyo., 1951).
d. Pellets of irregular shape (Alaska, 1951).
e. From moose calf (Wyo., Dec. 25, 1950).
f. Large pellets (Minn.).
g. From young cow moose (Jan. 21, 1952).
h. Soft pellets, some joined, from large bull (Wyo., Aug. 15, 1929).
 i. Pellets coalesced in soft mass, result of succulent feed (Wyo., Aug. 1951). H and i are only a small portion of the total sample.

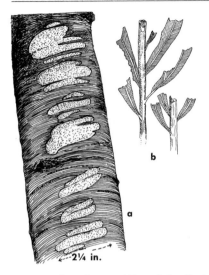

Fig. 148.   Moose sign

a. Tooth marks on aspen
   bark.
b. Fireweed nipped by
   cow moose (Wyo.,
   1952).

moose, when in a rutting state, that gives out a series of loud
sounds, which may be described as bawlings of a sort. On occasion
I have seen a pair together, at a moderate distance, when the
female gave out a distinct call, *Uh-u-ow-wa,* and I could see the
bull raise its muzzle slightly and open its lips a little. I knew he
was calling, but the grunt was so low that it failed to reach my
ears.

The cow and calf will call to each other, but the sounds are low.
The bleatlike call of the moose calf is in a lower tone than the
squeal-like call of the elk calf.

Caribou and Reindeer

This northernmost member of the deer family, of the genus
Rangifer, occupies, with its several species, the circumpolar regions
of the world. Those species occupying the Siberian and European
northland are known in the Old World as reindeer, and those
brought over to Alaska for domestication we are also accustomed
to speak of as reindeer. In America the caribou occupy most of
Alaska, though not continuously, and the northern tundra and the
boreal forests of Canada; formerly they ranged down into Maine,
northern Minnesota, and northern Idaho.

Caribou have the most distinctive track of all the deer, for their

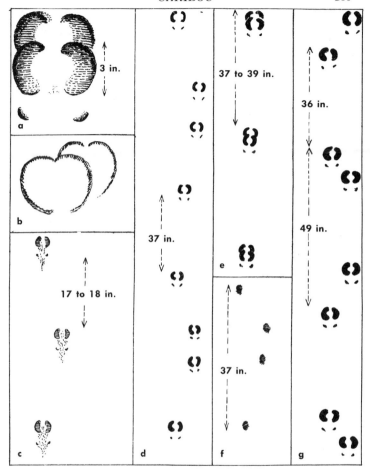

Fig. 149.   Caribou tracks, from Alaska

a. On wet sand. Hoof marks sometimes nearly 5 in. long.
b. On a layer of snow on ice, only the hoof edges making a mark.
c. Walking in shallow snow.
d. Slow gallop. Another trail showed 5-ft. leaps; leaps would be
   greater with speeding.   e. Walking, on wet sand.
f. Gallop of a young calf, 20-in. leaps.   g. Trotting, on sand.

Caribou

hoofs are rounded and tend to spread, the snowshoe-like effect thus helping somewhat to support the animal in snow. A track on a thin film of snow, as shown in *b* of Figure 149, is almost circular. Caribou tracks cannot be confused with moose tracks.

There is an interesting characteristic of the caribou foot that is often revealed in the tracks. In the front feet there is a considerable gap between the hoofs and the dewclaws, or pasterns. Moreover, the front hoofs tend to extend out forward of the vertical line of the front leg, and the dewclaws tend to come low to the

Rear and side view of left front foot of Caribou

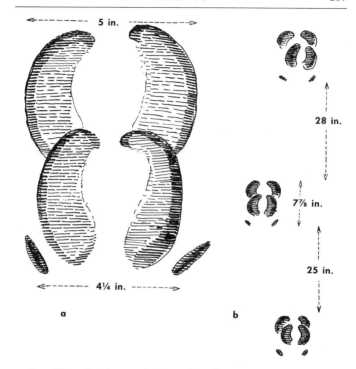

Fig. 150.   Caribou tracks in mud, walking gait, from Alaska

a. Smaller hind track slightly overlapping the larger front track; dewclaw marks go with the front track.
b. Walking trail pattern; straddle is 9¾ inches.

ground as the animal steps. The hind foot, on the other hand,
is more compact, with the dewclaws closer to the hoofs, and held
higher from the ground. Hence, in some tracks in mud or shallow
snow, when the hind foot partly covers the front track, only the
front dewclaw prints show, and these may be far enough back to
be associated with the hind track. This is shown in Figure 150.

    It has been observed also that with greater traveling speed the
dewclaw prints tend to be at right angles to the line of travel, being
more diagonal at the slower speeds.

    Caribou droppings are not as distinctive as the tracks, and more
nearly resemble those of other deer. The coalesced type resulting

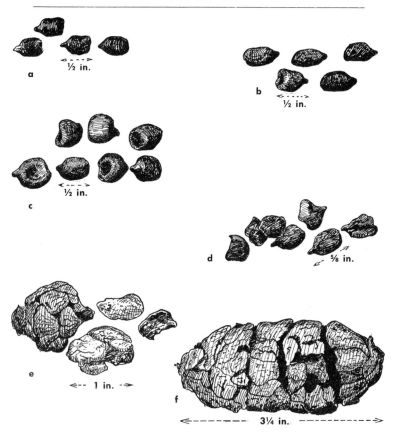

Fig. 151.   Caribou droppings, about ⅔ natural size (Alaska)

    a. From a young female (May 12, 1950).
    b and c. Other typical samples (May 10, 1940).
    d. Soft pellet type, from female (May 12, 1950).
    e. Pellets partly coalesced.
    f. Soft type. *E* and *f* both result from green food.

from succulent feed resembles the comparable types of mountain sheep and some of the other hoofed animals (see Fig. 151, e and f).

Traveling bands of hoofed animals generally produce vocal sounds as the female and young call to each other. We are all familiar with the baa-ing of sheep and the bawling of cattle under such circumstances. The caribou vocabulary is a short grunting sound, a low-pitched *a-a-w, a-a-w.*

The caribou also will thresh bushes or young trees with their antlers to remove the velvet. In winter you will find big pits in the snow where they have pawed down with their round flat hoofs to find the lichens underneath.

Whether it be in the Canadian northland or the mountains of Alaska, caribou sign is exciting, because it quickens the anticipation of possibly seeing the picturesque animal itself.

Wild Boar

Domestic Pig and Wild Boar

Pig tracks may be found near highways in the Middle West, but may also be found in some areas where they have gone wild, or where they forage in deer country. The wild boar of Europe, *Sus scrofa,* has been introduced into the United States, notably in the Cherokee National Forest and adjacent parts of North Carolina.

The tracks of domestic pigs, as well as those of the wild boar, are more rounded than those of deer. Also, the pig and boar dewclaws are more pointed, and extend farther out to the side (see Fig. 152, b).

The wild boar is of course more agile than the domestic pig,

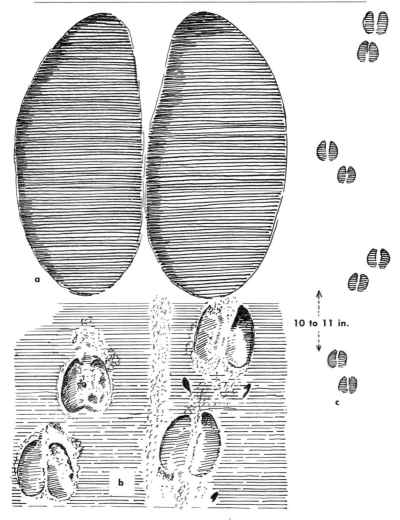

Fig. 152. Tracks of domestic pig

a. Adult track in mud, about ⅔ natural size (Iowa).
b. Tracks in snow (Wyo.).
c. Trail of adult sow, in mud (Iowa).

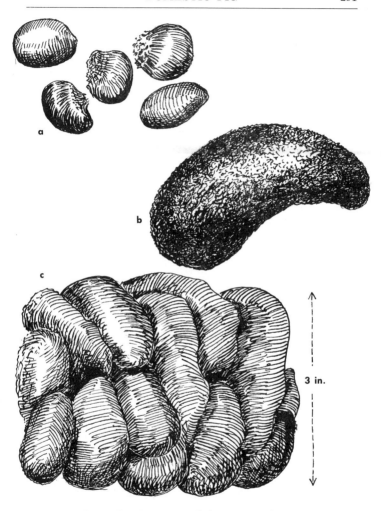

3 in.

Fig. 153. Droppings of domestic pig from a
Pennsylvania farm, about ⅔ natural size

a. Pellet form.   b. Unsegmented type.
c. Common type in which pellets are retained in a mass.

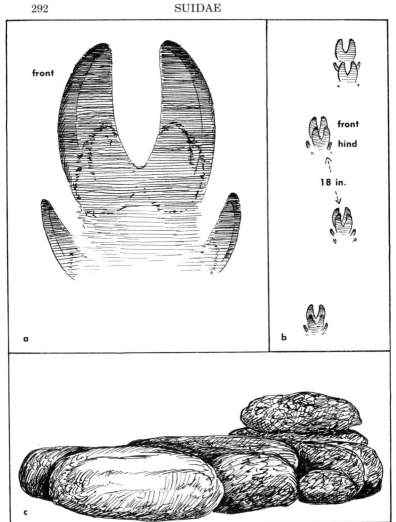

Fig. 154.   Wild boar tracks and scats (from Blue Mt. Forest Assoc.
hunting preserve, Newport, N.H.   Drawn by Carroll B. Colby)

Bottom and side view of right
hind foot of Domestic Pig
²/₅ size.

and has narrower hoofs and longer legs and strides. The wild boar, domestic pig, and peccary all root up the earth and more or less wallow, leaving signs of this activity in the earth. The wild boar also rubs on the trunks of trees and gouges them with its tusks. In all such places, as in the case of bear trees, one should look for telltale hairs and tracks (Fig. 154).

Mr. LeRoy C. Stegeman, who has studied the wild boar in Tennessee, tells us that wild boars have been known to rub trees to a height of 37 inches. He comments:

The trail of a wild boar is narrower than that of the domestic, the tracks being made almost in a single line. The tracks of the domestic hog are offset, forming two lines or a single zigzag line [see Fig. 152, c]. The wild boar will run or jump up banks too steep and high for the domestic hog to climb. The wild boar is a good jumper and will leap over obstacles such as down logs, that the domestic would go around or under. Wild boars frequently cross streams by walking across down logs, while

Fig. 154 (opposite)

a. Track of front foot. Hind feet are slightly smaller than front feet. Weight of animal causes the hoofs to spread. Dewclaws of front feet usually show in track but seldom those of hind feet. Natural size.
b. Tracks usually indicate a trot, with hind feet being placed in or partly over impression of front feet. In traveling, boars usually trot, even when moving but a short distance.
c. Droppings of wild boar influenced by diet, and of course by size of animal.

domestics would go through the stream. Wild boars are much taller than domestic swine. Therefore, the height to which trees are muddied may be good evidence of identity.

Domestic pig droppings are variable in form, depending on the kind of food eaten. They may be soft and almost formless, but on more solid food tend to form in pellets, either coalesced into one mass, as in Figure 153, c, or separate as in *a*. In *b* of this figure is a type of a more uniform consistency without segmentation. When feeding on grass the domestic pig produces pellets that are dry and have the appearance of miniature horse dung. Thus we find in the pig a type quite comparable to those of the elk and moose, with their seasonal variations.

Peccary or Javelina

The peccary, known in the Southwest as the javelina and in science as *Pecari angulatus,* is related to the pig family. Its home is in Central America and Mexico, but it has also established itself in southwestern Texas and southern Arizona, as well as in southeastern New Mexico.

The peccary inhabits the mesquite and cactus country, sometimes in sparsely wooded foothills, also high up in some of the southern mountains. It is known to use dens in the ground or hollow logs, sometimes caves in the rocky cliffs. In one trip to Arizona I found piles of droppings in such caves. Most were like those in Figure 155 but there were also many flat ones, like a rough pancake, deposited when semi-liquid. The food of the peccary consists of a great variety of things, including roots, fruit, cactus, nuts, insects, eggs, and any flesh that can be procured.

The hoof marks are smaller than those of pigs but are of the same general pattern (see Fig. 155). The peccary has only one

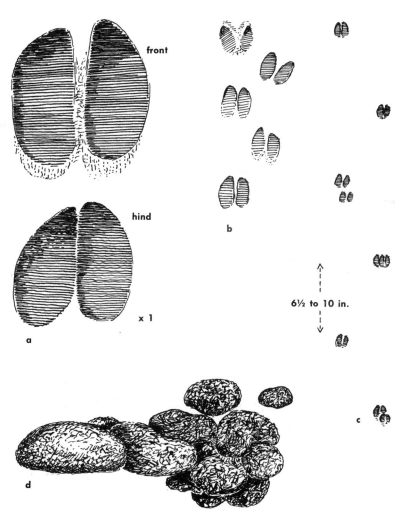

Fig. 155.   Peccary tracks and droppings

a. Typical tracks in clay, natural size. Front hoofs about 1½ in. long;
   hind, 1¼ in. (Fleishhacker Zoo, San Francisco).
b. Tracks in mud, showing variations (Tex. and Ariz.).
c. Track pattern, in mud. Width, or straddle, about 4 to 5 in.
   (Ariz.).
d. Dropping (Ariz.).

295

dewclaw on the hind feet but it does not show in the tracks found. An active animal, the peccary will readily leap a distance of 6 feet, and has been recorded as leaping as much as 10 feet 9 inches when startled.

When startled sufficiently or excited in any way, it produces a strong scent definite enough to be detected by the human nose and probably easily detected and interpreted by other javelinas or by enemies.

These animals express themselves with a grunt or squeal. Their presence is most readily detected, however, by their rooting places in the earth and by their tracks or by the piles of scats in caves.

Pronghorn or Antelope

The technical name, *Antilocapra americana,* suggests the unique character of this animal. The latter part of the genus name, *capra,* suggests goat, and so it was called by Lewis and Clark. It is a western plains animal, ranging from southern Saskatchewan

Fig. 156 (opposite)

a. Fawn track, about ⅔ natural size (Yellowstone Natl. Park, July 16, 1929).
b. Adult tracks, in mud, ⅔ natural size. Front track, 3¼ in. long; hind, 2¾ in. (Nev.).
c. Young pronghorn track, in mud (Nev.).
d. Adult track pattern, a slow run (Nev.).

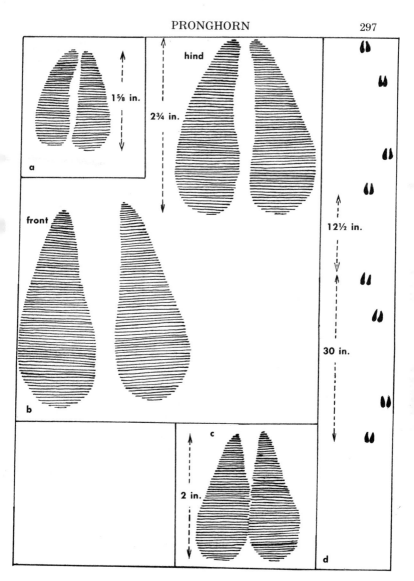

Fig. 156. Tracks of pronghorn

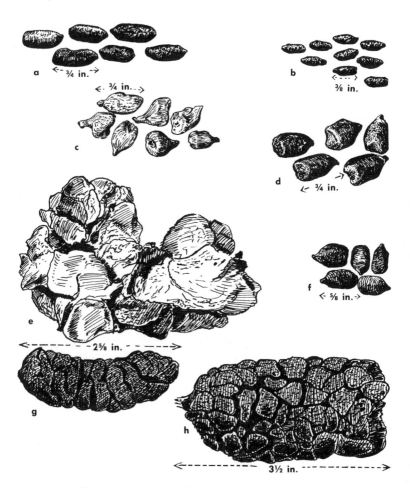

Fig. 157. Pronghorn droppings, about ⅔ natural size (Nevada)

    a. Pellet type, from adult (Aug. 15, 1939).
    b. Pellets of fawn (July 25, 1940).
    c. Semi-soft pellets, from adult (Sept. 15, 1939).
    d. Hard pellet type, from adult (Aug. 28, 1940).
    e. Soft mass type (Aug. 16, 1939).
    f. Pellet type, from adult male (Aug. 18, 1939).
    g. Soft type, from young animal (Aug. 18, 1939).
    h. Soft type, with pellet structure apparent.

298

south into northern Mexico, and is found in Montana and western North and South Dakota, western Nebraska, Wyoming, Idaho, Utah, Nevada, Colorado, eastern Oregon, and parts of California, Arizona, New Mexico, western Oklahoma and Texas.

This graceful animal is built for speed and loves to exercise this gift. Often I have seen a band take off on a swift race just for the sheer joy of running. Their running gait is smooth and level, with hardly any rise in the air at each bound.

Donald D. McLean of California recorded a jump of at least 27 feet: "I measured two such jumps in Lassen County where they cleared an open mud-bottomed cut." Other trails showed average leaps of 14 feet at high speed.

In calculating the 14-foot leap, Mr. McLean measured from right hind foot to right hind foot. Dr. Morris F. Skinner, who studied running pronghorn in Nebraska, found that the spread of the four feet when landing was 9 feet, with 6 to 7 feet to the next group of tracks — which comes pretty close to the same result.

Dr. Skinner followed a mature buck in Nebraska with a car at 40 to 44 miles per hour. A doe ran 38 to 42 miles per hour. At first the doe held her head high, then laid back her ears and stretched her head and neck forward as she went into high speed.

The pronghorn, or antelope, has no dewclaws, and therefore has the most streamlined foot of all, with the exception of the single-toed horse.

Pronghorn tracks are much like those of deer, but the hind border is usually broader. However, some tracks are difficult to distinguish. Figure 156 presents the general shape. In some areas mule deer share some of the range with pronghorn, and their tracks may be confused.

In many respects pronghorn droppings resemble those of deer and mountain sheep. The summer droppings tend to form an elongated narrow mass, very similar to certain scat types of the mountain sheep. (Compare, for example, Figures 157 and 159). On some occasions, a first hasty glance at such a sample in the sagebrush country reminded me of the coyote scat.

The pronghorn has an interesting habit of scraping the ground with a hoof, then depositing the dropping or urine on the bare spot of ground. This is the reverse of the bobcat's habit of *covering* its droppings by scratching dirt and debris toward it. Thus the two types of scratch signs can be distinguished, even without reference to the distinctive scats.

When startled or worried the pronghorn produces a loud whistling sound similar to that made by the whitetail deer, but it seems to me more musical, with almost a vocal quality — a fairly high-pitched *hieu-u-u-u!* The doe-to-fawn calls are a lower bleat. When annoyed or curious the pronghorn will stamp a foot as the deer do.

Mountain Sheep

The mountain sheep, of the genus *Ovis,* with several forms, inhabit the backbone of our continent, including the mountain ranges of Alaska and Yukon Territory down through the Canadian Rockies in British Columbia and Alberta, through Idaho and Montana, Wyoming, Nevada, Utah, Colorado, California, Arizona, New Mexico, western Texas, northern Mexico, and Lower California.

Mountain sheep tracks also resemble those of deer. Generally, however, the hoofs have straighter edges and the tracks do not so often take the traditional heart shape. In other words, they tend to be more blocky, somewhat less pointed. Nevertheless, it cannot be denied that certain samples are confusing. The tracks in Figure 158 were chosen as the most undeerlike.

As for the droppings, note the variety in Figure 159 and also the variety shown for the different kinds of deer. Tracking is not easy, and one must take into account the location of signs, whether among mountain sheep ledges or in deer forest.

The bighorn group, a variety of mountain sheep, make beds which may be looked for on jutting points above cliffs, wherever the animal has a good view. The animal scrapes at the dirt with a hoof to make a slight smooth hollow, then lies down. These beds are used often, and in areas long occupied by mountain sheep there will be a considerable accumulation of dung.

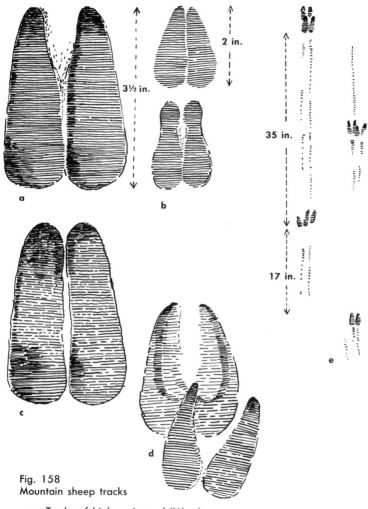

Fig. 158
Mountain sheep tracks

    a. Tracks of bighorn in mud (Wyo.).
    b. Bighorn lamb tracks, in mud (Wyo.).
    c. Track of desert bighorn, in mud (Death Valley, Cal.).
    d. Tracks of white (Dall) sheep (Alaska).
    e. Trail pattern of white sheep, in snow (Alaska).

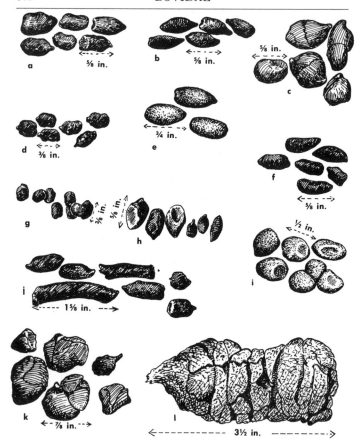

Fig. 159. Mountain sheep droppings, about ⅔ natural size

a. White (Dall) sheep ram (Alaska). d. Yearling white sheep (Alaska).
b. White sheep (Alaska).   e and f. Desert sheep (Texas).
c. Desert sheep (Texas).   g. White sheep lamb (Alaska).
h. Bighorn ewe and lamb (Wind River Mts., Wyo.).
 i. Bighorn clay droppings, from mineral lick (Jackson Hole, Wyo.).
 j. Bighorn, on soft feed (Wyo.).
k. Bighorn, soft pellet type (Wyo.).
 l. Bighorn scat, result of succulent feed (Wyo.).

The voice of the mountain sheep is the traditional *baa* like that of domestic sheep. However, bands of mountain sheep are generally rather silent, in contrast to the noisy domestic sheep.

My brother and I once took advantage of this call in photographing the white, or Dall, sheep in Alaska. I was on a ridge, waiting to photograph a group of sheep coming up toward me. They were down the slope, out of my view, and I was uncertain as to just where to expect them to appear on the ridge. My brother was at one side on the slope, where he could see me and the sheep, and, imitating the voice of the sheep so as not to alarm them too much, he guided my actions on top: "*Baa-a-a-a* — they're moving to your right — *baa-a-a-a* — now they're coming straight up."

Thus guided, I found myself in camera range when they came out on top.

If you are fortunate, you may have the experience of witnessing an interesting incident in mountain sheep activity. In the autumn, if you are in mountain sheep country, you may hear a loud *whack* as if someone had slammed two stout boards together, or had banged shut a car door. Follow the sound, and you may come upon two jealous rams fighting by simply banging their heads together.

Domestic Sheep

Tracks and droppings of domestic sheep may be confused with those of deer, mountain sheep, and goats (compare Figures 156 through 162). In the western plains and mountains domestic sheep travel in large bands. If you encounter a large mass of trails leading across the country, with hoofprints about as shown in Figure 160, you may be pretty sure that domestic sheep have traveled there. Deer are solitary or in small groups. Mountain

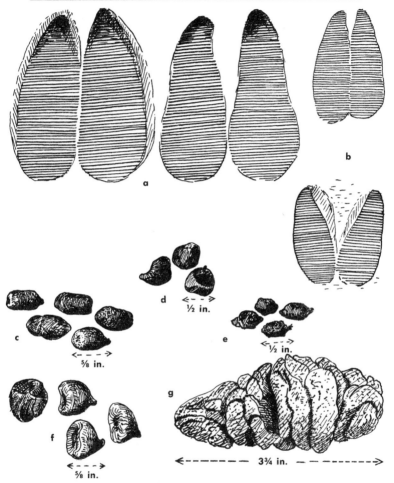

Fig. 160.   Domestic sheep sign

a. Two typical tracks of ewes, in mud. About ⅔ natural size (Utah).
b. Tracks of lambs, in mud. About ⅔ natural size (Utah).
c. Droppings of ewes, hard type (Wyo.).
d, e, f. Semi-soft pellet types (from Texas, California, and Utah respectively).
g. Dropping characteristic of succulent feed (Utah).

sheep and domestic goats also are pretty well scattered, or in groups of a few individuals.

With reference to individual trails, the deer is longer-legged than the domestic sheep and takes longer steps. That is one clue.

It is worth while to learn, if possible, whether or not there are domestic sheep ranging in a given locality. Their known absence simplifies the problem of identification of tracks and droppings. Field biologists often take advantage of such information in the hope of narrowing the search to only a few possibilities. On one occasion I found evidence in a part of the Teton mountain range, Wyoming, of occupancy by either domestic or mountain sheep. It was important to know which, in order to appraise a wildlife range problem there. I was unable to identify the abundant droppings that I found on a high mountain slope. It was only by finding the old remains of a dead mountain sheep and obtaining information on the ranges allotted to the grazing of domestic sheep that I could be reasonably sure the area in question had been occupied by mountain sheep.

Figure 160 shows what differences may exist in the tracks and droppings. It also, I fear, reveals confusing similarities.

Mountain Goat

The ace mountaineer of our big game animals is the mountain goat, *Oreamnos americanus,* which occupies high mountain crags, from southeastern Alaska south and east through British Columbia into the Cascade Range of Washington and the Rocky Moun-

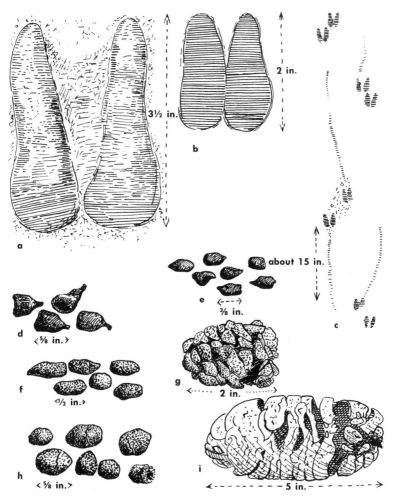

Fig. 161. Mountain goat tracks and droppings

a. Typical track in snow.   b. Track of kid, in mud.
c. Trail pattern, walking, in light snow.
d. Droppings, late summer or early fall.
e. Droppings of kid, late summer.   f and h. Winter droppings.
g. Summer droppings, late enough to form pellets, which, however, combine in a cluster.
i. Summer dropping when animal is on succulent feed.

306

tains in Idaho and western Montana. This animal has also become established in the Black Hills of South Dakota.

Tracks of the mountain goat resemble those of mountain sheep in that the toes tend to spread so as to present a somewhat square track form, as shown in Figure 161.

The droppings are easily confused with those of deer and sheep, as comparison with the illustrations for those animals will reveal, though they tend to be somewhat smaller. It is instructive to note the transition in form of the droppings, from the mass formed by succulent vegetation (Fig. 161, i), through the clustered pellets in *g*, the soft pellets of *d* and *e*, to the hard winter pellets in *f* and *h* when the animals are on dry feed. Note in *h* that the large samples appear to be made of two pellets combined.

As with other mountain dwellers, the mountain goat makes beds on rocky ledges, where the dusty beds and droppings can be found. Like mountain sheep, it also takes refuge in caves.

Domestic Goat

There are domestic goats of many breeds, and their tracks will vary accordingly in size. In general, their tracks and droppings are nearest in characteristics to those of the native mountain goat, as shown by comparison of Figures 161 and 162. Domestic goats do not occupy the present high ranges of the mountain goats in the Northwest, so there should be no confusion in the localities occupied by the latter. In the southwestern United States and in Mexico, however, domestic goats often range in the high country occupied by mountain sheep and deer. Consequently, in those areas the tracks encountered must be scrutinized carefully. The tracks shown here, especially — Figures 160, 161, and 162, should help to distinguish this domestic animal's track from those of the wild ones.

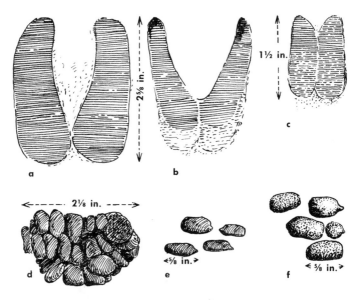

Fig. 162.   Domestic goat tracks and scats

a and b. Tracks in mud (Kanaga I., Alaska, 1937).
c. Track of kid, in mud (Kanaga I.).
d. Summer dropping (Kanaga I.).   e. Winter droppings (Wyo.).
f. Winter droppings (Texas).

Bison or Buffalo

The American bison, or buffalo, *Bison bison,* can now only be found in a few places: in northern Alberta, the Alaska Range south of Fairbanks, on the Bison Range south of Glacier National Park, in the Yellowstone and Wind Cave National Parks, in House Rock Valley in Colorado, and on the Wichita Mountains Wildlife Refuge in Oklahoma, and several other places.

The tracks are very similar to those of domestic cattle. On hard ground, where only the outer rim of the hoofs leave a clear mark the cloven-hoof effect is not prominent; the first impression may be that of a horse track. The droppings, too, are very

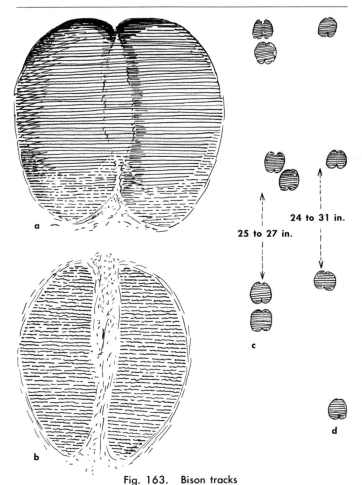

Fig. 163.   Bison tracks

a. Typical track in mud, 5 x 5 in. (Yellowstone Natl. Park).
b. Restored track of extinct superbison from Alaska (from plaster cast of left front foot of a young Pleistocene specimen obtained by Otto W. Geist).
c and d. Two track pattern variations in bison walking. Forefoot tracks are slightly larger than those of the hind foot (Yellowstone Natl. Park, 1929).

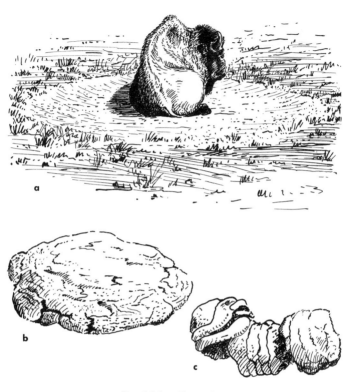

Fig. 164.   Bison sign

a. Buffalo wallow on the plains, where the animals roll and produce a slightly depressed bare place in the dirt.

b. Chips or droppings of the soft type, when diet is succulent, drying into a flat mass, diam. about 12 in.

c. Chips of the harder, layered type, with drier feed.

(Opposite) Trees rubbed by Bison, showing light-colored rubbed rings around the trunk

Bison

similar to those of cattle, both in the soft, formless, and harder
layered types. In Figure 163, b, is shown a "restored" track of
a young Alaskan Pleistocene superbison, obtained from a plaster
cast of the foot of a specimen recovered by Mr. Otto W. Geist.
Of course, the foot had shrunk considerably, an actual track would
be larger, but a close resemblance to the track of a modern bison
is revealed.

In Hayden Valley of Yellowstone, I came upon a pine growth
where bison had rubbed and horned trees extensively, so that
most of the trunks had a light-colored, worn ring. There were
the characteristic long, brown, somewhat kinky hairs of bison
clinging to the bark. In Oklahoma I have found isolated trees worn

so smooth in this way that they were finally killed. Bison will
also rub against big boulders, telephone poles, or any other convenient scratching place. You will find the trampled ground at the
base, and usually a few bison hairs.

The buffalo wallow has always been a feature of the plains (Fig.
164, a). Like horses, these shaggy animals are fond of rolling in
dust, but I have never seen one roll entirely over as a horse does.
I suppose the hump is in the way. It is reported that in early days
buffalo used to tear up a wet, soggy place with the horns, then
roll about until their bodies became caked with mud. This resembles the wallowing of bull elk in the rutting season, and may have
had the same significance.

Muskox

The muskox, *Ovibos moschatus,* has chosen the farthest-north
lands to live in, and few of us have the opportunity to find the
animal at home. But in 1936 I landed on Nunivak Island, in the
Bering Sea, where some muskoxen had been released. There among
the sand dunes was an old bull with all the appearance of bellig-
erence as I approached for pictures. There I found its tracks, so
much resembling the tracks of bison and domestic cattle.

The muskoxen are strange creatures that are content to live
on the Arctic tundra of northern Canada, in Greenland, and even
on some of the storm-swept islands of the Arctic Archipelago,
where their long warm coats serve them well. They have a unique
habit. When a band of muskoxen is approached by wolves, or
by human hunters, all the adults form a circle, with their horns
facing out against the enemy, and the calves are gathered in the

center behind this array of natural weapons. In earlier days, whenever an expedition desired to capture a muskox calf for a zoo, it was necessary to shoot down the defensive circle of parent animals before the calves could be taken.

The tracks shown in Figure 165 from Nunivak Island are much like those of cattle, but you will find no cattle on natural muskox range.

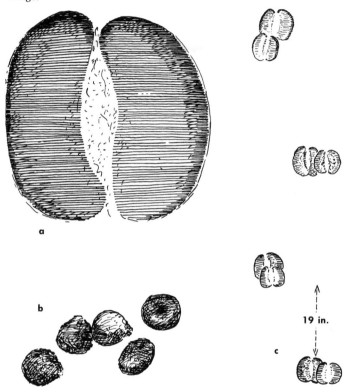

Fig. 165. Muskox tracks and droppings, from Nunivak Island, Alaska

a. Track in mud, about 5 in. length and width.
b. Droppings in pellet form.
c. Trail in sand. Straddle is about 10 in. Front-foot print is 5 x 5 in.; hind-foot print, 4 x 4 in.

Domestic Cattle

In many parts of the West domestic cattle occupy the same range as elk and other large mammals, and in some instances their tracks may be confusing. Domestic cattle tracks resemble those of bison and muskox. The track of a large calf or a yearling is easily confused with adult elk tracks. The mature domestic cow or bull track, however, is larger and more blocky than that of elk.

Cattle droppings also are similar to those of bison, with the same variations. It should be noted that certain elk droppings resulting from succulent feed in summer are very similar to those of cattle at that season. It would be difficult to distinguish them, except that on the average the size, or quantity, of an elk dropping is much smaller than that of domestic cattle. Compare Figure 166 with Figures 132 and 143.

Horse and Burro

Horse tracks can hardly be confused with anything else. The horse wrangler in the western mountains frequently has occasion to hunt up his saddle and pack animals when they stray from camp, and since he must often rely on fragmentary tracks his knowledge of the horse track is necessary. Typically, the horse track reveals the single round or oval hoof, with the V mark of the frog in the middle. A shod horse, of course, will make a track outlined rather strongly with the iron rim; in firm mud it shows the toe and heel calks. Mule tracks are smaller and narrower than those of a horse, and burro tracks are smaller still. The tracks shown in Figure 167, a and c, are those of unshod saddle horses,

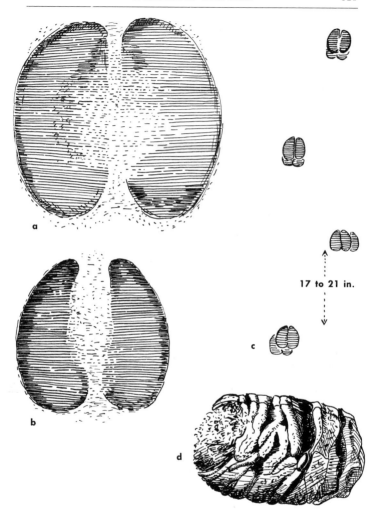

Fig. 166. Domestic cattle sign, from Wyoming

a. Adult Hereford track, in mud; length, 4¼ to 4¾ in.
b. Large calf track, length 3 in.
c. Hereford cow track pattern, 17- to 21-in. steps.
d. Dropping, firm type, 6½ in. long.

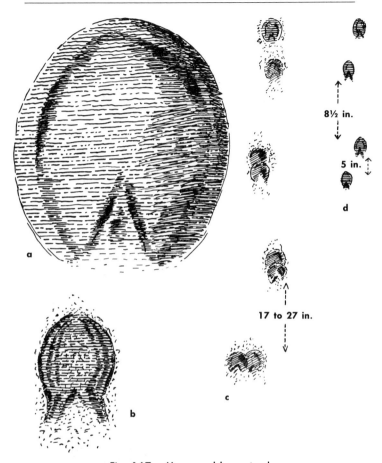

Fig. 167. Horse and burro tracks

a. Wyoming saddle horse track in snow. Front track was 6 in. long, hind track, 5½ in.
b. Young burro track in dust, about 2½ in. long (Nev.).
c. Track pattern of a saddle horse in light snow. Note the variations in the position of front and hind tracks. In this case the front track was forward or even with the hind track.
d. Track pattern of young burro shown in b.

Horses

the type one will find in the mountains. Obviously, the large work horses on farms, if any remain in this mechanized age, make much larger tracks.

Horse droppings are distinctive and familiar. There is an interesting observation that probably harks back to the days when wild horses first roamed the western plains many centuries ago. We once more have some wild horses in Wyoming and a few other western states, and wild burros in the Southwest. Among these wild horses it has been observed that when a stallion has established a local home range with a band of mares, it will leave droppings in the same spot repeatedly, until a considerable pile has accumulated. A male Indian rhinoceros, it is reported, will do the same. In view of this it is interesting to speculate that, after all, horse and rhinoceros are related, both being odd-toed ungulates!

In some places in the West it is still possible to hide at a water hole and see at the break of day the pronghorn and wild horses come in through the sage for a drink of water. It is a stirring sight when a band of horses strings along down a desert ridge, manes tossing, eyes looking here and there alertly — once again the wild animals that they were long before known human history.

Baird's Tapir

Tapirs are relatives of the horse and rhinoceros, and are found in the Malayan region and in the American tropics. The species that inhabits Central America and part of Mexico is *Tapirus bairdi,* an animal somewhat smaller than the other species.

In the Panama Canal Zone I found the distinctive three-hoofed tracks in the mud where the animal had crossed little streams. Sometimes the well-marked footprints followed the man-made jungle trails. The tapir may also have its own well-worn trail, resembling a cattle trail except for the three-hoofed tracks in the mud. Tapirs readily take to the water and are known to wallow in shallow pools.

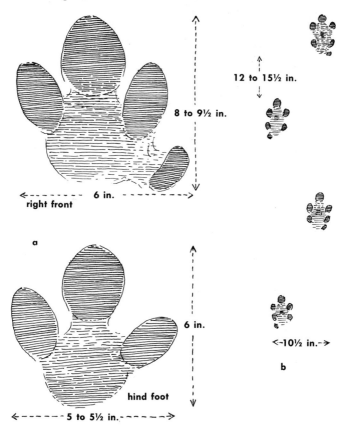

Fig. 168.   Tracks of Baird's tapir in mud (Panama Canal Zone)

a. Front and hind tracks.
b. Walking trail pattern. The hind foot appears to slightly overstep the front track.

Baird's Tapir

In Figure 168, a, the front track shows the fourth toe on the side, but this may not be easily seen in many of the tracks you find, especially when the hind foot steps into the front track. The straddle of the track pattern, as I found it, was slightly over 10 inches.

Birds

BIRDS, with their flight, songs, and bright colors, can be found and recognized without undue reliance on tracks and other sign. Yet a knowledge of a few of these signs is helpful, and in some respects necessary for certain studies. In the following pages are given a few tracks of representative bird groups, those most likely to be encountered on tracking expeditions, though one, the condor, can no longer be considered a likely find.

In general perching birds — those, like sparrows and a great many others that spend much of their time in the trees — tend to hop when on the ground, so their tracks appear paired. All game birds and those that spend much time on the ground, such as the raven, magpie, robin and pheasant, walk or run. Thus you will find the first group mostly hopping, leaving parallel tracks, and the second group leaving mostly alternating tracks. There are of course some exceptions—you will find some junco tracks alternating, for example. Also, the great horned owl, which lives mostly in trees, walks when on the ground. (See Figures 169 through 176.)

Bird droppings, a number of which are illustrated here (Figs. 177 through 179) are readily distinguished from those of mammals, yet some are not easily distinguished from each other. As with mammals, in some cases the hard dropping denotes dry food, such as twigs and buds for grouse, while the soft, semi-liquid ones result from succulent food. Bird droppings tend to be coated, at least at one end, with white calcareous material.

The pellets, or castings (Figs. 180–182), that are habitually regurgitated by some birds are at first glance similar to the scats of certain carnivores, but bird castings consist of pure feathers, fur, and bones, free from the digestive residue mingled with such remains in carnivore droppings. This residue in scats appears as crumbling, dirtlike material that serves as a matrix for the included hair and bones.

Bird pellets are extremely useful in studying the diet of certain birds. However, a study of the series illustrated here reveals so much variation in size and shape for each bird, depending on the kind of food eaten, that it is impracticable to identify the individual pellets without reference to a known nest or perch. Note, for example, the extreme variations in the pellets of the great

Willow Ptarmigan taking off. Grouse, and many other birds, often leave wing marks in the snow when taking flight.

horned owl (Fig. 182, c); note also the general similarity between those of this owl and those of the golden eagle. I have found it necessary to determine otherwise which bird uses a particular perch, or nest, where pellets are collected for study.

In spite of all these limitations, much natural history is revealed by a knowledge of bird sign. An accumulation of characteristic droppings (Fig. 178, e) on and beside a log reveals the drumming log of a ruffed grouse. Specific tracks concentrated about a bit of carrion in the woods disclose to you that the sharp-eyed ravens and magpies have found it. A mass of white guano streaks in vertical smears on a cliff face will point to the location of the aerie of certain hawks, falcons, owls, or raven. A splashing of similar white stains among the green vegetation in the woods should cause you to look overhead for a possible nest. There is satisfaction in reading the story of streamside loiterers by the tracks of goose, duck, or gull, especially if droppings or an occasional feather help you to make sure of the tracks. It is well to note whether it was a crane, with short hind toe, or a heron, with the long hind toe, which had walked in the soft mud.

You may be puzzled, as I was once, to know whether a crane or a wild turkey had walked on the shore of a pond. The crane foot is trim, with a fine "fingerprint" pattern. The turkey foot is coarser, with rougher under surface.

Thus, it seems worth while to give some passing attention to birds in this guide devoted principally to mammals.

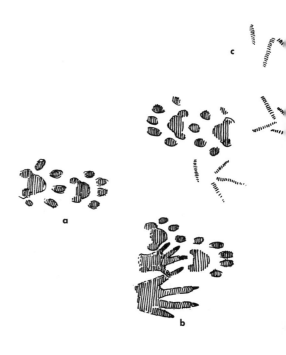

Fig. 169.   Riverbank record

Certain animals are wont to travel along riverbanks. Here, a mink (a) has happened along, in both directions. A muskrat (b) passed to the right. Spotted sandpipers (c) left their tracks. A Canada goose (d) has walked over the tracks of the sandpiper and muskrat. Part of the web shows in only one track, the upper one. And, in the upper right, are some marks that may possibly represent imperfect tracks of a toad (e). Here, then, is a traffic record that emphasizes the habits of a group of animals, which have mingled their footprints in a place that each one considers home ground. Notice that the goose footprint does not always show the web, and that the prints of the sandpiper do not always show every toe.

e

d

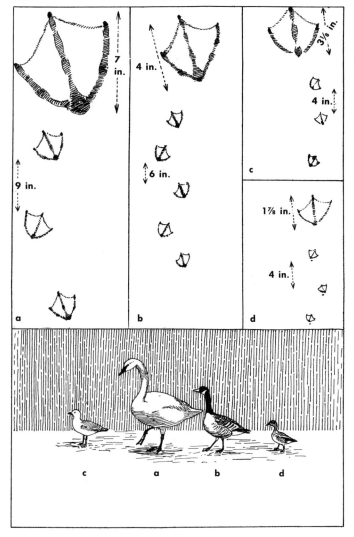

Fig. 170. Waterfowl tracks

a. Trumpeter swan, in mud (Wyo.).   c. Glaucous-winged gull (Wash.).
b. Canada goose, in mud (Wyo.).   d. Common teal (Aleutians).

Fig. 171. Tracks of grouse

a. Sage grouse, in mud.   c. Ruffed grouse, in mud.
b. Blue grouse, in snow.   d. Male ring-necked pheasant, in mud.
e. Rock ptarmigan: left, in mud; right, in snow, when toe feathers are
   well grown.

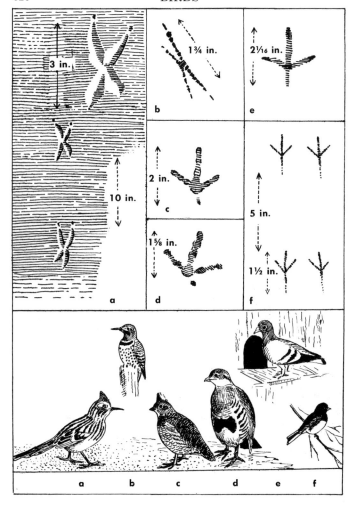

Fig. 172. Miscellaneous bird tracks

a. Roadrunner, in loose sand (Cal.).
b. Flicker, in mud.
c. Scaled quail, in dust (Texas).
d. Gray partridge, in dust (Nev.).

e. Domestic pigeon, in snow.
f. Junco, in snow.

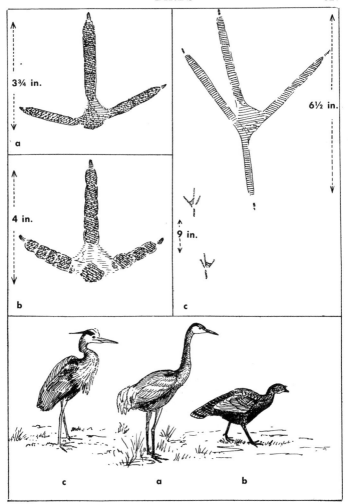

Fig. 173.   Tracks of crane, turkey, and heron

a. Sandhill crane, in mud (Okla.).   b. Wild turkey, in mud (Okla.).
c. Great blue heron, right foot, in mud. Below, the stride, almost in
a straight line (Yellowstone Natl. Park).

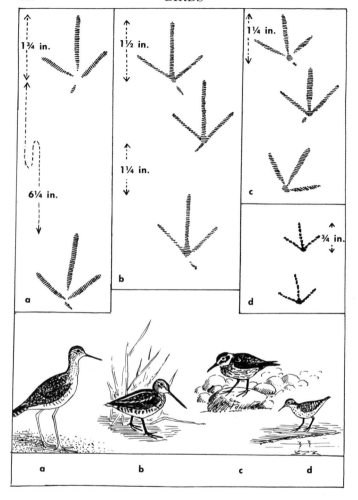

Fig. 174. Some shorebird tracks

a. Greater yellowlegs, in mud.   c. Rock sandpiper.
b. Common snipe, in mud.   d. Spotted sandpiper, in sand.

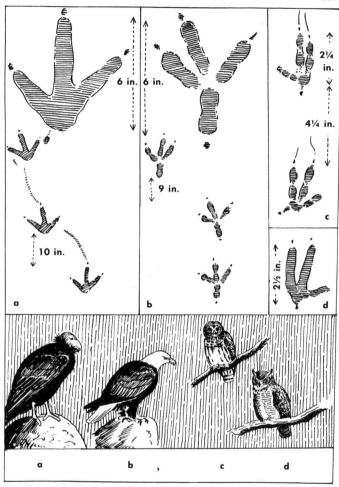

Fig. 175.   Some birds of prey tracks

a. California condor, in snow (Natl. Zoological Park, Washington, D.C., 1929).
b. Bald eagle, on sand (Aleutians).
c. Barred owl, in snow (Washington, D.C.).
d. Great horned owl, in snow (Natl. Zoological Park).

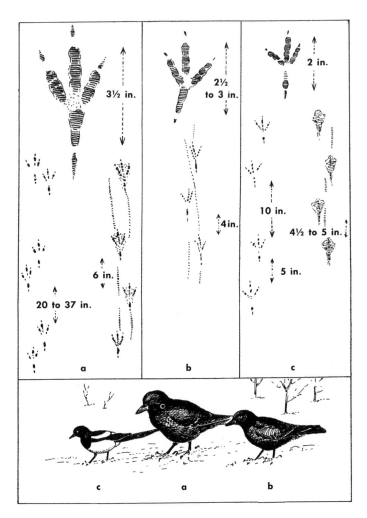

Fig. 176. Tracks of raven, crow, and magpie

a. Raven track, in sand (Aleutians). Left tracks, hopping to take flight;
    right, walking in snow (both from Wyoming).
b. Crow track in mud (Okla.). Below, walking gait.
c. Magpie track in snow (Wyo.). Left, hopping trail; right, walking,
    in deeper snow.

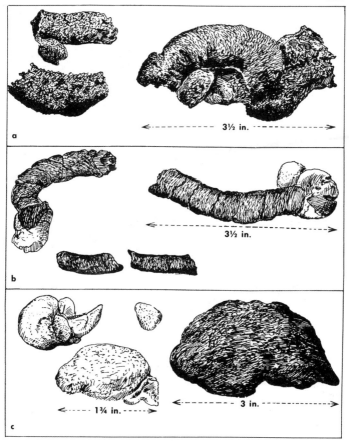

Fig. 177. Bird droppings, about ⅔ natural size

a. Trumpeter swan (Yellowstone Natl. Park).
b. Canada goose (upper left, Semichi I., Aleutians; upper right, Canada; lower, cackling Canada goose from Buldir I., Aleutians).
c. Great blue heron. This material is puzzling, for the largest specimen appears to be a disgorged pellet. The diet in this case is field mice (Wyo.).

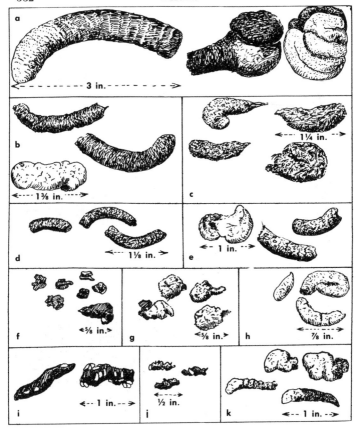

Fig. 178. Bird droppings, about ⅔ natural size

a. Wild turkey, hard-type scat (left, Ariz.) and the somewhat softer type from more succulent food (right, Okla.).

b. Blue grouse. The upper winter sample is old, dried out to smaller diameter. The middle sample is fresh, somewhat larger. The lower left is a summer sample, softer (all Wyo.).

c. Sage grouse.   d. Spruce grouse (Minn.).

e. Ruffed grouse. Left sample is from summer food.

f. Harlequin quail (Texas).   g. Lesser prairie chicken (Okla.).

h. Sharp-tailed grouse (No. Dak.). i. Bohemian waxwing, on berry diet.

j. Townsend's solitaire, on berry diet.   k. Chukar (Wyo.).

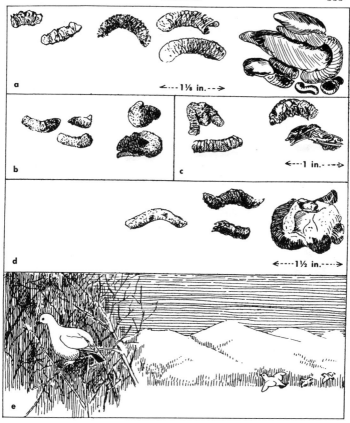

Fig. 179. Bird droppings, about ⅔ natural size

a. Rock ptarmigan (Alaska). Right, a soft-type summer specimen; two center ones (Mt. McKinley Natl. Park) and those at left (Aleutians), show variations of the hard type. b. White-tailed ptarmigan (Colo.).

c. Rock ptarmigan (left, Mt. McKinley Natl. Park; right, Alaska Peninsula).

d. Raven droppings (right, consisting of coiled material partly coated with white; left, shorter lengths).

e. Ptarmigan in northern landscape. Their winter feeding on buds and twigs produces the woody character of the droppings.

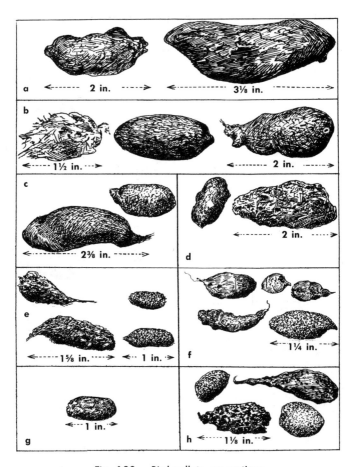

Fig. 180.   Bird pellets, or castings

a. Ferruginous hawk (Wyo.).
b. Red-tailed hawk. Left one contains feathers; the right, ground squirrel fur (Wyo.).

c. Prairie falcon (Wyo.).   f. Sparrow hawk (Nev.).
d. Swainson's hawk (Nev.).   g. Clark's nutcracker (Wyo.).
e. Shrike (left, Wyo.; right, Nev.).   h. Magpie (Wyo.).

Pellets of the gyrfalcon found at a nest on Savage River, Alaska, in 1951, were indistinguishable from those of the prairie falcon (c). That is, they had the same variations in size and shape that you will find at a prairie falcon nest. Both had fed extensively on rodents.

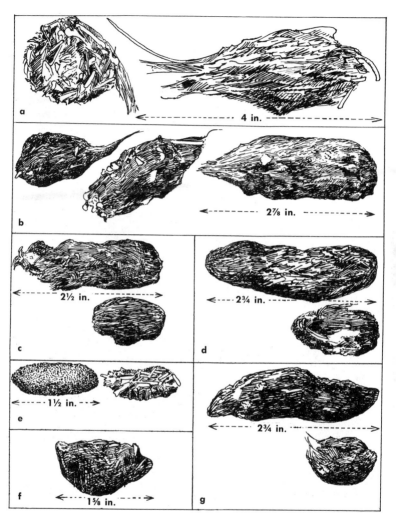

Fig. 181.   Bird pellets, or castings, about ⅔ natural size

a. Glaucous-winged gull. Left, bones and sea urchin fragments; right, feathers (Aleutians).
b. Raven (Wyo.).
c. Long-eared owl (Wyo.).
d. Short-eared owl (Alaska).
e. Burrowing owl. Left, insect remains; right, rodent remains.
f. Great gray owl (Wyo.).
g. Goshawk (Wyo.).

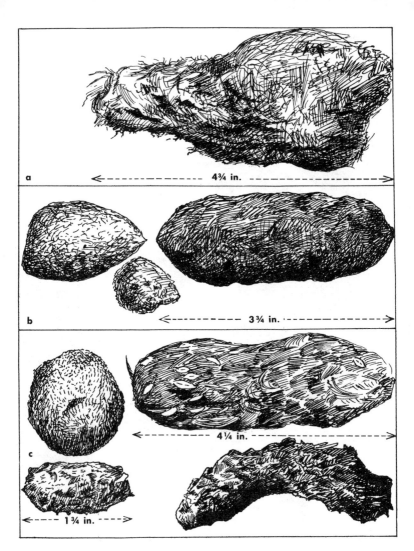

Fig. 182.   Pellets, or castings, of birds of prey, about ⅔ natural size

a. Bald eagle (Aleutians).
b. Golden eagle. These variations could be found at a single nest
   (from Nevada, Wyoming, and Alaska respectively).
c. Great horned owl (Wyo.).

336

Amphibians and Reptiles

AMPHIBIANS AND REPTILES too leave signs of their presence. As a matter of fact, in some places when you read the early morning record on a dusty road, you will find toad tracks prominent in the story. You will find, also, that when left to itself and not disturbed a toad walks and does not hop (see Fig. 183). However, I have not seen evidence of the frog's walking.

On the desert sands you will find many trails, including those of the lizard. Tortoises dig burrows, some of which are later used by burrowing owls. The gopher tortoise of Florida digs a burrow many feet long, with an opening as much as 8 by 12 inches.

There are at least three species of tortoises of the genus *Gopherus* which have accustomed themselves to living in dry, or even desert, areas, and to digging burrows in the ground for shelter.

Gopherus polyphemus is the species you will find in the Southeast, from southern South Carolina south through central Florida and west along the Gulf Coast to southeastern Texas. This species is colonial, and burrow openings are oval in shape, flattened in the proportions of the tortoise itself, approximately 6 by 9 inches in diameter, sometimes larger, and they often extend underground for distances of more than 20 feet.

There is another one, *Gopherus berlandieri*, a little smaller in

Gopher Tortoise, emerging
from its burrow

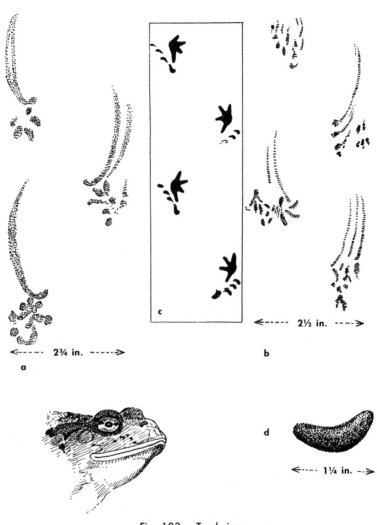

Fig. 183. Toad sign

a and b. Toad tracks on a dusty road, walking, with the feet dragging. The exact form of the footprints is hard to determine in dust.

c. Toad footprints in wet mud. Here the toed-in front feet are clearly indicated, as well as the row of toe prints of the hind foot.

d. Toad dropping, about ⅔ natural size.

338

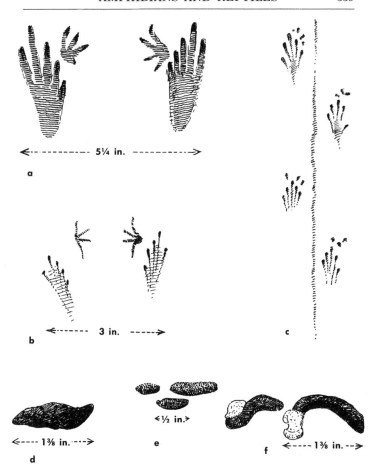

Fig. 184. Frog and lizard sign

a. Tracks of bullfrog in mud.
b. Tracks of frog, about size of leopard frog.
c. Lizard track, in sand. The marks of front toes are obscure (Nev.).
d. Dropping of leopard frog (Minn.).
e. Droppings of small horned lizard.
f. Droppings of collared lizard that had been feeding on insects (Okla.).

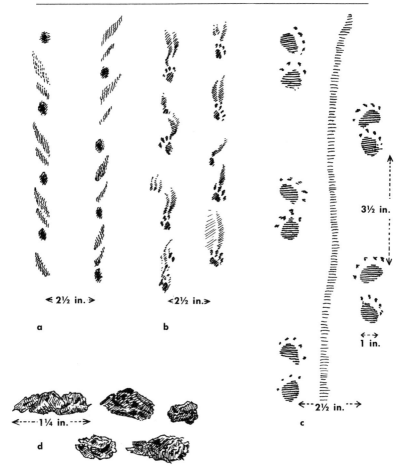

Fig. 185.   Tracks and scats of turtles, of unknown species (Okla.)

a. Tracks in loose sand that rolled into the imprints to obscure their
   form.
b. On firmer sand, where details are a little more clear.
c. In mud, showing details of feet, and the tail drag.
d. Scats, about ⅔ natural size, black or dark green in color.

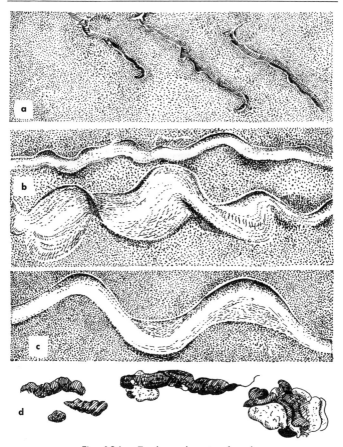

Fig. 186.   Tracks and scats of snakes

a. Track of sidewinder, *Crotalus cerastes*, in sand; direction of rattlesnake's travel is to the left (from published photograph by Walter
   Mosauer).
b. Garter snake tracks in dust, moving to right. Above (diam. ⅝ to
   ¾ in., moving leisurely; below (diam. ¾ to 5 in.), moving fast,
   with strong side loopings.
c. Track of kingsnake in dust; diam. 1 in.
d. Two samples at right, droppings of hognose snake. At left, droppings
   of unknown snake species.

size, which lives only in parts of southern Texas and in Mexico.

Still another is called the desert tortoise, *Gopherus agassizi,* which lives in the Southwest: "Deserts of southeastern California, the southern tip of Nevada, the extreme southwestern corner of Utah, western and southern Arizona, and Sonora, Mexico" (from Pope). The burrows of the desert tortoise are not as deep as those of the eastern species and apparently these are also more solitary. In fact, some of them find shelter without digging a burrow.

Among the many kinds of burrows you may find within the areas listed here, along the southern belt from South Carolina and Florida to southern California, there are certain oval or somewhat flattened ones that are likely to be those of the gopher tortoise. When you find a burrowing owl at its underground home, or an opposum, rattlesnake, or other animal in its subterranean refuge, the hole it is living in may be one that was originally dug by a tortoise.

Reptile droppings are interesting in that, at least among snakes and lizards, you will find a capping of white calcareous deposit at one end, as in the case of birds. Compare Figures 184, f, and 186, d, with Figures 177, b, 178, a, and 179, d, to mention only a few.

These few illustrations of amphibian and reptile sign are only a suggestion of what can be found in this particular realm of nature.

Insects and Other Invertebrates

INSECTS leave signs, too, even footprints and droppings. In Florida during the spring of 1952 we found in the sand the raised ridges, the rope-like tubes, that mark the tunnels of the mole cricket (see Fig. 188, a). These were much like mole runways, though only a scant inch in diameter. There were also little mounds, like miniature molehills, which I learned were the "throw-ups" of certain burrowing beetles of the genus *Geotrupes*. Some mounds were as much as 6 inches in diameter, and when fresh showed a lumpy surface, just as certain fresh molehills do. However, after wind or rain or drying out, they leveled off into a smooth surface. Other beetles that throw up mounds are *Bolboceras* (shown in Fig. 188, b), *Bolbocerosoma*, and *Phanaeus carnifex*. Some of these mounds are even more inconspicuous. You may also become familiar with the burrowings under the bark of trees, which present characteristic tracery in dead trees when the bark has fallen off.

As could be expected, the big, bumbling Mormon cricket leaves a distinct trail in dust or sand, as shown in Figure 189, a and b. The grasshopper, too, makes a somewhat similar trail, when it is not hopping or flying, and of course it comes in many sizes with its many species. One day in sand dune country of the Southwest, I took a walk to see what had been about. There were tracks of lizards, kangaroo rats, and desert foxes — and many little fine traceries that could only be made by insects. There before me was a shiny black beetle making one of those trails (Fig. 189, c). Notice the similarity of pattern in trails of crickets, grasshoppers, and beetles. Apparently it is the hind leg that trails behind and leaves the backward-pointing mark, and one of the forward pairs, probably the middle pair, that makes the cross mark. You will notice in Figure 189, b, which has a more exact cross mark than *a*, that each print-cluster consists of three parts, accounting for the three feet on each side.

Here is a curious problem. Several of us were lounging on the shore of Jackson Lake in Wyoming. In the fine sand were many tracks, including the trail shown on the next page. A deer track? Impossible to imagine an elfin deer that leaves a footprint one third of an inch long! At least it served to lead our thoughts into the realm of fairies. When you learn the identity of the creature, the author of this would be interested to hear about it.

343

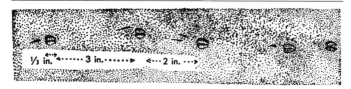

Mysterious tracks

D, e, and *f* of Figure 189 show droppings of the Mormon cricket, caterpillar, and grasshopper, respectively, with enlargements to show the minute structure. In *f* the grasshoppers had fed on vegetation that produced as droppings packets of stiff bristle-like fibers neatly stacked together. In 1934 grasshoppers were extremely numerous on the dry lands along the Missouri in Montana, where these specimens were collected. The ground was strewn with the droppings that looked like seedheads of grass scattered about.

The caterpillar droppings in *e* are peculiar in being longitudinally segmented into hexagonal form, as shown in the cross section.

One day outside our kitchen window, under some tall plants, I found a scattering of these crinkly pellets, or frass, as caterpillar droppings are called. Searching among the leaves directly above I found the large caterpillar industriously chewing at the border of a leaf. Such frass can be a guide for the entomologist, not only to locate the caterpillar but to identify the insect, once a more complete knowledge of such material can be classified. A good method toward that end is to capture an insect or caterpillar, then collect and record by drawing and description the droppings or frass deposited in the cage soon after capture. By this means I obtained positive identification of some of the samples shown in the accompanying figures.

In addition, there are the little drops of pitch on conifer bark, the little tufts of sawdust here and there, the many indications that mark the hidden work of insects.

The world of insects has much room for exploration.

When my brother and I were in school in western Minnesota we used to find small holes in the muddy bottom of the Red River. Always in pairs, they were in the shallows near shore and were big enough for us to put our fingers into. Quite often when we poked a finger into one hole a crayfish would shoot out of the other end of the tunnel, tail first. After we had learned about this, and wanted to catch the crayfish to have a look at it just for fun, we put a finger in each entrance, got the crayfish between them, and lifted it out through the soft mud.

Later, along slough banks in North Dakota and in other places, I found the little mud chimneys along the shore, not far from the water, and learned that these mounds, with a vertical tunnel down through the center, were also constructed by crayfish.

Sand crabs have burrows on the ocean beach and, as reported on page 205, on the east coast of Florida such burrows may be confused with the burrows of the species of white-footed mouse, *Peromyscus polionotus phasma,* that lives there.

Through the shallow water along the banks of the Red River we also saw the freshwater clams and the trails or grooves they left in the mud as they walked along on the fleshy "foot" they put out through the partly opened shell. On certain sandy ocean beaches we are accustomed to locate marine clams at low tide by the slight mounds on the sand. Clam and crayfish sign are shown here in Figure 187.

Everything that crawls makes a track sooner or later, somewhere. You may have noticed an unusual number of earthworms about after a rain, sometimes crawling over the sidewalk. It has even been said that they fall with the rain.

The fact is that after a heavy rain earthworms tend to come out to the surface of the ground, and in muddy spots you may see the network of their trails, such as those shown in Figure 190. If you look closely you will notice that in the softest mud their trails are the widest, over ⅛ inch. When they come to firmer ground their trail is narrower (they don't sink as deep there), and where they strike drier spots you will find gaps in the trails, where the soft bodies made no impressions.

You will also find holes in the mud, with the diameter of the wider portions of the trail, where the earthworms came out for air. At some of these holes, or covering them, will be a tiny pile of very small soft mud pellets left there by the worm (see Fig. 190).

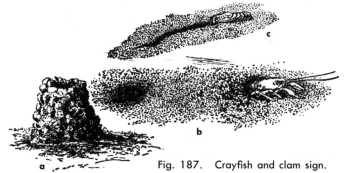

Fig. 187.   Crayfish and clam sign.

a. Hollow dirt column thrown up by crayfish on shore.
b. Crayfish burrow with two entrances, in mud under water.
c. Clam and its trail in mud.

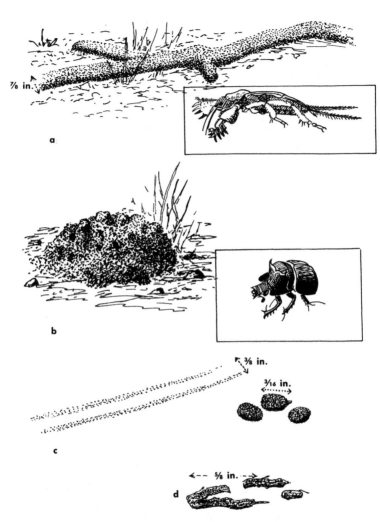

Fig. 188.   Insect sign

a. Runway of mole cricket, *Gryllotalpa.*
b. Mound of earth thrown up by a burrowing beetle, of the genus *Geotrupes.* Mound sometimes has diam. of 6 in. Another mound-maker, *Bolboceras,* shown at right.
c. Centipede tracks and, at right, droppings of millipede, *Spiro-bolus* (Fla.).   d. Droppings of katydid, *Pterophylla.*

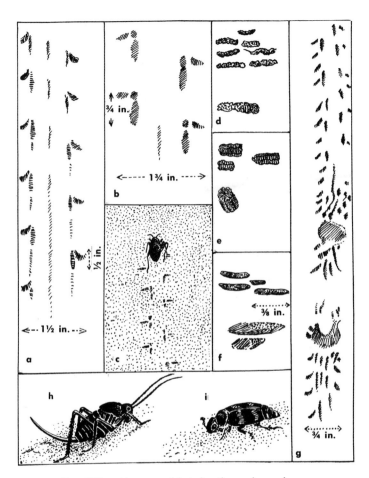

Fig. 189.   Mormon cricket, beetle, and grasshopper

a and b. Tracks of Mormon cricket in dust (Wyo.).

c. Beetle leaving tracks in desert sand.

d. Droppings of Mormon cricket, about natural size; enlarged figure below shows structure.

e. Caterpillar frass, probably one of the swallowtails; enlarged figure below shows hexagonal cross section.

f. Grasshopper droppings, about natural size, with enlarged samples below.

g. Grasshopper trail in sand; a shuffle with one short hop.

h. Mormon cricket.   i. Carrion beetle.

347

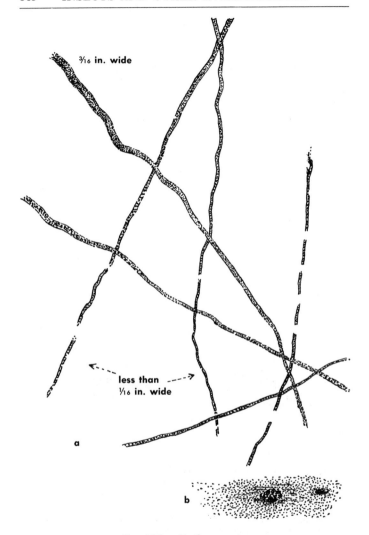

Fig. 190.   Earthworm sign

a. Trails in wet mud.
b. Burrows, one plugged by tiny mud pellets.

Twigs and Limbs

ANIMAL LIFE depends ultimately on vegetation for existence and it is to be expected that shrubs and trees should furnish a share of this nourishment. One spring in Wyoming, when the snow had melted away, I found an extensive patch of buffaloberry bushes in a river bottom, conspicuously encircled by a light-colored band where meadow voles had eaten the bark. Often you will find the bark of wild rose bushes eaten, under the snow, and the stems cut into lengths (Fig. 191, a). The tooth marks are tiny, less than ¹⁄₁₆ of an inch.

One fall in Wyoming an early snowfall came while the aspens and cottonwoods still had their leaves. As a result, they held so much snow that the woods were filled with broken trees and limbs. Next spring when the snow melted away we found that the dwellers under the deep snow had fared very well indeed. Cottonwood and aspen bark is palatable to many animals, and the fallen limbs everywhere indicated evidence of winter feasting. Figure 191, c, shows cottonwood-limb markings left by pocket gophers, which had tunneled through the snow and left some of their earth cores over and beside the limbs. Note the smooth surface of the mouse work in *b* and the coarse appearance of *c*, where the pocket gophers had eaten the bark and also gouged into the wood. The gopher tooth marks were about ¹⁄₁₆ of an inch, some smaller, others considerably larger.

Moose and elk help themselves to bark, especially on aspen and to some extent fir, and occasionally alder and large willow trunks. Usually the gnawings are vertical or diagonal stripes on the trunk (see Figure 148). Occasionally on a slanted or horizontal large limb you will find a few moose bites, as in Figure 191, d. These marks measure from ¼ to ½ an inch in width.

Of course the master lumberman is the beaver, who sometimes fells trees as large as 2 feet in diameter. Figure 191, e, shows a twig stripped of bark; the tooth marks here are about ⅛ inch wide. In *f* the beaver has severed a willow stem, leaving tooth marks about ⅛ to ¼ inch wide. *G* shows a cottonwood limb stripped of bark by a beaver, with a few gouges in the wood from ¹⁄₁₆ and ⅛ to ¼ inch in width. Where beavers have been working you will also find beaver gnawings on the tree itself, bark being removed as high as 6 feet above the ground. The explanation of this is that the beaver was out working on the surface of deep snow.

349

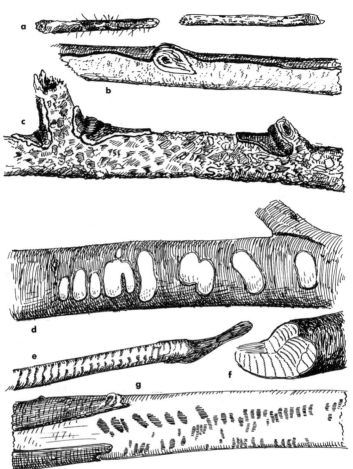

Fig. 191. Gnawed twigs and limbs

a. Wild rose twigs gnawed by meadow voles in winter. Note that
   the slanted cut at the end is not done by a single bite, but by
   successive tooth cuts. See also Fig. 107, b.
b. Cottonwood limb gnawed by meadow voles under the snow.
c. Cottonwood limb gnawed by pocket gophers under the snow.
d. Aspen limb bitten into by moose. See also Fig. 148.
e. Bark eaten off willow twig by beaver.
f. End of willow stem severed by beaver.
g. Beaver gnawings on a cottonwood limb. See also Fig. 87, c.

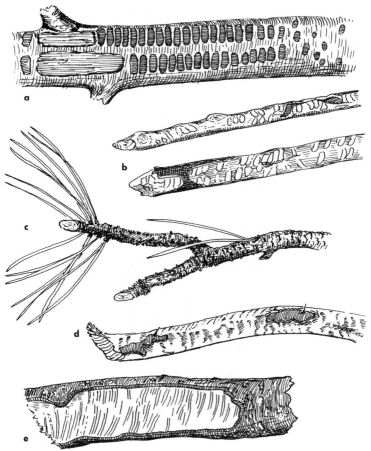

Fig. 192.   Gnawed twigs and limbs

a. Pits of sapsucker in a willow stem. Pits are up to ⅛ in. wide.
b. Cottontail gnawings. Tooth marks vary from a little less than ⅟₁₆ to a little less than ⅛ in. (Wisc.).
c. Tips of lodgepole pine nipped by snowshoe hare (Wyo.). See also illustration on pages 245 and 354.
d. Porcupine gnawing of bark. Smaller tooth marks up to ⅟₁₆, larger ones ⅛ in. wide (Idaho).
e. Very old gnawings of porcupine on spruce limbs (Wyo.). Tooth marks about ⅟₁₆ in. wide. See also illustrations on pages 184 and 186.

Woodpeckers leave neat rows of pits in the bark (see Fig. 193), and there are many other scars left on trees by insects or accidents. Lightning marks are among the most common of these. Lightning leaves long vertical streaks on trees, often somewhat spiral and generally neatly healed over on aspens. At other times you will find trees broken and splintered by lightning.

A mark that all woodsmen must learn to recognize is the "blaze" (see Fig. 194, a), made by slashing a small patch in the tree's bark with an ax. This is a sign left by man to indicate his trails through the forest. Knowledge of it can often save you from an unexpected night outdoors.

Fig. 193.   Tree borings of the pileated woodpecker. These are made by the bird when seeking out ant colonies in the trunks of trees or stumps. The openings may be in many sizes, some upward of a foot in length, others small, very often in groups as shown here. Generally they are elongated, and square off at the ends, but there are variations in size and shape, all depending on the way the bird adapts its work to the need for reaching the insects within.

It is interesting to notice that very often the holes drilled by the sapsucker also tend to be square or oblong in shape.

Fig. 194

a. An old blaze drawn by Paul Brooks (Lincoln, Mass.). This mark is
   often hard to tell from the scar left by sawing off a branch.
b. Aspen trunk with an old, healed lightning strike; a blaze mark has
   similar rough edges but is much shorter in length.

Fig. 195. Spruce grouse and blue grouse both feed on spruce and fir twigs, and leave partially denuded twigs such as here shown.

Snowshoe hares sometimes leave twigs in this same condition (see also page 245).

Bone and Horn Chewing

ONE WINTER DAY when I drove with dog team to a reindeer herd in the Kuskokwim country of Alaska, I saw intensified to a remarkable degree a habit that is fairly common among the deer. We know they like to nibble at antlers. The reindeer I saw were not only chewing the shed antlers, but were eating them off the owners' heads! Many of those who still carried their antlers had them chewed down to smaller size by their neighbors. The females, especially, were feeding on the spike antlers of their fawns.

Antler chewing has been noted in several places among the deer, and the habit is very prevalent among the Wyoming elk herds. Such chewing is done by the molariform teeth, or grinders, and the rough marks made by those teeth are distinctive. Note the antler tips in Figure 196, c, with their appearance of having been gouged and "worn" off in a clumsy manner.

Note by contrast the neat carving effect in b, the work of rodents, equipped with gnawing teeth. These rodents no doubt include mice, possibly ground squirrels, certainly the porcupine. I have not been able to identify properly the specific rodents who do this work, but I do know that they are extremely efficient. Figure 196, b, shows all that remained of a large elk antler, and a, the nearly finished horn of a mountain sheep. I also found a large leg bone of a horse pretty well trimmed down.

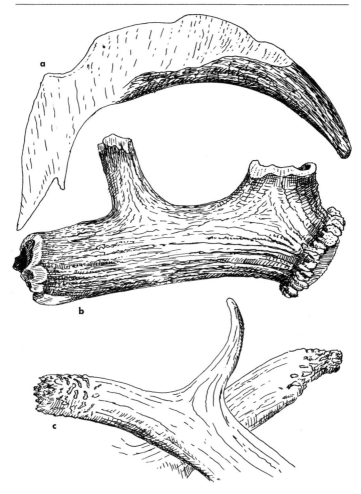

Fig. 196. Horn-chewing sign

a. All that is left of a mountain sheep horn eaten by rodents.
b. All that is left of a large elk antler, almost completely consumed
   by rodents.
c. Tips of two elk antlers chewed by elk.

Bibliography
and Index

Bibliography

Aiken, Russell
  Tracks: a unique method of collecting them. Nature Magazine, 15 (3):170 (1930). Describes plaster cast method.
Alcorn, J. R.
  On the decoying of coyotes. Journal of Mammalogy, 27 (2): 122-26 (1946).
Allen, A. A.
  A Christmas walk with birds and beasts. American Forestry, 25 (312): 1526-30 (1919).
Allen, Durward L.
  Notes on the killing technique of the New York weasel. Jour. Mamm., 19 (2):225-29 (1938).
Anthony, Harold E.
  The bat. Natural History, 25 (6):560-70 (1925).
――――
  Field book of North American mammals. Putnam, 1928.
Arlton, A. V.
  An ecological study of the mole. Jour. Mamm., 17 (4):349-71 (1936).
Audubon, John James, and John Bachman
  The quadrupeds of North America. V. G. Audubon, 1851-54.

Bailey, Vernon
  Biological survey of Texas. U.S. Dept. of Agric., Biological Survey. No. Am. Fauna 25 (1905).
――――
  Capturing small mammals for study. Jour. Mamm., 2 (2):63-68 (1921).
――――
  Mammals of New Mexico. U.S. Dept. of Agric., Bur. of Biological Survey. No. Am. Fauna 53 (1931).
――――
  Trapping animals alive. Jour. Mamm., 13 (4):337-42 (1932).
Benson, Seth B.
  Decoying coyotes and deer. Jour. Mamm., 29 (4):406-9 (1948).
―――― and Adrey E. Borell
  Notes on the life history of the red tree mouse, *Phenacomys longicaudus*. Jour. Mamm., 12 (3):226-33 (1931).
Bergtold, W. H.
  Unusual nesting of a raccoon. Jour. Mamm., 6 (4):280-81 (1925).
Blair, W. Frank
  Notes on home ranges and populations of the short-tailed shrew. Ecology, 21 (2):284-88 (1940).
――――
  Some data on the home ranges and general life history of the short-

tailed shrew, red-backed vole and woodland jumping mouse in northern Michigan. American Midland Naturalist, 25 (3):681–85 (1941).

Brunner, Josef
Tracks and tracking. Outing Pub. Co., 1909.

Burt, William H.
The mammals of Michigan. Univ. of Michigan Press, 1946.

—— A simple live trap for mammals. Jour. Mamm., 8 (4):302–4 (1927).
—— and Richard P. Grossenheider
A field guide to the mammals. 3rd ed. Houghton Mifflin, 1975.

Cahalane, Victor H.
Mammals of North America. Macmillan, 1947.

Chubb, S. Harmsted
How animals run. Natural History, 29 (5):543–51 (1929).

Clark, Harold W.
Records of night: the ramblers are revealed. Nature Magazine, 14 (4):222 (1929).

Crabb, Wilfred D.
The ecology and management of the prairie skunk in Iowa. Ecological Monographs, 18:201–32 (1948).

—— Food habits of the prairie spotted skunk in southeastern Iowa. Jour. Mamm., 22 (4):349–64 (1941).

Dalquest, Walter W.
Mammals of Washington. Mus. of Natural History, Univ. of Kansas Pub., 2:1–444 (1948).

Davis, William B., and Leonard Joeris
Notes on the life history of the little short-tailed shrew. Jour. Mamm., 26 (2):136–38 (1945).

Davis, William B., and Walter P. Taylor
The bighorn sheep of Texas. Jour. Mamm., 20 (4):440–55 (1939).

de la Croix, P. Magne
The evolution of locomotion in mammals. Jour. Mamm., 17 (1):51–54 (1936).

Dixon, Joseph S.
Notes on the life history of the gray shrew. Jour. Mamm., 5 (1):1–6 (1924).

Eadie, W. Robert
A contribution to the biology of *Parascalops breweri*. Jour. Mamm., 20 (2):150–73 (1939).

Errington, Paul L.
An analysis of mink predation upon muskrats in north-central United States. Iowa State Coll. of Agric. Research Bull. No. 320 (1943).

Fry, Walter
The wolverine. Cal. Fish and Game, 9 (4):129–34 (1923).

Giles, LeRoy W.
Food habits of the raccoon in eastern Iowa. Jour. Wildlife Management, 4 (4):375–82 (1940).

Glass, Bryan P.

The black-footed ferret in Oklahoma. Jour. Mamm., 31 (4):460 (1950).

Glover, Fred A.

Killing techniques of the New York weasel. Penn. Agric. Exp. Sta., Paper No. 1147 (1942).

—— A study of the winter activities of the New York weasel. Penn. Game News, 14 (6):8–9 (1943).

Grinnell, George Bird

Mountain sheep. Jour. Mamm., 9 (1):1–9 (1928).

Grinnell, Joseph

Bats as desirable citizens. Cal. Fish and Game Commission, Teachers' Bull. No. 6 (1916).

—— Disgorgement among songbirds. Auk, 14 (4):412 (1897).

—— and Joseph S. Dixon and Jean M. Linsdale.

Fur-bearing mammals of California. Univ. of California Press, 1937.

Hall, E. Raymond

Breeding habits of the short-tailed shrew, *Blarina brevicauda*. Jour. Mamm., 10 (2):125–34 (1929).

—— Food of the *Soricidae*. Jour. Mamm., 11 (1):26–39 (1930).

—— Habits of the star-nosed mole, *Condylura cristata*. Jour. Mamm., 12 (4):345–55 (1931).

—— Mammals of Nevada. Univ. of California Press, 1946.

—— Notes on the life history of the sage-brush meadow mouse (*Lagurus*). Jour. Mamm., 9 (3):201–4 (1928).

—— A revised classification of the American ermines with description of a new subspecies from the western Great Lakes region. Jour. Mamm., 26 (2):175–82 (1945).

—— The weasels of New York: their natural history and economic status. Am. Midland Naturalist, 14 (4):289–344 (1933).

Hamilton, William J., Jr.

Activity of Brewer's mole (*Parascalops breweri*). Jour. Mamm., 20 (3):307–10 (1939).

—— American mammals. McGraw-Hill, 1939.

—— The biology of the little short-tailed shrew *Cryptotis parva*. Jour. Mamm., 25 (1):1–7 (1944).

—— The biology of the smoky shrew. Zoologica, 25 (4):473–92 (1940).

—— Exploring the world of "whistle pig." Audubon Magazine, 52 (2):96–101 (1950).

Hamilton, William J., Jr. (*contd.*)
  Life history notes on the northern pine mouse. Jour. Mamm., 19 (2):163–70 (1938).
Handley, Charles O., Jr., and Clyde P. Patton
  Wild mammals of Virginia. Virginia Commission of Game and Inland Fisheries, 1947.
Harper, Francis
  The Florida water-rat (*Neofiber alleni*) in Okefenokee Swamp, Georgia. Jour. Mamm., 1 (2):65–66 (1920).
Hartman, Carl G.
  Possums. Univ. of Texas Press, 1952.
Herlocker, Emmett
  Mountain beaver — biological curiosity. Audubon Magazine, 52 (6):387–90 (1950).
Hickie, Paul
  New developments in a small mammal trap. Jour. Mamm., 16 (1):71–73 (1935).
Hisaw, Frederick L.
  Observations on the burrowing habits of moles (*Scalopus aquaticus machrinoides*). Jour. Mamm., 4 (2):79–88 (1923).
Hooper, Emmet T.
  The water shrew of the southern Allegheny Mountains. Mus. of Zoology, Univ. of Michigan, Occasional Papers No. 463 (1942).
Howell, Arthur H.
  Description of a new race of the Florida water-rat (*Neofiber alleni*). Jour. Mamm., 1 (2):79–80 (1920).
  ———
  A revision of the American Arctic hares. Jour. Mamm., 17 (4):315–37 (1936).

Ingles, Lloyd Glenn
  Mammals of California. Stanford Univ. Press, 1946.
Ivey, R. DeWitt
  Life history notes on three mice from the Florida east coast. Jour. Mamm., 30 (2):157–62 (1949).

Jackson, Hartley H. T.
  A review of the American moles. U.S. Dept. of Agric., Biological Survey. No. Am. Fauna 38 (1915).
  ———
  A taxonomic review of the American long-tailed shrews. U.S. Dept. of Agric., Biol. Sur. No. Am. Fauna 51 (1928).
Jaeger, Ellsworth
  Tracks and trailcraft. Macmillan, 1948.
Jewett, Stanley G.
  Notes on two species of phenacomys from Oregon. Jour. Mamm., 1 (4):165–68 (1920).
Johnson, C. Stuart
  Tracks from the Pleistocene of west Texas. Am. Midland Naturalist, 18 (1):147–52 (1937).

Klugh, A. Brooker
Notes on the habits of *Blarina brevicauda*. Jour. Mamm., 2 (1):35 (1921).

Lang, Herbert
Position of limbs in the sliding otter. Jour. Mamm., 5 (3):216–17 (1924).
Lay, Daniel W.
Ecology of the opossum in eastern Texas. Jour. Mamm., 23 (2):147–59 (1942).
Liers, Emil E.
Notes on the river otter (*Lutra canadensis*). Jour. Mamm., 32 (1):1–9 (1951).
Lucas, Frederick A.
Fossil footprints. Evolution, No. 10 (Nov. 1928), p. 5.

McCabe, Robert A.
Notes on live-trapping mink. Jour. Mamm., 30 (4):416–23 (1949).
McLean, Donald D.
The prong-horned antelope in California. Cal. Fish and Game, 30 (4):221–41 (1944).
Marshall, William H.
Mink displays sliding habits. Jour. Mamm., 16 (3):228–29 (1935).

——— A study of the winter activities of the mink. Jour. Mamm., 17 (4):382–92 (1936).
Mason, George F.
Animal tracks. Morrow, 1943.
Mills, Enos A.
The grizzly. Houghton Mifflin, 1919.
Moore, A. W.
Improvements in live trapping. Jour. Mamm., 17 (4):372–74 (1936).

——— Notes on the sage mouse in eastern Oregon. Jour. Mamm., 24 (2): 188–91 (1943).

——— Notes on the Townsend mole. Jour. Mamm., 20 (4):499–501 (1939).
Murie, Adolph
Cattle on grizzly bear range. Jour. Wildlife Management, 12 (1):57–72 (1948).

——— Ecology of the coyote in the Yellowstone. U.S. Natl. Park Service, Fauna Ser. No. 4 (1940).

——— Following fox trails. Mus. of Zoology, Univ. of Michigan, Misc. Publications No. 32 (1936).

——— Some food habits of the black bear. Jour. Mamm., 18 (2):238–40 (1937).

——— The Wolves of Mt. McKinley. U.S. Natl. Park Service, Fauna Ser. No. 4 (1940).
Murie, Olaus J.
The elk of North America. Stackpole Co. and Wildlife Management Institute, 1951.

Murie, Olaus J. (*contd.*)
  The mink—brown mischief. Home Geographic Monthly, 1 (7):43–48
  (1932).

  Notes on the sea otter. Jour. Mamm., 21 (2):119–31 (1940).

Nelson, Edward W.
  Bats in relation to the production of guano and the destruction of insects.
  U.S. Dept. of Agric., Dept. Bull No. 1395 (1926).

  Report upon natural history collections made in Alaska. U.S. Army
  Signal Service, 1887.
  —— and Louis Agassiz Fuertes
  Wild animals of North America. Natl. Geographic Society, 1930.
Newman, H. H.
  The natural history of the nine-banded armadillo of Texas. Am. Natu-
  ralist, 67 (561):513–39 (1913).

Palmer, E. Laurence
  Larger mammals. Cornell Rural School Leaflet, 19 (2):1–44 (1925).

  A talk on winter animals. Cornell Rural Sch. Leaf. 13 (3):83–130 (1920).
Pearce, John
  Identifying injury by wildlife to trees and shrubs in northeastern forests.
  U.S. Fish and Wildlife Ser., Research Report No. 13 (1947).
Pettigrew, J. Bell
  Animal locomotion. Appleton, 1874.
Polderboer, Emmett B.
  Habits of the least weasel (*Mustela rixosa*) in northeastern Iowa. Jour.
  Mamm., 23 (2):145–47 (1942).
  —— and Lee W. Kuhn and George O. Hendrickson
  Winter and spring habits of weasels in central Iowa. Jour. Wildlife
  Management, 5 (1):115–19 (1941).
Proctor, Thomas
  Disgorgement among songbirds. Auk, 14 (4):412 (1897).

Quick, Edgar R., and A. W. Butler
  The habits of some Arvicolinae. Am. Naturalist, 19 (2):113–18 (1885).
Quick, H. F.
  Habits and economics of the New York weasel in Michigan. Jour.
  Wildlife Management, 8 (1):71–78 (1944).

Reed, Charles A., and Thane Riney
  Swimming, feeding, and locomotion of a captive mole. Am. Midland
  Naturalist, 30 (3):790–91 (1943).
Reynolds, Harold C.
  Some aspects of the life history and ecology of the opossum in central
  Missouri. Jour. Mamm., 26 (4):361–79 (1905).
Rollings, Clair T.
  Habits, foods and parasites of the bobcat in Minnesota. Jour. Wildlife
  Management, 9 (2):131–45 (1945).

Rossell, Leonard
  Tracks and trails. Pub. by Boy Scouts of Am., distr. by Macmillan,
  1928.
Rutherford, Ralph L., and Loris S. Russell
  Mammal tracks from the Paskapoo beds in Alberta. Am. Jour. of Science,
  5th ser., 15 (87):262–64 (1928).

Scheffer, Theophilus H.
  The common mole of eastern United States. U.S. Dept. of Agric.,
  Farmers' Bull. 583 (1917).
——
  Hints on live trapping. Jour. Mamm., 15 (3):197–202 (1934).
——
  Trapping moles and utilizing their skins. U.S. Dept. of Agric., Farmers'
  Bull. 832 (1917).
Schmidt, F. J. W.
  Mammals of western Clark County, Wisconsin. Jour. Mamm., 12-
  (2):99–117 (1931).
Scott, Thomas G.
  The secrets of the trail. Country Life in America, 8 (2):202–5 (1905).
——
  Some food coactions of the northern plains red fox. Ecological Mono-
  graphs, 13 (4):427–79 (1943).
——
  Stories on the tree-trunks. Country Life in America, 6 (1):37–39, 90
  (1904).
Seton, Ernest Thompson
  Lives of game animals. Doubleday, 1929.
——
  The mole-mouse, potato mouse, or pine-mouse. Jour. Mamm., 1 (4):185
  (1920).
——
  On the study of scatology. Jour. Mamm., 6 (1):47–49 (1925).
Severinghouse, C. W., and John E. Tanck.
  Speed and gait of an otter. Jour. Mamm., 29 (1):71 (1948).
Shaw, William T.
  Alpine life of the heather vole (*Phenacomys olympicus*). Jour. Mamm.,
  5 (1):12–15 (1924).
Shull, A. Franklin
  Habits of the short-tailed shrew. Am. Naturalist, 61 (488):495–522
  (1907).
Silver, James
  The European hare (*Lepus europaeus* Pallas) in North America. Jour.
  Agricultural Research, 28 (11):1133–37 (1924).
—— and A. W. Moore
  Mole control. U.S. Fish and Wildlife Ser., Conservation Bull. No. 16.
Simpson, Sutturland Eric
  The nest and young of the star-nosed mole. Jour. Mamm., 4 (3):167–71
  (1923).
Skinner, M. P.
  Bears in the Yellowstone. McClurg, 1925.

Smith, Clarence F.
Notes on the habits of the long-tailed harvest mouse. Jour. Mamm., 17 (3):274–78 (1936).

Sooter, Clarence A.
Habits of coyotes in destroying nests and eggs of waterfowl. Jour. Wildlife Management, 10 (1):33–38 (1946).

Stegeman, LeRoy C.
The European wild boar in the Cherokee National Forest, Tennessee. Jour. Mamm., 19 (3):279–90 (1938).

Stephainsky, H.
Mit der Kamera im Spurschnee. Der Naturforscher, 6 (6):211–17 (1929).

Stickel, Lucille F., and William H.
A *Sigmodon* and *Baiomys* population in ungrazed and unburned Texas prairie. Jour. Mamm., 30 (2):141–50 (1949).

Svihla, Arthur
Life history notes on *Sigmodon hispidus hispidus*. Jour. Mamm., 10 (4):352–53 (1929).

—— Life history of the Texas rice rats (*Oryzomys palustris texensis*). Jour. Mamm., 12 (3):238–42 (1931).

—— The mountain water shrew. Murrelet, 15 (2):44–45 (1934).

—— and Ruth D. Svihla
Mink feeding on clams. Murrelet, 12 (1):22 (1931).

Svihla, Ruth D.
Habits of *Sylvilagus aquaticus littoralis*. Jour. Mamm., 10 (4):315–19 (1929).

Taber, F. Wallace
Contribution on the life history and ecology of the nine-banded armadillo. Jour. Mamm., 26 (3):211–26 (1945).

Tappe, Donald T.
Natural history of the Tulare kangaroo rat. Jour. Mamm., 22 (2):117–48 (1941).

Tevis, Lloyd P., Jr.
Summer activities of California raccoons. Jour. Mamm., 28 (4):323–32 (1947).

Walker, Alex
Notes on the forest phenacomys. Jour. Mamm., 11 (2):233–35 (1930).

Walker, Lewis Wayne
Passers-by. Outdoor Life, 70 (1):50–52 (1932).

Warren, Edward R.
The mammals of Colorado. Putnam, 1910.

Whitney, Leon F.
The raccoon and its hunting. Jour. Mamm., 12 (1):29–38 (1931).

Wilson, Clifford
Animal trackers. Rod and Gun in Canada, 36 (8):20–21 (1935).

Wood, Rodney C.
Animal tracking for Boy Scouts: hints on animal tracking. Canadian General Council for Boy Scouts Assoc. 1924.

Wright, William H.
  The grizzly bear. Scribner, 1909.

Yeager, Lee E., and R. G. Reunels
  Fur yields and autumn foods of the raccoon in Illinois River bottomlands.
  Jour. Wildlife Management, 7 (1):45–60 (1943).

Index

THE READER will find it practical to go directly to the illustrations; in most cases it will not be necessary to consult the text for identification of tracks.

Page numbers in **boldface type** refer to the illustrations. In instances where the identifying common or scientific name appears in the caption opposite the illustration, the boldface number gives the *actual location* of the drawing. Continuous pagination **(156-59)** indicates that no text interrupts successive illustrations.

369

"If I were to make a study of the tracks of animals and represent them by plates, I should conclude with the tracks of man."

Henry David Thoreau